MEDIEVAL TEXTS AND STUDIES

General Editor

John A. Alford

The child Silence between her nurse and a seneschal (from MS Mi .LM.6, folio 203 recto A, courtesy of the University of Nottingham, with the kind permission of Lord Middleton).

Silence

A THIRTEENTH-CENTURY FRENCH ROMANCE

Newly Edited and Translated

with Introduction and Notes

by

SARAH ROCHE-MAHDI

EAST LANSING
COLLEAGUES PRESS

Medieval Texts and Studies: No. 10

ISBN 0–937191–31–0
ISBN 0–937191–32–9 (pbk.)
Library of Congress Catalog Card Number 91–77546
British Library Cataloguing in Publication Data available
Copyright © 1992 Sarah Roche-Mahdi

Published by Colleagues Press Inc.
Post Office Box 4007
East Lansing, MI 48826

Distribution outside North America
Boydell and Brewer Ltd.
Post Office Box 9
Woodbridge, Suffolk IP12 3DF
England

Printed in the United States of America

CONTENTS

For Rachel and Rebekah,

mulieribus fortissimis

PREFACE

THE TRANSLATION THAT FOLLOWS had its origins in the sheer delight I experienced in discovering *Silence* during Joan Ferrante's 1981 NEH Summer Seminar on "Woman in Life and Literature in the Middle Ages." All of us participants were dismayed that an Arthurian romance so intrinsically significant and so undeservedly neglected was practically unknown even among specialists in medieval literature. It seemed imperative to make it available in a better edition and also accessible to more than the few who can read a relatively difficult Old French text. The bilingual format that follows is meant to do both. The Old French text has been newly edited on the basis of the latest scholarship and careful reexamination of the unique manuscript. The facing translation is meant to serve as an aid to those learning Old French or to be read on its own. *Silence* should be of particular interest to teachers and students of medieval and comparative literature and women's studies, as well as to anyone who loves a first-rate story. I have attempted to keep introduction and notes brief and yet indicate the literary-historical questions and philological problems raised by the work. For those interested in a comparison of motifs, I have included a plot summary of "Grisandole," the major analogue and likely source for the final episode of *Silence*, since *L'Estoire Merlin* is not yet available in translation.

I wish to express my profound gratitude to Prof. Anne Iker-Gittleman of Vassar College, who gave so generously of her time and expertise in Old French at an early stage in this endeavor. The mistakes that remain in this version are mine alone. Thanks to Rebekah Gerstein for her proof-reading and valuable stylistic suggestions, to Jane Lindfors and Jane Spickett, who gave me friendship, refuge, and solace, and to Michele, Bee, Beth, Betsy, Charlene, Diane, Jane, Myke, Laura and Lilybeth, without whose collective and individual support I would never have finished this project. I wish to thank the staff of the Library of the University of Nottingham, who have been unfailingly cordial and helpful. I am most grateful to the Keeper of Manuscripts, Dr. Dorothy Johnston, and I owe special thanks to Lord Middleton, the very generous owner of the manuscript of *Silence*.

INTRODUCTION

SINCE THIS ROMANCE is only beginning to recover its voice after a silence of more than seven hundred years,[1] it seems appropriate to introduce the text and briefly summarize its contents before discussing its literary sources, linguistic play and ideological stance. The very existence of the manuscript containing *Silence* — a well-worn anthology that must have been the property of a professional entertainer — was unknown to the scholarly world until 1911, when it was discovered in the manor house of a British nobleman in a box marked "old papers — no value," together with letters from Henry VIII and other documents (Cowper 1959, 17). The poem itself, ignored after that except for Gelzer's brief treatments (1917, 1925, 1927), was edited for the first time by Lewis Thorpe in the 1960s and first published separately in 1972. This volume is now out of print. The language, Old French with many Picard features, is of the second half of the thirteenth century. The author, Heldris of Cornwall, is otherwise unknown.[2]

The plot, reduced to a minimum, is that Silence, daughter of Cador and Eufemie of Cornwall, is raised as a boy because Eban, king of England, will not allow women to inherit. When she reaches adolescence, Nature and Nurture appear as vituperative allegorical figures who torment her. Reason tells her to

---

[1] In the face of the dearth of secondary literature on *Silence* in general and the almost total lack of rigorous literary analysis (but cf. Bloch 1983, 1986), the discussion that follows owes much to the feminist issue of *Yale French Studies* (1981), especially Felman's article, and to conversations with Maria-Eugenia Lacarra during the NEH Summer Seminar (1981). Thanks also to Kathryn Slott for her insightful linguistic comments. I should also mention that the main points of my linguistic analysis of the women's names as well as other key portions of this introduction (which is in part a heavily revised version of a paper I wrote in 1981 and presented on a number of public occasions) appear without my permission and without acknowledgment in the afterword to a Spanish version of *Silence* published in 1986 — a translation based on, not simply in accord with, earlier drafts of this one, which began, at my invitation, as a collaborative effort.

[2] As Gelzer (1927, 99) has convincingly argued, "Master Heldris" seems to be a name picked from the pages of Geoffrey of Monmouth because of its connection with Cornwall: Cheldricus, a Saxon leader defeated and slain by Cador, duke of Cornwall (*History of the Kings of Britain* 9:1–5). Is this *Lokalpatriotismus* (as Gelzer suggests), the desire to please a patron (e.g., Richard of Cornwall)? Is the author, like the heroine, a transvestite she? Or does he just want to make us think so?

continue her life as a male. She runs away to learn the art of minstrelsy and then becomes a famous knight. Having repeatedly rejected the advances of Eban's highly sexed wife, Eufeme (who fakes a bloody rape attempt), Silence is sent on a supposedly hopeless quest: the capture of Merlin, who has prophesied that he can be taken only by a woman's trick. She succeeds, but is unmasked by Merlin, as is the queen and the queen's latest lover, disguised as a nun. Justice is done, women's right to inherit is restored, and Silence becomes queen of England through marriage with Eban.

Major Sources and Analogues

Thorpe took the story of the warrior maiden "Grisandole" in *L'Estoire Merlin* (Sommer 2:281–92) to be the "only real literary source" (14) for *Silence*, assuming more or less free invention for the rest, with details gleaned mainly from Geoffrey of Monmouth and Wace (17, 32–34). Gelzer (1927) and Lecoy (1978) have stressed that "Grisandole" fails to provide the Potiphar's wife motif as a motive for the disguised maiden's quest for Merlin; they note that Lucy Paton (1907), in a study published before the discovery of *Silence* and apparently unknown to Thorpe, posited that both "Grisandole" and a group of later tales that include the satisfyingly ironic motif of the vengeful queen who insists on the quest that will undo her derived from a more complete earlier source. Gelzer, after a tabulated comparison of motifs, concluded that *Silence* must derive from something like Paton's X; Lecoy sees *Silence* as providing striking confirmation of Paton's hypothesis.

I would argue that "Grisandole," with its imperfections and prejudices, is as likely a source as any hypothetically more complete X for an author as spirited and original as Heldris to have used, greatly improved upon, and reacted against. But "Grisandole" (or X) is hardly the only major source. At least two other romances are important: the *Roman d'Eneas* and some version(s) of the "Seven Sages of Rome.[3] Alain de Lille is everywhere, as is the matter of Tristan. Saints' lives, other tales and ballads[4] of warrior maidens and women musicians also deserve mention. Here again, what is interesting is how Heldris reworked existing material for his/her own purpose: to refute the definition of woman as

---

[3] Whether the author could have known the *Roman de la Rose* of Jean de Meun is uncertain. We cannot date the manuscript of *Silence* with sufficient accuracy, let alone determine the actual date of Heldris's composition. But whether the fact that both Oiseuse and Eufeme are called *huissiere* indicates literary influence — to cite only one example — it is certainly important to note the coincidence and the negative implications the word has for women.

[4] For example, the very popular Spanish ballad "La doncella guerrera," certainly old (although not attested in the standard *cancioneros*), which survived into the twentieth century in more than a hundred versions (Menendez-Pidal 1939, 221; 1973, 71).

defective male and to challenge the allegedly "natural" foundations of the social order.

To begin with the *Roman d'Eneas*, it seems clear that the three female characters in *Silence* owe a good deal to Dido, Lavine, and Camille (Lasry 1985). Eufeme is far inferior to Dido, sharing her passion and scheming, but possessing none of her nobility and dignity—nor her pangs of guilt. Eufemie is far superior to Lavine, but equally emboldened by and subject to love. But most importantly, Camille, the warrior queen of Vulcane, serves as both model for and contrast to Silence:

> She was marvellously beautiful and of very great strength. There was no other woman of her wisdom. She was very wise, brave and courteous and possessed great wealth and ruled her land wonderfully well. She had been raised always amid warfare, so that she loved chivalry greatly and upheld it her whole life. She had no interest in women's work, neither spinning nor sewing, but preferred the bearing of arms, tourneying and jousting, striking with the sword and the lance: there was no other woman of her bravery. During the day she was king, but at night, queen. No chambermaid or handmaid went about her during the day, nor ever in the night did any man enter the chamber where she was. She governed herself so wisely, both early and late, that no one could detect any folly in her, either in deed or in appearance, or feel any envy toward her.
>
> (Yunck 1974, 3959–86)

Both Silence and Camille are noble, loyal and courageous warriors, but Camille is queen in her own right and feels no tension between womanhood and the practice of chivalry. Both are also beautiful blondes, described (as Dido, Lavine, Eufeme and Eufemie are not) according to the tradition of *effictio* (Lasry 1985). But again, the contrast is significant: while Camille's blonde beauty is depicted in a military context (just as the beauty of a male warrior might be described to heighten the pathos of his death), Heldris stresses Silence's tension by separating the description of her as lovely maiden, Nature's masterpiece, from the scene in which she is armed for battle. Similarly, Silence's internal conflict, expressed by Nature's admonitions and her own self-examination echoes the external verbal and ideological confrontation of Camille with a Trojan warrior in battle. He taunts her:

> Enough of this arrogance: put down the shield and lance and hauberk, which cuts into you too much, and stop exhibiting your prowess. That is not your calling; you must spin, sew, and clip. The place to do battle with a maiden like you is in a beautiful chamber, behind the bed-hangings. Did you come here to show off?
>
> (7081–89)

And he ends by offering to pay for her sexual services, even though, he says, a hundred Trojans couldn't satisfy her lust. Camille retorts—after killing him:

I did not come her to show off or indulge in debauchery, but to practice chivalry. I want none of your deniers: you have made a very foolish bargain. I know better how to strike down a knight than to embrace him or make love to him; I do not know how to do battle on my back. (7117–25)

Silence reflects, after Reason has persuaded her to remain a man:

> I have a mouth too hard for kisses
> and arms too rough for embraces.
> One could easily make a fool of me
> in any game played under the covers.
> (2646–49)

Camille, who represents an ideal that Silence, through no fault of her own, achieves but is unable to sustain, dies a hero's death in battle. As Heldris makes painfully clear, Silence is not so fortunate: our *mulier fortis* must dwindle into a wife.

The third major vernacular literary source for *Silence*, the very popular story of "Dolopathos" ("he who suffers sorrow") or the "Seven Sages of Rome," offers a cluster of essential motifs: the question of inheritance, the vow of silence, the lustful queen, the accusation of rape, and the theme of nature and nurture. (The indecisiveness of the king, who shifts the responsibility for a judgment of life or death onto his advisers, is transferred to the French king in *Silence*.) In the best-told version, Herbert's *Dolopathos* (Brunet and Montaiglon 1856), the king sends his heir, Lucemien, to the great sage Virgil, who is head of an exclusive private school outside of Rome. The boy, favored by heredity and environment, learns the seven arts so well that his schoolmates are jealous and try to poison him (just as the minstrels plot to kill Silence). He reads in the stars that his mother is dead and his father has remarried. He swears to Virgil as an act of unquestioning obedience that he will not speak until he sees him again. Naturally, his silence destroys the *joie* of the court. There is much involved play with speech and silence; Dolopathos speaks as King David: "my harp is rent and broken." The queen tries everything to break the boy's silence, including seduction. One of her ladies gives evil counsel: Lucemien is her enemy because he is heir; she should stage a rape scene. The queen appears before the court all bloody and her dress torn to the waist. The prince's guilt seems obvious, and of course he does not speak to defend himself. No one wants to pronounce sentence, but the king insists justice must be done. Lucemien is stripped naked and about to be burned at the stake when a rider from afar appears—a distinguished old man, the first of the seven sages—to begin the process of storytelling that saves the hero's life. (Similarly, when Silence, disguised as a minstrel, is in danger of being executed by her father, a wise old man, Merlin in disguise, appears as rescuer.) The tales include warnings against too hasty judgment, incidents of rescue, and examples of the treachery of women. Finally Virgil appears (with a story as well) and Lucemien can speak. The queen is suitably punished: she and her damsels are burnt. Lucemien becomes a model ruler, a philosopher king, and is finally converted to Christianity by a wandering preacher.

The "Seven Sages" undoubtedly goes back to a story of the education and temptation of an Eastern ascetic (Roloff 1973), however much the original spiritual purpose may be obscured in certain variants; it remains fundamentally misogynist in all its extant versions. Speech and sensuality are identified with woman; the final test on the path to virtue is the command or vow of silence. The stories told (in other versions the queen gets a chance to reply) are of the deceitful deeds of women. Attacks on women abound, from two-liners to full-blown tirades.[5] The queen and her ladies, described as a nest of serpents, are

---

[5] One or two examples from Herbert's version — by no means the most virulent — will suffice to demonstrate the misogyny of the tradition:

> Crois tu chose ke fame die?
> Certes, tu fais trop grant follie.
> C'onkes, par mon cors ne par m'arme,
> N'oi parler de saige dame;
> Mal savoir n'est pas ciance.
> Mais je vos dis tot en fiance,
> Et bien saichiez ke je di voir,
> Que de mal puet fame savoir
> Plus ke nule autre criature.
> Teilz est ses sanz et sa nature.
> Je sai aikes de lor covine.
> (10,238–48)

> (Do you believe anything a woman says?
> Then you are truly stark, raving mad.
> For never, upon my body and soul,
> have I heard of a wise woman.
> Knowledge of evil is not wisdom.
> But I tell you this confidently,
> and know well that I speak the truth,
> that a woman can know more of evil
> than any other creature alive.
> That is her essence and her nature.
> This I know about the way they are.)

Virgil's attack on the queen leaves no doubt that she stands for woman:

> . . . . .Folle criature,
> Farsie de mal et d'ordure,
> Plainne de grant forsenerie
> Et d'outrage et de lecherie,
> La plus desloial riens ki vive. . .
> (10,252–56)

> (Lascivious creature,
> bloated with evil and corruption,
> bursting with fury,
> outrage and lechery,
> the most disloyal thing
> on the face of the earth.)

Neither walls nor towers nor war machines can prevail against her, in short,

> N'est malx ke par feme ne vegne.
> (10,292)

> (There is no evil that does not come from women.)

hardly counterbalanced by the first good queen. And as the tale spreads in Europe, titles such as the thirteenth-century Spanish *Libro de los enganos y los asayamientos de las mugeres* ("Book of the Treachery and Cunning of Women") focus not on the wise men, but on the evil stepmother wanting to do in her stepson for the inheritance.

Heldris transforms both motif and message, chiefly, of course, by making the pure and silent hero a she. The question of inheritance becomes a case of sex discrimination: the king's unjust and irrational decision to punish women for the greed of men. The wise and just monarch becomes the shallow, scheming Eban, who rules by terror and distribution of political favors, disloyal to his wife and to his most faithful vassal and rescuer, Silence. Certain graphic details of the "rape" scene are followed closely, but the accusation takes place in private, and the king covers up the entire incident. Considering the boy's social status, Eban explains to Eufeme (4234–36), this is to everyone's advantage. After all, boys will be boys—what Silence did was due to the impetuous nature of youth (4237). A pity to spoil the lad's good record. Besides, it will look bad if word gets around that the king found him in the queen's chamber. To pacify her, he promises to have the boy killed abroad, but he is lying. Statements regarding nature and nurture, now applied to a woman disguised as a man, go beyond social convention to ask what is really natural. But this last point needs to be discussed separately.

The chaste female in male dress who does not reveal her sex recalls many popular accounts of holy virgins, saints and martyrs. The "lives" of saints Marina and Eugenia are particularly relevant: both are blameless, as opposed to the "reformed prostitute" type, and both are accused of crimes that, given their sex, they could not have committed.[6] Marina, whose father disguised her sex, is raised in his monastery as the monk Marinus and accused of fathering a child; her sex is discovered only after her death. Eugenia runs away to a monastery, becomes abbot, is accused of adultery, comes before the judge, who is her father, rends her garments to show she is a woman, converts her father and is eventually martyred. Saints Apollinaris, Euphrosyne, Pelagia, and Theodora are other examples of disguised females. And as Bloch (1987) suggests, the life of the male saint Alexis, son of Euphemian, may have influenced the names of characters as well as provided another example of disguise. Again, however, the contrast is striking: Silence's reward for her loyalty, purity and perseverance is an all-too-earthly crown.

---

[6] For this and related motifs, see Stith Thompson, *Motif-Index*, e.g., K 2113 (princess disguised as man accused of illicit relations with Queen); K 1837 (disguising of women in men's clothes); also K 310, 514, 1321, 1836.

As for the theme of girl as minstrel,[7] Thorpe suggested (1972, 33) that the idea came from Geoffrey of Monmouth (IX:1), where the Saxon leader Badulf, defeated by Cador, enters York dressed as a minstrel. This is certainly possible, since many other details seem to come from these few pages concerning Cador; yet the closest parallel is Nicolete, who dyes her face, disguises herself as male minstrel, and seeks passage on a ship. There is also Tharsia, daughter of Apollonius of Tyre (Tarsiana *la juglaresca* in the thirteenth-century Spanish version, the *Libro de Apolonio*), who saves her chastity by persuasive speech and by performing as a street musician, whose father thinks she is dead and with whom there is a moving scene of recognition. And when she tells her brothel-keeper, "studiis liberalibus erudita sum et in genere musicali possum modulari. Duc me in forum!" (Singer 1895, 93 [the *Gesta Romanorum* version]), she is, as it were, a combination of Euphemie and Silence. Like the people of Cornwall, all come running to hear the gifted musician (omnis populus cucurrit ad virginem videndam). The Spanish version includes a good deal of verbal play with the contrast of speech and silence. Yet Silence acts out of loyalty and devotion to family, not romantic love or the need to preserve her maidenly virtue. And she experiences intense inner conflict between her womanhood and her male upbringing.

Nature and Nurture

Nature appears frequently in Old French romance as creator of the most beautiful girl in the world (for example, Gelzer 1917, Malkiel 1977, Lasry 1985). As such, and so she first appears in *Silence*, she is clearly a trivialized version of the goddess Nature in Alain de Lille's *Anticlaudianus*, the *vicaria Dei*, *artifex* and arbiter of morals who wants to create the perfect human being. And when she appears to complain and nag Silence about the perversion of her work, she is an obvious parody of Alain's heroine in *De planctu Naturae*, who laments the unnatural behavior of humans and the degeneration of the world. Nature, as *procreatrix*, abhors the transvestite: misuse of the organs of generation threatens the survival of the species. "The association of sophistry and sodomy which lies at the core of Alain's thought" (Bloch 1987, 86) pervades Heldris's witty and sophisticated play with linguistic forms and sexual perversion.

---

[7] The article by Rokseth (1935), despite its title, is disappointing in general and does not mention Silence.

"Nature passe noreture" (and, rarely, the contrary) is a common Old French proverb (Gelzer 1917, 56; cf. Tobler-Lommatzsch 6,2:807–8, *norreture*); for example:

> Et par tant, ce dist l'escripture
> Nature passe nourreture.
> Voirs est, nourreture vilaine
> Souvent bonne nature amaine
> A ordure et a vilenie,
> Dont ele est destruite et hounie.
> Et si revoit on le contraire.[8]

> (And thus, as Scripture says,
> does nature surpass nurture.
> It is true that a bad upbringing
> often leads a good nature astray
> into vileness and base conduct,
> by which it is dishonored and destroyed.
> And one also sees the opposite.)

Herbert says of Lucemien (*Dolopathos* 1367–78):

> Moult fu de bone norreture
> Et de bon sens fu par nature;
> Par lui se semont et esmuet
> Li biens qui de nature muet;
> Li hons puet a peine endurer
> Qu'on li puist desnaturer;
> Nature sormonte et trespasse
> Tout ce ke norreture amasse,
> Et quant la bonne norreture
> S'aconpaigne a bone nature
> Dont est bone la conpaignie;
> Li uns biens fet a l'autre aie.

> (He had a very good upbringing
> and was intelligent and prudent by nature;
> environment arouses and stimulates
> natural endowments;
> the human being can scarcely

---

[8] Tobler-Lommatzsch 6,2:808 cites A. Scheler, ed. *Dits et contes de Baudoin de Conde et de son fils Jean de Conde*, Brussels 1836, 2:264,83.

be dis-natured;
nature overcomes and surmounts
everything that nurture can mass against it,
and when a good upbringing
is harmoniously combined
with good character,
one good reinforces the other.)

Another formulation, "Nature et noreture mainent grant tencon" (Gelzer 1917, 57), is lively personification bordering on more. It seems to have been Heldris's original idea to allegorize this tension into a lively debate. But beyond that, the author is asking a much more profound and difficult question than which counts more, heredity or environment: what is "natural" and what is acquired male or female behavior? With exquisite irony, Heldris has Nature employ deviant speech (sophistry) and argue precisely from a conventional view of what is natural in both her major and minor debate with Nurture, as well as in lesser textual skirmishes. In the major debate (2500–64), Nature tells Silence that sex determines one's social role: give up romping in the woods (it's bad for the complexion); go to a chamber and learn to sew. Nurture wins with the help of Reason, a personification of Silence's inner voice, who demonstrates that no one in their right mind would choose to live as a woman. Masculinity means freedom of movement, having a voice, being on top. Silence concludes, "I'm on top; why should I step down?" (2641). In the second debate (5996–6090), Nature argues that man is naturally carnivorous, and wins when Merlin abandons nuts and roots for a large roast of prime rib. But if Nature is arguing in terms of acquired characteristics, that is, environmental determinism, Nurture's argument is perverse as well: she claims to be able to dis-nature people permanently, to change supposedly innate characteristics through remedial training. Each blames the other for Adam's fall (note that Eve's guilt is underplayed here). Nature triumphs by means of a theological argument: God created man entirely good; snake and apple were environmental factors. In contrast to their sophistry, a key authorial intrusion (2295–2342) argues that one's true nature is one's moral nature (the heart). Innate proclivity for evil can be only temporarily and superficially modified by Nurture for the good, but her capacity for harm is enormous. The harm done to a good nature by even a small amount of bad upbringing far outweighs the good that any amount of good upbringing can impose upon a bad nature. This lays the foundation for the provocative statements with which the author concludes the poem: women who do bad things are less culpable than men; given their circumstances, it is a wonder there are any good women at all. Woman's upbringing gives her no motivation to be good — indeed, she rarely has a chance to choose.

Euphemism and Silence

Whatever the constellation of female characters may owe to the *Eneas*, it is Heldris who wittily and tellingly makes them into figures of speech. And whatever the equation of grammatical and sexual deviation may owe to Alain de Lille, only Heldris raises such profound questions, predicated on the primary opposition of speech and silence, concerning women's voice and men's discourse, women's place in or absence from the social contract, whether verbal, economic or political — matters that the modern reader might reasonably expect to find expressed so explicitly and with such emphasis on linguistic play in French feminist criticism of the 1970s rather than in a medieval romance. To be sure, the question of women's speech and silence is a commonplace of medieval literature but mainly in misogynistic utterances, and the moral issues raised by Enide's silence in *Erec* are quite different (Roloff 1973, Ruberg 1978, McConeghy 1987).[9]

The women's names are examples of liminal language with a not-so-subliminal message.[10] Eufeme ("Alas! Woman!") represents the female as socially defined: the object of male lust and male barter, with no voice in determining her fate. Her body ends a war. Her name hardly conceals *feme*; she embodies all the negative stereotypes traditionally associated with her sex: she is lustful, scheming, disloyal, and vengeful; she speaks only to deceive. Eufemie ("use of good speech") is also defined by convention: as typical romance heroine, she sustains the linguistic and ideological code of courtly ideals. Despite the medieval equivalent of the best private schools, Ph.D. and M.D., she, too, is defined by desire. To be sure, hers is a reciprocated *grande passion* for an eminently suitable beloved, rather than the crude and undiscriminating sexuality of Eufeme. She makes good use of her powers of speech to communicate with Cador until the language of the body can take over. But if she is the initiator of dialogue before her marriage, she speaks only to acquiesce

---

[9] Briefly, Enide has failed to speak out of fear: her atonement consists in being forbidden to speak and having to find the courage to break silence when appropriate. A wife must demonstrate not blind obedience but sound judgment; she must act not out of fear, but love. Good marriage is a partnership. This is a laudable position (very much like Cador's in *Silence*), particularly in contrast to the wife-beating of Oringles. *Erec's* stress on the need for integration of public and private spheres and also its essentially conservative if positive view of woman's place are typical of courtly romance.

[10] In contrast, the men's names, except for some obvious Arthurian associations, seem to yield no particular significance for this text. Cador is of course prominent in the Arthurian material; besides slaying the Saxon leader, he raises Guinevere at his court. Evan's name may have been inspired by that of King Evrain in *Erec et Enide*. I suggest that the names Renaut and Beghes are simply lifted from the *Quatre Fils Aymon*, where Renaut de Montauban defeats "Beges li Sarrazin" (note the reference to Aimon, lines 5892–94). Thorpe tried unsuccessfully to trace Silence's three French knights with convincingly realistic names. Gelzer (1927, 98) notes that the form 'Fortigierne' for Vortigern otherwise occurs only in the English *Arthour and Merlin*.

afterwards. Good speech, temporarily denied Cador by the torments of love, is now his characteristic, while the brilliant and articulate Eufemie is reduced to a silent spouse, subsumed under Cador's identity ("the countess, his wife"). Only one letter separates one euphemism from the other, "bad" *femme* from ideal *femme*; in fact, Eufeme is once called Eufemie for the sake of rhyme (5206), but also to indicate their interchangeability.

Euphemia/Euphemism gives birth to Silence, who transcends both real-life role and literary convention, whose naming and upbringing challenge the very foundations of the social order: by engaging in deviant naming, her parents subvert the cultural procedure that normally assures propriety and property: the naming by the father of the male with a name signifying male. She is a live metaphor that opens up revolutionary possibilities for the redefinition of male and female. As human metaphor, Silence experiences a semantic and personal clash within herself at puberty, the time in life when the human being becomes aware of sexuality and of the possibilities of metaphorical language — a double loss of innocence that precipitates the perverse debate between heredity and environment.

The narrator engages in highly complex play with the rhetorical possibilities and social implications of the "boy" named Silence, not the least of which is the consistent use of grammatical inconsistency: masculine pronouns to refer to a being we know to be female. The text itself thus interferes with the functioning of language as a code that upholds conventional distinctions, constantly challenges the legitimacy of social classification by gender. As linguistic counterpart to Silence's transvestism, this usage exposes a supposedly essential, natural distinction as one of social role-playing. Heldris's punning on -*us* and *us* usage (noted by Gelzer 1917, Bloch 1986) emphasizes that societal norms are masculine. The play with Silentius/Silentia demonstrates that woman cannot be seen as a minus of man: the root is the same, the endings are grammatically (if not socially) equi-valent. This indicates an unsettling proximity, the possiblity of a unity so fundamental that the metaphor will collapse. When male and female are reduced to an arbitrary gender distinction marked by minute grammatical suffixes, what does a minute difference in the genitalia signify? The narrator plays with these questions most explicitly in lines 2476–79:

> Il a us d'ome tant use,
> Et cel de feme refuse,
> Que poi en falt que il n'est malles.
> Quanque on en voit est trestot malles.

> (He was so used to men's usage
> and had so rejected women's ways
> that little was lacking for him to be a man.
> Whatever one could see was certainly male!)

By revealing that relations between the sexes are based on masking, the author has undercut the surface contrast between Silence and Eufeme as heroine and villainess before their ultimate confrontation. The king's praise of Silence as a "good woman" (6631–34) and his patriarchal admonition to Eufeme, "a woman should keep silent" (6398), are equally distasteful. If a good woman is hard to find, the reason lies in convention, not in the innate wickedness of the female sex—nurture, not nature.[11]

Merlin's Laughter

In reality, Silence has proved that a woman can hold her tongue; figuratively, she is speaking loudly: Silence as *sprechender Name* evokes the idea of woman. It evokes popular and clerical "wisdom" regarding women (they have no right to a public voice / the last thing they ever are is silent). Silence herself is a refutation of this tradition, a statement concerning women's very real silence: their exclusion from language and culture. She has unmasked the problem of women's silence in a man's world. The contrast between the opening up of revolutionary possibilities and the narrative closure (justice is done, evil queen and lover are executed, girl gets king), which sustains the conventions of romance, is deeply disturbing.

Weary of trifling with mortal fools, bored with his roles of friendly helper and buffoon, Merlin takes command of the story. Under the control of the great magician, supreme trickster and shapeshifter, the denouement takes the ironic form of tricheur / euse triché(e). Merlin, in *Silence* as elsewhere, "knows very well how the story will turn out" (6160). Here as elsewhere, he is, as Bloch has so incisively put it, the "spoiler of family fictions" (1983, 213). In one sense, Eufeme has the last laugh, as Silence states in her final interior monologue (6457–60):

> I thought I was tricking Merlin,
> but I tricked myself. I thought
> to abandon woman's ways forever,
> but Eufeme has ruined any chance of that.

Yet Merlin laughs more than anyone,[12] and he has the last laugh after all.

---

[11] As Natalie Zemon Davis has noted, "defects of the males were [traditionally] thought to stem not so much from nature as from nurture," whereas "female disorderliness" went back to the Garden of Eden (1975, 124).

[12] The incidents of laughter on the way to court (peasant, leper, burial) are traditional; cf., e.g., Paton (1907), Gelzer (1927), Lecoy (1978).

At the close of his *Etymologies and Genealogies*, Bloch says that medieval romance

> serves as a virtual guidebook, a manual of instruction for the integration of the hidden self within the public sphere. The romance hero is precisely he who, having lived through a series of internal crises, either achieves — like Erec, Yvain, Cliges — a balance between personal desire and social necessity, or who — like Tristan — is excluded from society altogether. . .Medieval poetry served to found a vision of man that will for centuries to come inform his notion of of what he is and govern his rapport with others. (1983, 226)

But if this serves as a good working definition of standard romances, one must ask how it applies to *Silence*. The story of the woman called Silence offers no solution, despite the narrative resolution. We are left with Merlin's mocking laughter.

Note on the Text and Translation

The only extant copy of *Silence* is contained in folios 188 recto to 223 recto of what is now MS. Mi.LM.6 of the University of Nottingham. Because the manuscript has been thoroughly described by Thorpe in the introduction to his edition, I will briefly summarize here. Before it ended up forgotten in its box, the manuscript may have been copied for a noble lady, Beatrice de Gavre, on the occasion of her marriage to Guy IX de Laval, ca. 1286 (Cowper 1959, 6). It undoubtedly fell into the hands of the English during the Hundred Years' War, when town and castle were sacked in 1428. It ended up as the property of Lord Middleton at Wollaton Hall, where W. H. Stevenson discovered it. The text of *Silence* seems to be the work of a single, rather careless scribe. There are fourteen endearingly clumsy miniatures, eleven of which appear to be the work of one artist. The language, a mixture of francien and picard, includes several unusual vocabulary items.[13]

Lewis Thorpe must be congratulated for being the first to have undertaken and accomplished the challenging task of editing the unique manuscript of *Silence*. However, like most pioneer efforts, his work stands in need of considerable revision. It is particularly marred by faulty morpheme boundaries and an inadequate and frequently fanciful glossary. I have corrected Thorpe's printed

---

[13] Lecoy (1978) has listed most of them. Several are not in Godefroy or Tobler-Lommatzsch, e.g., *fural* 5946 "flint." In the same line, *esce*, "tinder," is not in Godefroy. Both are wrong in Thorpe, who glossed the first as "tinder" and failed to recognize the second. Markedly picard are, e.g., *agaise* 5889, *fordine* 790, *pire* 3332, *tercuel* 1822.

text on the basis of a careful comparison with the original manuscript, considered and adopted most of Lecoy's suggestions (1978), and in several cases made my own emendations. In certain instances, my examination of the manuscript itself, in good light and with a magnifying glass, yielded a different reading from that of Lecoy, who relied on a photocopy. I have also adopted several of the astute suggestions made by Prof. Iker-Gittleman of Vassar College, to whom I am very much indebted. Undoubtedly, many problems remain. If, after listing thirteen pages of corrections, Lecoy could say that "the text still offers a good number of difficulties likely to tax the reader's wits," I offer this assessment as a plea for leniency in my own case.

In rendering the text into modern English, I aimed at a reasonably literal version. Three stylistic peculiarities of Old French are particularly challenging: the frequent repetition with variation characteristic of poetry intended for oral recitation, and the syntactic independence and verbal sparseness of the brief poetic line. Because Old French lines generally stand on their own, with relatively rare and sometimes, to the modern reader, baffling use of subordinating conjunctions, the sequence of lines — and thoughts — within a given passage can be determined not so much by logic as by exigencies of rhyme, the use of repetition, or intellectual and aesthetic delight in deliberate interference with, or suspension or interlacing of, ideas. I have on occasion felt it necessary to take liberties with the sequence of phrase or line and to supply subordination. The individual Old French phrase is notoriously spare: this native elegance can sometimes fall flat or cause mystification if rendered literally; yet, on the other hand, expansion or qualification can destroy ambiguity. It is precisely for these reasons that I find a bilingual format so important.

Silence

A THIRTEENTH-CENTURY FRENCH ROMANCE

[M]aistres Heldris de Cornuälle
Escrist ces viers trestolt a talle.*
A çals quis unt conmande et rueve,
El conmencier dé suns qu'il trouve,
Que cil quis avra ains les arge   5
Que il a tels gens les esparge
Que,* quant il oënt un bon conte,
Ne sevent preu a quoi il monte.
Ne violt qu'espars soiënt par gent
Qui proisent mains honor d'argent,   10
N'a gent qui tolt voellent oïr
Que si n'ont soing c'om puist joïr
De gueredon qu'il voellent rendre.
Uns clers poroit lonc tans aprendre
Por rime trover et por viers,   15
Tant par est cis siecles diviers
Qu'ançois poroit rime trover
Qui peüst en cest mont trover
Blos solement un sol princhier
U il peüst sol tant pinchier   20
Dont il eüst salve sa paine,
Ne le traval d'une sesmaine.
Volés esprover gent avere?
Servés le bien, come vo pere:
Dont serés vus li bien venus,   25
Bons menestreus bien recheüs.
Mais, puis qu'il venra al rover,
Savés que i porés trover?
Bien laide chiere et une enfrume,
Car c'end est tols jors la costume.   30
Avere gent, honi et las,
Ja n'est cis siecles c'uns trespas.
Vos le paravés desjué
Q'or n'i a mais ris ne jué,
Que vos en vivrés mains assés   35
Quant vos, caitif, tant amassés.
Jo n'ai preu dit, car n'est pas vivre
D'avere gent, car tolt sont ivre,

2

Master Heldris of Cornwall
is writing these verses strictly to measure.
As for those who possess them, he commands and requests,
right here at the beginning of the work he is creating,
that anyone who has them should burn them   5
rather than share them with the kind of people
who don't know a good story
when they hear one.
He does not wish to have his verses circulated
among those who prize money more than honor,   10
or among people who want to hear everything
but do not care to make a man happy
with some reward they might wish to give.
A learned man might study long
to fashion rhyme and verse,   15
but things are so bad in these times
that it's a lot easier to write poetry
than to find in this world
one single solitary prince
from whom he might pinch   20
even so little that he might have saved himself the trouble—
not a week's wages.
Do you want to see how stingy people are?
Serve them well, as if they were your father:
then you will be most welcome,   25
judged a fine minstrel, well-received.
But when the time comes to ask for something,
do you know what you will find?
Very bad cheer and a sour face,
that's what you'll always get from them.   30
You greedy, nasty, petty people,
this world is but a transitory place:
you have so robbed it of all pleasure
that there is no play or laughter any more.
You'll profit far less from it   35
while you pile up riches, you fools.
No, I haven't got it right—you can't call that living,
what stingy folk do; they are all drunk,

Que, enbevré en Avarisse,
Qui est lor dame et lor norice,   40
Honor lor est si esloignie
Que il n'en ont une puignie. /
Doner, joster et tornoier,
Mances porter et dosnoier
Ont torné en fiens entasser;   45
Car qui violt avoir amasser,
Quant il n'en ist honors ne biens?
Assés valt certes mains que fiens.
Li fiens encrassce vials la terre,
Mais li avoirs c'on entreserre   50
Honist celui ki l'i entasse.
S'il a .m. mars en une masse
Trestolt icho tient il a nient,
Et neporquant perdre le crient;
Et om qui crient n'est pas a ase,   55
Ains vit a dol et a mesaase.
Li avoirs fait l'ome lanier,
Et sans preu faire travellier.
Il ne fait el fors soi sollier.
Si ne croit mie sa mollier: 60
Il n'a cure qu'ele le balle,
Car s'i faloit une maälle
Dont avroit il desparellié
Les .m. mars por cui a villié.
Ne sai que dire des haïs   65
Por cui cis siecles est traïs—
De honte ont mais lor cort enclose.
Chi n'a mestier metre de glose,
Car jo n'i fas nule sofime.
Jal savés vus tres bien meïsme: 70
Losenge est mais en cort oïe,
Amee i est et conjoïe.
Ens el prologhe de ma rime
Grans volentés me point et lime.
Il me prent moult grans maltalens   75
Qu'a force se honist la gens.
Ainz que jo m'uevre vus conmence,
M'estuet un petit que jo tence
Por moi deduire en bien penser,
Car jo me voel tost desivrer,   80
Que quant venra al conte dire

intoxicated with Avarice,
their sovereign lady and wet nurse.   40
Honor is so scarce with them
that they haven't a fistful of it.
Generosity, jousting and tourneying,
wearing ladies' sleeves and making love
have turned to heaping up mounds of dung.   45
What good does it do one to pile up wealth
if no good or honor issues from it?
Assets are worth much less than manure:
at least dung enriches the soil,
but the wealth that is locked away   50
is a disgrace to the man who hoards it.
If a man amasses a thousand marks,
he soon thinks this is nothing,
and yet he's afraid of losing it.
And a man afraid is not at peace,   55
he is miserable and ill at ease.
Wealth only makes a man mean-spirited
and makes him toil without profit.
All he does is soil himself.
He doesn't trust his wife any more: 60
he doesn't want her to spend any of it,
for one missing penny
would mar the perfection of
those thousand marks he lost sleep over.
I don't know what to say of those hateful men   65
who thus abuse this earthly life —
thye have enclosed their courts with shame forever.
There's no need to supply a gloss for this,
for I don't deal in sophistry.
Indeed, you yourselves know very well   70
that False Praise is preferred at court,
she is cherished and enjoyed there.
In this prologue to my poem
I feel tremendously compelled, stung, goaded [into talking
    about this].
It bothers me terribly   75
that people are driven to disgrace themselves.
Before I begin my story for you,
I really have to let it all out a little
in order to get into the proper frame of mind.
I want to get it all out of my system beforehand,   80
so that when it's time to tell the tale,

N'ait en moi rien qui m'uevre enpire.
Or dirai donques ma gorgie.
Mar fust la morjoie* ainc forgie
Dont sont honi tant roi, tant conte,   85
Tant chevalier, n'en sai le conte.
Avere gent! ahi! ahi!
Par Avarisse estes traï!
Lassciés ester et dites fi,
U, se cho non, jo vos desfi. /   90
Formens valt miols de gargherie,
Et rosse miols de margerie,
Et l'ostoirs de falcon muier,
Et li falcons miols del bruhier,
Et bons vins miols d'aigue awapie,   95
Et li butors miols de la pie:
Autant valt povertés honeste
Miols de .m. mars sans joie et feste,
Et volentés gentils et france
Qu'avers a iestre et rois de France.   100
Ausi valt miols honors de honte.
Dé or revenrai a mon conte
De mon prologhe faire point,
Car moult grans volentés me point
De muevre rime et conmencier,   105
Sans noise faire, et sans tenchier.

Ebans fu ja rois d'Engletiere,
Si maintint bien en pais la terre.
Fors solement le roi Artu
N'i ot ainc rien de sa vertu   110
Ens el roiame des Englois.
Li siens conmans n'ert pas jenglois,
Car n'avoit home ens el roiame,
De Wincestre trosqu'a Durame,
S'il osast son conmant enfraindre   115
Nel fesist en sa cartre enpaindre,
Par tel covant n'a droit n'a tort
N'en issist point trosqu'a la mort.
Il ot justice en sa ballie;
La soie gens n'ert pas fallie.   120
Il maintenoit chevalerie,
Si sostenoit bachelerie
Nient par falose mais par dons.
Par lor service et en pardons

there'll be nothing left in me to spoil the telling.
So now I'm going to get it off my chest!
Cursed be the day the strongbox was ever forged,
for which so many kings and counts   85
have disgraced themselves I can't keep count.
O greedy people, alas! alas!
You are betrayed by Avarice!
Let her be and say fie upon her,
for if you don't, I will defy you.   90
Just as wheat is worth more than weeds,
and rose worth more than daisy,
and goshawk more than molted falcon,
and falcon more than buzzard,
and good wine more than stagnant water,   95
and bittern more than magpie,
so honest poverty is of greater worth
than a thousand marks without joy and festivity,
and it's better to be gracious and frank
than to be stingy and King of France.   100
Just so is honor worth more than shame.
Now I will return to my tale
and end my prologue at this point,
for I feel a tremendous urge
to begin to tell my story   105
without a lot of fuss and bother.

Once upon a time Evan was king of England.
He maintained peace in his land;
with the sole exeption of King Arthur,
there never was his equal   110
in the land of the English.
His rules were not just idle talk—
there wasn't a man in his kingdom,
from Winchester to Durham,
whom he wouldn't have thrown in jail   115
if he dared to break his law,
on such terms that, right or wrong,
he wouldn't get out till he was dead.
He upheld justice in his realm;
his people were no criminals.   120
He maintained chivalry
and sustained young warriors
by gifts, not empty promises.
For their service and gratuitously

Lor dona il tols jors assés.   125
N'ert pas de bien faire lassés:
Son cho qu'il erent de valoir
Les honera et dona loir.
Del sien lor donoit liëment
Et moult apparelliëment;   130
Car cho doit cascuns prodom faire:
*Doner et garder** cui retraire.
Si violt doner moult liëment,
Car ki done derriänment
Il n'i a gré, ains piert son don   135
Et plus avoec, son los, son non:
Si venroit il miols escondire,
Mais en prodome n'a que dire./

Moult ot prodome en roi Ebain
Ki ot les Englois en se main.   140
Il ensauça tols ses amis.
A grant anor si les a mis
Et quant cho vint al grant besoing
Sel misent moult bien fors del soing.
Cho parut moult bien al roi Bege   145
Ki tint la tiere de Norwege.*
De lui et del roi d'Engletiere
Dura moult longes une guerre,
Et sorst par petite oquoison.
Puis en arst on mainte maison,   150
Tante vile en fu mise en flamme,
Et colpé tant pié, tante hance,
Et tante gens caitive esparse
Dont la contreë en est arse
Que nel vos puis demi conter.   155
Li mals se prist si a monter
Que Norouege en fu priés gaste,
Atainte de fain et de laste.
Et morte en fu la gens menue
Et li autre priés confundue   160
Quant des prodomes li plus sage
Esgarderent un mariäge
D'Ebain, qu'il ont trové felon,
Et de la fille al roi Begon.
La fille Beghe ot non Enfeme: 165
El mont n'avoit plus biele gemme.
Dient [al roi] qu'ont esgardé.

8

he gave them plenty every day. 125
He never tired of doing the right thing.
Aside from any question of their worth,
he honored them and gave them gifts.
He gave freely and unstintingly
of his possessions, 130
and that is what every wise man should do:
give and be careful about taking things back.
He must be willing to give gladly,
for he who hesitates to give
receives no thanks; on the contrary, he loses his gift 135
and more than that — his fame and reputation:
he would do better to refuse.
But a wise man is above reproach.

This King Evan who ruled over the English
was a very wise man indeed. 140
He enriched all his friends
and placed them in positions of great honor,
so that when the hour of greatest need came,
they got him out of any trouble.
This was quite clear to King Begon,* 145
who held the realm of Norway.
Between him and the king of England
a war had lasted a very long time.
It began over something trivial;
then many houses were set on fire, 150
and so many cities were put to the torch,
and so many feet and haunches sliced,
and so many people wretchedly scattered,
that the country was so devastated
I can't tell you the half of it. 155
The damage began to mount up so
that Norway was nearly destroyed,
afflicted with hunger and misery.
The lower classes had died of it,
and the others were almost finished off, 160
when the wisest of the counselors
thought of arranging a marriage
between Evan, whom they had found a dreadful foe,
and the daughter of King Begon.
Begon's daughter was named Eufeme: 165
the world never held such a beautiful gem.
They told the king what they had in mind.

9

Il lor respont: "Segnor, par Dé,
Par vostre consel li donrai,
Ma fille; et si l'en somonrai,   170
Por acorde et por aliänce,
Qe la pais soië a fiänce."

Rois Beghes fait Ebain savoir
S'il violt qu'il puet sa fille avoir
Por acordance de la guerre,   175
Et qu'il ait mis en pais la terre.
Quant il l'entent, si est haitiés.
Respont as més com afaitiés:
"Or ai ge moult bien guerriié
Et bien mon traval emploié   180
Se jo a feme puis avoir;
Il n'a el mont si chier avoir,
Que jo tant aim et tant desir
Par us d'eglise od li gesir.
Piece a l'amors de li me poinst."   185
Dient si home: "Dex le doinst/
Qu'encor l'aiés en vo saisine,
Car moult est franche la mescine."
"Et voire soi," cho dist Ebains,
"Ne ruis el mont ne plus ne mains."   190

Li rois ne s'est pas atargiés.
Ses briés a ses cor*l*ius* cargiés.
Envoie por .ii. archevesques,
Por son clergié, por ses evesques;
Mande barons, contes palais,   195
Car il ne finera jamais
S'ara esposé la puciele
Dont a oïe la noviele.
Il fait apparellier ses nés,
Ses mas, ses sigles et ses trés;   200
Et mettre i fait et amasser
Quanqu'est mestiers por mer passer,
Que quant cil venront que il mande
Es nés truissent preste viände.
Atant s'i vienent li mandé,   205
Car li rois l'avoit comandé.
Et quant il furent tolt emsanble,
Li rois lor dist cho que lui samble
Qu'a mollier prendra la Noroise.

10

He replied to them, "Lords, by God,
I'll follow your advice and give him my daughter,
and I will tell him I'm ready to do so,   170
in exchange for accord and alliance,
so that peace may be guaranteed."

King Begon let King Evan know
that he could have his daughter if he wished,
on condition that he end the war   175
and leave the land in peace.
When Evan heard this, he was overjoyed,
and replied to the messengers like the well-bred man he was,
"Now I have fought a good fight indeed:
it was well worth the hard work   180
if I can have this woman to wife,
for there is no greater treasure on earth;
I want and desire above all
to wed her and bed her properly.
I have suffered long for love of her."   185
His men said, "May God grant
that you get possession of her,
for the girl comes from a very good family."
"And may it be so," said Evan,
"That is the only thing in the world I want."   190

The king didn't delay.
He charged his messengers with letters.
He sent for two archbishops,
for his clergy, for his bishops;
he sent for barons, counts of the palace,   195
for he would never be at rest
until he married the girl
he has had such welcome news of.
He had his ships made ready,
masts and sails and spars,   200
and had collected and placed there
whatever was needed for an ocean voyage,
so that when those he had summoned arrived,
they would find provisions ready aboard the ships.
Then those whom the king had summoned came,   205
for he had so commanded.
And when they were all assembled,
the king told then he was planning
to marry the Norwegian princess.

Il n'i a celui cui en poise, 210
Qu'avoir en cuident grant redos
Et de la guerre estre en repos
Ains dient: "Sire, bien sarons
Ains .xv. dis se nos l'arons."
"Vostre merchi," li rois a dit. 215
"Vos en avrés moult grant porfit.
Apparelliés vos donc en oire,
Car bien matin tenrés vostre oire.
Atornés vos endementiers."
Cil li respondent: "Volentiers." 220

Al matinet .ii. archevesque
Entrent es nés et .iiii. evesque,
.ii. duc avoec et .iiii. conte.
Que valt, segnor, d'aslongier conte?
Li maronier en mer s'espagnent, 225
Et de l'esploitier ne se fangnent.
Tant font qu'il vienent e[n] Norwege.
Contre aus al port fu li rois Bege
Et sa fille Enfeme lor carge,
C'onques plus longe n'i atarge. 230
Cil prendent la fille al Norois
Et maint cheval avoec morois,
Et ors et ostoirs et lyons.
Ne sai que plus vos en dions. /
Cange li vens, si s'en retornent, 235
C'onques plus longes n'i sojornent.
En Engletiere prendent port.
Li rois Ebains n'a nient de tort
De cho qu'il vint contre sa drue.
Quant il le vit, gent le salue; 240
Cele li rent moult biel salu,
Cho a le roi moult bien valu.
Li rois demeure a li baisier
Et puis sil fait bien aäsier,
Car son cuer ot un poi amer 245
De la lasté et de la mer.
Tier jor apriés l'a esposee,
Car forment l'avoit golosee.
Noces i ot grans et plenieres
Od més et daintiés de manieres, 250
Ne sai que conte la despense,
Car plus i ot que nus ne pense.

12

No one was opposed to this,   210
for they thought they would have great relief
and respite from war.
And so they said, "Sire, we'll know
within two weeks whether she's ours or not."
"My thanks to you all," the king said,   215
"you shall benefit greatly from this.
So now prepare yourselves quickly,
for you shall set out early tomorrow morning.
In the meantime, get ready."
They replied, "Gladly."   220

At the crack of dawn, two archbishops
and four bishops boarded the ships,
together with two dukes and four counts.
My lords, what's the use of prolonging the story?
The sailors set out upon the sea,   225
and made every effort to make good time,
so that they arrived in Norway.
King Begon awaited them at the port
and entrusted his daughter Eufeme to them
without further delay.   230
They took the Norwegian king's daughter
and many black horses as well,
and bears and fowlers and lions, too.
I don't know what else to tell you.
As soon as the wind changed, they returned;   235
they didn't stay there any longer.
They reached the English port.
King Evan omitted none of the niceties
when he came to greet his beloved.
When he saw her, he greeted her gallantly;   240
she returned his greeting courteously,
which was most pleasing to the king.
The king lingered to kiss her
and then saw to her comfort,
for her heart was a little bitter   245
from the tiring journey across the sea.
Three days later he married her,
for he had yearned for her a long time.
The wedding was magnificent,
with all kinds of elegant and dainty dishes.   250
I don't know how much it cost—
more than anyone could imagine.

13

Les noces durent .xii. mois,
Car tels estoit adonc lor lois.
Entiere avoit adonques joie;   255
Mais li aver, cui Dex renoie,
Ont enpirie la costume.
Grans maltalens m'art et alume
Qu'il l'ont cangie et remuee.
Car fust la pute gens tuee   260
Par cui honors est abascie,
Et li plus halt [qui] l'ont lascie —
Si ne vivent mais c'un poi d'eure,
Mais li diäbles lor cort seure!
Il vivent mais que faire suelent,   265
Et por quant com plus ont plus welent.
Certes, j'en ai moult grant engagne.
Ausi est d'auls com de l'aragne:
El ordist tel,* painne et labore;
Et si se point ne voit on l'ore   270
Enmi sa toile qu'a ordi,
Si font li pusnais esdordi
Et clerc et lai et conte et duc
S'enprendre, mois ne altre buc.
Cui caut? Car trop i a a dire: 275
Repairier voel a ma matyre.
Grans fu la fieste en Engletiere.
Atant vint uns cuens en la tiere
Ki avoit .ii. filles jumieles.
.jj. conte esposent les puchieles.   280
Cho dist cascuns qu'il* a l'ainsnee;
Por quant li uns a la mainsnee./
Mellee i ot por son avoir,
Car cascuns [violt] la terre avoir.
Li uns le violt par mi partir;   285
Li altres dist qu'il iert martyr
Et vis recreäns en batalle
Ançois qu'il a plain pié i falle.
Cui caut? Li plais a tant alé
Que jor ont pris de camp malé.   290
Par l'esgart de cels del païs,
Del roi, de ses barons naïs,
A Cestre fu li jors només:
La sera li plais assomés.
Li jors fu d'ambes pars tenus,   295
Car cascuns i est bel venus.

14

The wedding festivities went on for a year:
that was the custom in those days,
they lived life to the fullest then.   255
But avaricious men — God curse them —
have spoiled the old ways.
I'm really incensed
to think they've changed things so!
I'd really like to kill the bastards   260
who have so abased honor.
And as for those of highest rank who have abandoned it —
they only live a short time anyhow,
and with the devil always on their tail at that!
They live less well than they used to,   265
and yet the more they have, the more they want.
This really makes me very angry.
It's as if they were caught by a spider:
thus she stretches her web, labors and works;
and just as one doesn't see the design   270
that she has worked into her web,
the dazzled stinking fools are trapped,
cleric and layman and count and duke,
no less than any other dupe.
What's the use? There's too much too say.   275
I want to get back to my story.
The festivities in England were magnificent.
Then a count with twin daughters
came to the land.
Two counts married the girls.   280
Each one claimed to have the older,
but one of the two must have had the younger.
There was a quarrel over the inheritance,
for both of them wanted to have the land.
One wanted to share it equally;   285
the other said he would be a martyr
and vile coward in battle
before he would yield an inch of it.
Why say more? The case went so far
that they set a date for hand-to-hand combat   290
to be judged by the nobles of the country,
the king and his native barons.
The trial was set for Chester;
there the case would be decided.
The appointed date was kept by both parties;   295
each arrived in good time.

Li rois, li baron s'entremettent
Del acorder et painne i mettent.
Mais cil s'aficent d'ambes pars,
Que niënt ne valt lor esgars.   300
Et sunt andoi par lor pechié
En la batalle si blecié
Qu'il en sunt mort par lor verté.
Ne cil ne cil ne l'*ot* reté.
Ki donc veïst duel enforcier!   305
Alquant se voelent esgrocier
Por duel des contes et ocire.
Or a li rois Ebayns grant ire.
"Ahi! ahi!" fait il. "Chaieles!
Quel duel por .ii. orphenes pucieles!   310
Que mes barons en ai perdus
J'en sui certes moult esperdus:
Mais, par le foi que doi Saint Pere,
Ja feme n'iert mais iretere
Ens el roiame s'Engletiere,   315
Por tant com j'aie a tenir tiere.
Et c'en iert ore la venjance
De ceste nostre mesestance."
L'asise fait a tols jurer
Por bien le sairement durer.   320
Alquant le font ireëment
Et li plusor moult liëment,
Qui n'en donroiënt une tille.
Mais cil qui n'a mais une fille
Et a ballier grant teneüre,   325
Cuidiés qu'il n'ait al cuer rancure?
Li rois fait les mors enterrer,
En .ii. sarqus bien enserrer.
Escrire i fait: "Par covoitise
Tolt a maint home sa francise, /   330
Et plus avoec — quant s'i amort
Troter le fait jusque a la mort."
Li rois n'i violt plus demorer.
Li vif lasscent les mors ester,
Qu'autre confort n'en puet on faire.   335
Cascuns s'en vait a son repaire.

Li rois Ebayns se part de Cestre
Et si s'en vint viers Eurincestre.
Dont ert castials, or est cités.

16

The king and his barons did their best
to arbitrate and reach an agreement,
but both parties were adamant,
so negotiations came to nothing.   300
Each one had the bad luck
to be so severely wounded in the fight
that they both died trying to prove themselves right.
Neither one nor the other could prove his claim.
Then one could see sorrow increased!   305
Some wanted to start fights and do more killing
out of grief at the counts' death.
Then King Evan flew into a terrible rage.
"Oh! Oh!" he cried, "Great heavens!
What a loss on account of two orphaned girls!   310
What a way to lose good men —
I am certainly very upset about this.
But by the faith I owe Saint Peter,
no woman shall ever inherit again
in the kingdom of England   315
as long as I reign over the land.
And this will be the penalty
for the loss we have suffered."
He had everyone swear to uphold the decree,
to confirm the validity of the oath.   320
Some did it in anger,
but most did it quite gladly —
the ones who had nothing to lose.
But as for those who had only daughters
and huge holdings to bequeath,   325
don't you think their hearts were filled with rancor?
The king had the dead men properly buried,
laid to rest in two solid tombs.
On each of them he had inscribed:
"Greed has robbed many a man of his freedom,   330
and more than that if he gets hooked —
she makes him trot till he is dead."
The king didn't want to stay any longer;
the living left the dead in peace,
since they could give them no other comfort,   335
and everyone left for home.

King Evan left Chester
and headed for Winchester.
Winchester was a castle then; now it is a city.

Forjes i a d'antiquités.   340
Illuec sojorne la roïne,
Od li mainte france mescine.
Li rois i vait grant aleüre.
Oiés mervellose aventure!
A cho qu'il passent par le bos,   345
Si vint uns serpens grans et gros
Par le foriest viers als siflant,
Et li alquant s'en vont ciflant,
Tant qu'il se fiert ens en la rote
Et point les o sa choe et tolte.*   350
Geite venim parmi la bouche:
Honist et tue quanque touche.
Li serpens vole entor a rue.
N'i a un qui estordre en pue
Se Dex quis forma nes garist.   355
L[i] rois Ebayns fort s'esmarist.
Li serpens vole tolt entor,
Et, quant il a parfait son tor,
Fu lor espant par les narines
Ki des chevals bruist les eschines.   360
Apriés le fu geite fumiere
Ki lor enconbre le lumiere,
Si qu'il ne pueënt veïr goute.
Or a li rois Ebains grant doute.
Li serpens lor en tue .xxx.   365
Li rois se trait viers une sente
Amont el bos, deviers le vent,
Por le bruïne quis soprent.
Li altre vont apriés batant,
Et li serpens remest atant: 370
Manguë les mors, sis devore.
Et li rois Ebayns plaint et plore.

Li .xxx. sunt el bos estraint,*
Et li rois a son duel estraint.
Dist a sa gent: "Quel le feron?   375
S'a tant remaint, honi seron
Se nos ensi nos en tornomes.
Mais s'il i a nul de mes homes
Ki le serpent osast requerre,
Si le peüst vaintre et conquerre,   380
Qu'en lui eüst tant de bonté,
Jo li donroie une conté:

18

There are smithies there from ancient times.   340
The queen was in residence there,
and with her many noble damsels.
The king was traveling there at top speed.
But wait till you hear the amazing thing that happened then!
While they were passing throught the woods,   345
a great big dragon came
whistling through the forest towards them.
They were ambling along, joking and chatting,
when it rushed into the midst of their company
and stung them with its tail and grabbed them.   350
It spewed forth venom from its mouth
that harmed and killed whomever it touched.
The dragon flew about in circles.
Not one of them will be able to escape
unless God who made them saves them!   355
King Evan was greatly disconcerted.
The dragon flew around and around,
and when it had finished its rounds,
it threw forth flames from its nostrils
that charred the horses' backs.   360
After the flames it breathed clouds of smoke
that hid the light from view,
so that they could scarcely see a thing.
Now King Evan was really worried.
The dragon killed thirty of his men.   365
The king headed for a path
that led above the woods, upwind,
because of the fumes that were stifling them.
The others followed him, still fighting.
Then the dragon stopped and took a break: 370
it ate the dead, gobbled them up.
And King Evan wept and lamented.

Those thirty men in the woods were done for.
The king restrained his grief somewhat
and said to his men, "What shall we do?   375
If things stay like this, we shall be disgraced
if we return home in such a state.
But if there is any man among you
who dares to take on the dragon.
and if he overcomes and kills it,   380
if he is valiant enough to do this,
I will give him a county

19

Et feme li lairai coisir
En mon roiame par loisir.   385
Ki miols li plaira, celi prengne,
Mais solement soit sans calenge."
N'i a nul ki ost mot soner,
Por quanque il promet a doner,
Por quanque il sot dire et canter,
Qui del envaïr s'ost vanter.   390
Un vallet o le roi avoit,
Cador le preu, ki moult savoit.
Il ert li plus vallans de tols,
Li plus amés et li plus prols.
Cil amoit moult une meschine   395
Ki venue ert a la roïne.
Fille ert Renalt de Cornuälle.
N'a feme el regne qui li valle.
Li cuens n'avoit enfant que li:
Tols ses païs en abeli,   400
Qu'el mont n'avoit plus bele mie,
Et si l'apielent Eufemie.
Des .vii. ars ert moult bien aprise,
D'amer Cador forment esprise.
Cil l'aime et dire ne li oze,   405
Ainz a s'amor si fort encloze
Que nuz ne l'aperçoit en lui.
Tant suefre Cador fortre anui.
Li fus sans flame bruïst plus
Que se flame en issçoit u fus: 410
Si fait amors, que li covierte
Agoisse plus que li aperte.
Amors tolt Cador l'esmaier:
Il se volra ja assaier.
Del roi se part moult bielement: 415
El bos se pert isnielement.
Un escuier qu'a plus sené
A son ceval od lui mené:
Ne violt qu'altres fors Deu le sace.
Descent el bos en une place.   420
Il fait ses armes aporter,
Qu'il ne s'en puet preu deporter.
Arme soi tost et kiolt aïr,
Car le serpent volt envaïr.
Ne violt la longes demorer;   425
Comence Deu moult a orer. /

20

and I will let him have his choice
of any woman in the kingdom.
Let him take the one he likes best,   385
except, of course, if she's already pledged."
Nobody dared to utter a word,
no matter how much he promised to give,
no matter how much he cajoled and wheedled,
nobody dared boast that he would attack it.   390
But the king had a young follower,
Cador the brave, an accomplished youth.
He was the bravest knight of all,
the best-loved and most valiant.
He was very much in love with a girl   395
who had come to serve the queen.
She was the daughter of Renald of Cornwall.
Not a woman in the realm was her equal.
She was the count's only child,
the crowning glory of his estates,   400
the most beautiful girl in the world,
and they called her Eufemie.
She was well versed in the seven arts,
and she was deeply in love with Cador,
who loved her and did not dare to say it.   405
He hid his love so deep inside
that no one could perceive it in him.
Cador suffered anguish all the more,
for fire without flame burns more fiercely
than if flame and fire issue from it.   410
That is the nature of covert love:
it hurts much worse than when out in the open.
Love took Cador's fear from him.
He would be ready to prove himself immediately.
He contrived to disappear from the king's sight   415
and vanished into the woods at once.
A squire more seasoned than most
brought him his horse:
he didn't want anyone but God to know.
He went to a certain spot in the woods,   420
and had his arms brought to him there,
for he could hardly fight without them.
At once he was armed and ready to do battle,
for he wanted to attack the dragon.
He didn't want to wait around for long.   425
He began to pray fervently to God:*

21

"Bials sire Dex, ki formas home,
Ki peça por mangier la pome;
Et del tien saint avenement
Fesis par angele anoncement;   430
Et en le Virgene te mesis,
Humanité en li presis;
Por nos, bials Sire, te bassas.
Com ains fu, virgene le lassas;
Et circoncis fus tu apriés,   435
Que Judeu font encor adiés;
Et el flum Jordan baptiziés,
Li cresmes i fu envoiés
Del ciel, tés fu ta volentés.
Puis fus el temple presentés,   440
Et geünas por nos pechiés,
Car enemis nos ot bleciés;
Des Juïs fus vilment penés,
Et en le crois a mort penés,
Car nostre lois est tels escrite   445
Que tu en as la mort eslite
Por faire satifatiön
Contre nostre dampnatiön.
Angeles nel puet faire a delivre
Car prendre, morir et puis vivre,   450
Et s'angeles eüst, bials dols sire,
Por nos sofiert en crois martyre,
(Mais jo sai bien cho ne puet estre)
Qui seroit donques nostre miestre,*
Et volroit avoir signorie   455
Sor nos et grant avoërie.
Et tu avoies dit que hom
Seroit d'altresi grant renom
Come li plus haus de tes angeles
Et qu'il seroit pers as archa[n]geles,   460
Et home et angele en un leu
T'aoërroiënt come Deu.
Por cho t'est*iu*t nos rachater,
Morir et puis resusciter:
Cho ne puet nus faire sans toi.   465
Ta vertus soit hui dedens moi!
Tolt cho fesis tu sans dotance.
Si com c'est, Sire, me creänce,
Issi me soies tu aidiere
Encontre ceste beste fiere!   470

22

"Dearest Lord God, who made mankind,
who sinned through eating the apple,
and announced your blessed coming
by means of an angel,   430
and placed yourself within the Virgin,
taking on human form in her—
for us, sweet Lord, you humbled yourself.
Virgin she was, virgin you left her;
and you were circumcized thereafter,   435
as the Jews still do today,
and baptized in the river Jordan,
for which the chrism was sent
from heaven, such was your will.
Then you were presented in the temple.   440
You did penance for our sins,
for our enemy had wounded us.
You were vilely misused by the Jews
and put to death on the cross,
for it is written in our law   445
that you elected to suffer death
to make satisfaction
for our damnation.
An angel couldn't have done it freely—
become flesh, die and live again—   450
and if an angel had, dear Lord,
suffered martyrdom on the cross for us,
(but I know this cannot be)
he would then be our master,
and would wish to have power   455
and complete dominion over us.
But you had said that man
would have such renown
as the highest of your angels
and would be equal to the archangels,   460
and man and angel would adore
you as God on equal footing.
For that reason you had to redeem us,
die and be resurrected:
no one but you could do it.   465
May your strength be within me today!
All this you did without hesitation.
As truly as this is my belief, Lord,
be my aid in like manner
against this ferocious beast.   470

23

Sainiés soie de vertu Deu!
N'est pas creänce de Judeu!"
Saut el cheval, moult bien a armes
Et prent l'escu par les enarmes. /
Çainte a l'espee ki bien talle,   475
Reciut son dart, dist: "Dex i valle!"
Li chevals saut entre les cesnes.
Il li a acorcié les resnes.
Viers le serpent vint une voie
Tolt coiëment que il ne l'oie,   480
Car ne li violt pas faire cuivre
Ainz qu'il le voïs[t] del sanc ivre.
Il voit le serpent ja si fars
De ces mors homes demis ars
Qu'il vait ja faisant un dangier   485
De boivre sanc, de car mangier.
Anchois qu'il ait Cador veü
L'a Cadors de son dart feru
Que l'une joë li desserre.
Li serpens vint Cador requere.   490
Fiert le ceval u il sist sus
Qu'il l'esboiele. Cil chiet jus
Sor le serpent, por poi nel crieve.
Et Cador d'altre part se lieve,
Recuevre en meësme l'eure.   495
Trait a le branc, se li cort seure,
Trence l'eschine par mi oltre.
Et li serpens el sanc se woltre,
Et brait et crie; et li rois l'ot,
Et dist adonc un cortois mot: 500
"Ba! Ust Cadors li amorols?
Set le, va! nus? ne *vos*, ne nols?"
Cho dist li rois: "Sainte Marie!
Com est ma gens hui esmarie!
Com ele est hui mal atornee!   505
Las! com ai fait pesme jornee!
Se Cador perc ensorquetolt,
Dont sui jo bien honis del tolt!"
L'escuiers Cador dist: "Bials sire,
Se jo le vos osoie dire,   510
Au serpent est alés, par foi,
Cador li pros, mais nient par moi."
Li rois le cheval esporone
E les resnes li abandone.

24

May I be strengthened by God's power!
This is not the creed of a Jew."
He leapt to his horse, he was well armed,
he took his shield by both its straps,
he girt his sword that strikes so well,   475
he took his lance and said, "God prevail!"
The horse leapt forward between the oaks,
he drew the reins up short.
He made his way toward the dragon
very quietly, so that it wouldn't hear him,   480
for he didn't want to attack it
until he saw it drunk with blood.
He saw the dragon already so stuffed
with those half-charred dead men
that it was already having trouble   485
drinking blood and eating flesh.
Before it caught sight of Cador,
he had struck it with his lance
so that one jowl was torn open.
The dragon came after Cador.   490
It struck the horse on which he sat
and disemboweled it. Cador fell right
near the dragon, who nearly skewered him.
But Cador got right up again
and rallied at once.   495
He drew his sword, rushed at the dragon,
and sliced its spine completely through.
The dragon weltered in its blood
and brayed and shrieked. The king heard this
and then exclaimed in a courtly manner: 500
"Oh! Where is my beloved Cador?
Who knows? No one? Nobody at all?"
(thus the king spoke) "Holy Mary!
How distraught my men are today!
How badly things have turned out for them!   505
Lord, I've had a dreadful day.
If I lose Cador on top of everything,
that will be the absolute height of misfortune."
Cador's squire said, "Good Sir,
if I may make so bold as to tell you,   510
truly, Cador the brave has gone to seek the dragon,
but it isn't my fault."
The king spurred his horse onward
and gave it free rein.

25

U soit a vivre u a morir   515
Cador verra qu'il fist norir.
Trestolt est ja fait del serpent.
Li rois est a demi arpent,
Se li escrie: "Amis! amis!
Com ceste beste vos a mis   520
A grant torment, ma gent et toi!
Ne sai que faire, las, de moi!"
Cadors l'entent et dist: "Venés,
Et vostre gent i amenés."
Li rois i vint avoec sa gent;   525
Et Cadors, qui le cors a gent,
De son serpent soivre la tieste.
Cil criement moult le morte bieste.
La tiest met en son sa lance.
Al roi a dit: "Me covenance,   530
Car li serpens est mors par moi!"
"Et vos l'arés, bials niés, par foi."

Del serpent moult grant joie funt.
La tieste o auls porté en ont.
Li rois a puis tant esploitié   535
Et tant alé et tant coitié
Que al quart jor qu'il mut de Cestre
Vint de halte hore a Herincestre.
Tuit s'esmervellent de la tieste;
Del roi et des siens font grant fieste.   540
Cadors est forment bien venus
De cho que si est contenus.
Li rois en vint a la roïne
Et Cadors vait a la mescine
Por cui amors a travellié   545
Et mainte nuit longe vellié.
Entre la roïne et le roi
Mainnent grant joie et ont de quoi.
Cador parole a Eufemie
Ki pas ne li est enemie,   550
Car se il li osast proier
Bien se lairoit amoloier.
Tost venroit a l'amor doner,
Mais n'i pensast de viloner.
El l'ainme moult, mais ne set pas.   555
Et het l'il dont de rien? Het? las!
Ja n'a il cose en nule terre

26

Whether he lives or dies,   515
he will seek Cador, whom he brought up.
The dragon was already dead.
The king was halfway down the slope.
He shouted to Cador, "My friend! My friend!
What terrible suffering this beast   520
has caused you and my men!
I don't know what to do, alas!"
Cador heard him and shouted, "Come here,
and bring your men with you."
The king came there with his men,   525
and Cador the handsome
severed the head of his dragon.
The others were very much afraid of the dead beast.
He put the head on the tip of his lance,
and said to the king, "Grant me a boon,   530
for I'm the one who killed the dragon."
"And you shall have it, dear nephew, upon my word."

All rejoiced greatly at the dragon's death.
They carried its head away with them.
Then the king made such haste   535
and traveled and pushed on so quickly
that on the fourth day after he had left Chester
he arrived in good time at Winchester.
Everyone marveled at the head.
They prepared a great feast for the king and his men.   540
Cador was given a very warm welcome
because of his valiant conduct.
The king went in to greet the queen
and Cador went to see the maiden
for whose love he had suffered so   545
and lain awake many a long night.
The king and queen are delighted,
and they have reason to be.
Cador speaks to Eufemie,
who is certainly not his enemy,   550
for if he dared to ask her,
she would let her heart be softened.
She would give herself at once,
provided that his intentions were honorable.
She loved him dearly, but he didn't know it.   555
And did he hate her at all? Hate? Alas!
There is nothing in the whole world

Qu'il amast tant, s'il l'osast quere.
Cho parut el bos de Malroi;
Et s'il nel rueve donc al roi   560
Puis qu'il puet feme prendre a chois,
Nel puet on bien tenir a mois?
Rover al roi? Ainme donc si?
La u se siet dejoste li,
Pense en son cuer que par halsage   565
Ne venra ja a mariäge;
Mais s'il s'aperçoit qu'el* l'ait chier,
Et que son cuer n'ait viers lui fier,
Et que l'amor i quist trover,
Dont le volra al roi rover./   570
Acointier le violt sans trestor
Que por s'amor sofri*t* estor;
Dont se porpense n'osera
Si tost, mais un poi soferra.

Li rois se colce quist lassés   575
Quant a mangié et but assés;
Et li pros Cador s'est colciés.
Grans mals li est al cuer tociés.
.j. petitet devant le jor
Il taint et plaint, mue color,   580
Par le venim, par le fumiere,
Que li gieta la bieste fiere.
Uns camberlens, qui a non Ades,
A dit al roi qu'il est malades.
Il n'oï noviele en l'an nule   585
Dont tant li pesast. Tost s'afulle
Et vint corant ens en la sale
Et voit Cador et taint et pale.
Quant il le vit issi ataint
D'ansdeus ses bras l'acole et çaint.   590
Fiert soi el pis, ses mains detuert,
Si a tel dol por poi ne muert.
Envoie lués por Eufemie:
El païs n'a si sage mie.
Et ele i vint moult tost en haste.   595
Ses bras manie, son pols taste,
Puis dist al roi qu'el* le garra
Ainz .xv. jors qu'il n'i parra.
"Et jo vos donrai riche don,
Amie, et moult gent gueredon."   600

28

he would love more, if only he dared to ask.
This was clear in the woods of Malroi.
And if he doesn't ask her of the king,   560
now that he has his choice of wife,
won't he look the perfect fool!
Ask her of the king? Is this how he loves her?
There, seated beside her,
he thought in his heart that such haughty behavior   565
would never persuade her to marry him.
But if he perceives that she likes him,
and that her heart is not proud toward him,
and that he might find love in there,
he will ask her of the king.   570
He wants to tell her without delay
that he is suffering terribly for love of her.
But he won't do this right away:
he still has to suffer a little, first.

The king retired, all tired out,   575
after he had eaten and drunk his fill,
and valiant Cador retired, too,
his heart afflicted with terrible pain.
A little bit before daybreak,
he moaned and groaned and changed color   580
because of the venom and the fumes
that the fierce beast had spewed at him.
A chamberlain named Ades
told the king that Cador was ill.
He never in a whole year heard news   585
that upset him more. Immediately, he got dressed
and came running into the room
and saw Cador lying there all pale and wan.
When he saw him stricken thus,
he took him and held him in his arms.   590
He beat his breast and wrung his hands,
he suffered so he nearly died.
At once he sent for Eufemie:*
she was the wisest doctor in the land.
She arrived in the greatest haste.   595
She took his arm and felt his pulse,
then she told the king she would cure him
within two weeks, so well that there would be no trace of illness.
"And I will give you a rich gift,
my friend, and a fine reward."   600

29

.iii. barons mande isnielement,
Si lor a dit moult bielement
Qu[e] en tote se regiön,
U il a mainte legiön,
N'i a prince si riche mie   605
Qu'a baron ne l'ait Eufemie
Celui que miols desire et ainme,
Por c'altres forçor droit n'i clainme,
Mais que son neveu li garisse
Que il de dol ne se marisse.   610
Cele l'en merchie et encline.
Un lit fait faire li mescine
En une des plus maistres canbres.
Li pavemens estoit fins lambres:
Selonc le cambre ert li vergiés   615
U li mie et li clergiés
Ont fait planter erbes moult chieres
Qui viertus orent de manieres. /
Bials est li viergiés les les estres.
Entre l'odors par les fenestres   620
Ki plus söef iolt de piument.
La ne gira il pas vilment.
Li lis est fais, Cador s'i colce.
Por noise faire nus n'i touce,
Ne mais li meschine et li sien;   625
Et ele le parfait si biem,
Que dedens .viii. jors par verté
L'a si gari de s'enferté
Par le grasse nostre Segnor.
Mais ele l'a mis en gregnor,   630
Car li alers et li venirs,
Li maniiers et li tenirs
Qu'ele i a fait, com a malage,
A fait l'amor en li plus sage.
Amors l'*a*siet* plus que ne siolt: 635
Com plus le voit et plus le violt,
Et el voloir de li veïr,
Puis que cho vient al voir jehir,
Sent il son cuer forment amer.
"E las!" fait il. "Vient cho d'amer,   640
Si grans mals et tels amertume?
Or est malvaise sa costume,
De primes bien et puis mal faire.
Trestolt cho fait il por atraire.

30

He quickly sent for three barons,
and announced to them most solemnly
that in his entire kingdom,
where he had legions of followers,
there was no prince so rich   605
that Eufemie couldn't have as lord and husband
the one she most desired and loved,
as long as there was no prior claim,
provided that she cure his nephew,
so that he, the king, wouldn't die of sorrow.   610
She thanked him for this and bowed low.
The girl had a bed prepared
in one of the very finest chambers.
The pavement was made of beautiful marble.
Next to the room was the garden,   615
where both physicians and clerics
had planted many precious herbs
with many healing virtues.
The garden outside the room is beautiful.
Through the windows comes the scent of perfume   620
that smells sweeter than nectar.
Cador will rest most pleasantly there!
The bed was made ready; he was placed in it.
For fear of doing him harm, no one touched him
except the girl and her own servants.   625
And she did her work so perfectly,
that within a week, truly,
she had cured him of his infirmity,
by the grace of our Lord.
But she had made him worse as well,   630
for her comings and goings,
the way she handled and held him
when he was sick,
made love for her grow stronger in him.
Love laid siege to him more than before.   635
The more he saw of her, the more he wanted to.
And from his desire to see her,
to tell the truth,
he felt his heart grow very bitter.
"Alas!" he said. "Is that what comes of love?   640
Such dreadful pain and such bitterness?
Then Love's ways are truly wicked—
first to to good and then to do evil.
All this he does to manipulate lovers.

31

Li mals que li serpens me fist   645
N'ert pas si gregnor comme cist.
Il n'ert pas honteus a veïr.
Cestui n'os jo nului jehir.
Amors m'a moult acoärdi
Viers une feme, fait hardi   650
Por emprendre grant fais por soi.
Cis mals se tient moult entor moi.
Jo li puis bien amor rover,
Mais or me poroit reprover
Son traval et sa medecine,   655
Et poroit penser la mescine
Que folie ai en li veüe,
Que por cho ruis que soit ma drue.
Ele m'a fait d'un mal delivre,
Mais d'un moult gregnor voir m'enivre,   660
Car ivres sui et esmaris
Quant jo languis, si sui garis.
Ne li os, las! amor rover,
Nel taisir ne puis bien trover.
Et puet si estre ele ot altre ami   665
Ainz qu'ele mesist painne a mi. /
Et feme rest de tel afaire,
Ne fait pas al miols que puet faire,
Sa volenté tient por raison,
De soi honir quiert oquoison.   670
Son voloir trait contre nature,
Contre raison, contre droiture:
Ne prent garde u s'amor desploie
Et puet sel estre se desroie
Que mariër puet a plaisir.   675
Mais mioldres pooirs est taisir.
Amors m'a mis en marison,
Nen ai confort de guarison."
Cador se plaint qu'Amors le grieve.
Amors que fait? .i. dart soslieve   680
Qui plus est trençans d'alemiele,
Si l'a feru sos la mamiele.
"H[e]las!" fait il, "qui si me point?"
Et Amors priés del cuer se joint
Et tant li grieve l'envaïe   685
Qu'il gient, et crie: "Aïe! aïe!"
Et en l'altre cambre par sontre
Estoit li rois illuec encontre.

The hurt the dragon gave me*   645
wasn't as serious as this;
it wasn't shameful to see.
But I don't dare reveal this one to anybody.
Love has made a mighty coward of me
before a woman, when it had given me   650
the courage to perform a mighty deed for her.
This hurt has a strong hold on me.
I could reveal my love to her,
but her efforts and her medicines
might then be a reproach to me: 655
the girl might think
that I had found her behavior unseemly,
and that I want her for my mistress.
She has saved me from one malady,
but now, truly, a much worse one poisons me,   660
for I must be drunk or mad
if I still languish now that I am cured.
Alas, I do not dare reveal my love to her,
but I don't think it's a good idea to conceal it, either.
And maybe she had another friend   665
before she started taking care of me.
Yes, that's the way a woman is:
she doesn't do the best she can,
she holds her will to be reason,
she seeks occasion to dishonor herself;   670
her will works contrary to nature,
contrary to reason and to convention.
She doesn't care where she deploys her love,
and can easily stray out of bounds
if allowed to marry where she pleases.   675
But it's better to be silent.
Love has caused me great distress;
I have no hope of being cured."
Thus Cador complained that Love was giving him grief.
And what did Love do? He took up a dart   680
sharper than a lance's point,
and struck Cador just beneath the breast.
"Alas!" he cried. "What has pierced me so?"
And then Love pressed him close to the heart,
and this attack hurt him so   685
that he moaned and cried, "Ah! ah!"
The king was close by,
in the next chamber.

33

Quant ot la vois Cador le preu
Moult tost en vint a son neveu.   690
Se li a dit: "Bials niés, qu'avés?"
"Sire," fait il, "vos ne savés?
Jo me dormoie meriane,
Si sonjai qu'ens el bos d'Ardane
Estoie alés por deporter.   695
Ne vol nule arme o moi porter,
Ne vol ne lance ne escu:
Si vi mon serpent revescu
Que jo par pieces esmiäy.
Il me chaça et jo criäy.   700
Sire, or vos ai jo dit mon songe,
Mais Dex le me tort a mençoigge."
"Bials niés, cho dist ne plus ne mains
Mais que foibles estes et vains,
Car vos avés moult wit le cief,   705
Et en dormant vient derecief
Devant tolt cho que vos fesistes
Ainz que ceste enferté presistes."
Li rois son neveu moult enorte
Qu'il se rehait et reconforte;   710
Mais ne set u li mals li tient
Ne de l'enferté qui li vient
Dont nen avra la medecine
Se Dex nel fait et la mescine/
Quil gari de l'autre enferté.   715
Volés vos oïr la verté?
Quant il parvint a l'anuitier
Adonc estut Cador luitier,
Vellier la nuit, jaindre, pener,
Qu'Amors le prent a demener,   720
Fai le fremir, suer, tranbler.
Pis que fievre li puet sambler:
Car fievre est lués de tel nature
C'om le piert sovent par froidure
U par bien durement suer;   725
Mais Amor *ne* violt remuer
Ne por grant froit, ne por calor;
Ne n'espargne home por valor,
Ne por fierté, ne por promesse.
Ne li est plus d'une contesse   730
Que d'une soie camberiere.
A Cador pert bien qu'ele est fiere.

When he heard the voice of Cador the brave,
he went to his nephew at once.   690
He said to him, "Dear nephew, what's wrong?"
"Sire," he said, "don't you know?
I was taking a noonday nap.
I dreamt I went riding
in the forest of Arden,*   695
simply for pleasure. I had no wish to wear weapons,
neither lance nor shield.
Then I saw my dragon revived—
the one I had hacked to pieces.
It was chasing me and I cried out.   700
Sire, now I have told you my dream,
but may God keep it from coming true!"
"Dear nephew, this means no more and no less
than that you are frail and weak,
for you are still very light-headed,   705
and when you sleep,
everything you did
before you got sick comes back to you."
The king exhorted his nephew
to take heart and be comforted,   710
but he didn't know where the malady had struck
or that he had succumbed to an illness
for which there is no cure
except from God and the girl
who healed him of his other hurt.   715
Do you want to hear the truth?
Every night, when it grew dark,
that's when Cador's struggle began.
He was awake all night, suffering, groaning,
for Love had seized control of him,   720
made him shiver, sweat and tremble.
It was worse than the symptoms of a fever,
for fever is such that
a man often loses it through chill
or by sweating copiously.   725
But Love refuses to give way
to extreme heat or cold;
he doesn't spare a man for valor
or yield to threats or promises.
A countess is the same to him   730
as any of her chambermaids.
Love seemed very fierce to Cador.

35

De la meschine vus voel dire.
Esté li ot en liu de mire.
Sovent rala, sovent revint   735
Por veïr com li mals li tint.
S'anchois l'ama, or l'ainme plus,
Ne mervalt ja de cho nus.
Vos avés veü bien sovent
Fus et estoppe avoec le vent   740
Vienent assés tos a esprendre
Que n'i estuet ja painne rendre.
Altretels est d'Amor l'orine.
Puis qu'ele aferme une rachine
Que puist amans nes tant doter   745
Que lor soit boin d'oïr conter
L'uns d'als a l'autre cho que fait?
Tres donques croist l'Amors a fait
Par bien la parolle asseïr,
Et par sovent entreveïr.   750
Se plus i a a volenté
Tant croist l'Amor plus a plenté,
Car puis qu'en parler ont delit
Si croist l'Amors moult de petit
Por cho que il ensanble soient.   755
Mais amant* qui ne s'entrevoient
Et forssalent que d'an en an,
N'ont mie d'assés tel ahan
Que d'iestre apriés et consirrer.
Car cho fait Eufemie irer,   760
Que cascun jor voit que desire
Et de son desir se consire. /
Ele desire qu'il seüst
Qu'ele altre ami que lui n'eüst:
Mais qu'en li tant de cuer n'a mie   765
Que die a lui qu'ele est s'amie.
Dirai jo dont qu'ele ait delit
Quant el ne fait, grant ne petit,
De quanque li siens cuers desire,
Fors lui amer sans ozer dire?   770
S'ele a delit en son amer
En la sofrance a tant d'amer
Que jo nen os nomer delit.
S'ele en a rien, cho est petit.
De la dolor qui dont le tient   775
Et de l'amor dont li sovient

Now I want to tell you about the girl
who served as his physician.
She came and went often   735
to see how the patient was doing.
If she loved him before, she loved him more now —
no one should be surprised at this!
You've seen so many times before
how embers and stubble can catch fire   740
without the slightest effort,
where there is wind.
Such is Love's origin.
As soon as he takes root,
how can lovers possibly doubt   745
that it is good for both of them
to tell each other what they are doing?
Then love grows very quickly,
through well-chosen words,
by keeping frequent company.   750
The more there is mutual consent,
the more luxuriantly love grows.
For where there is delight in speech,
love grows from very small beginnings,
as long as lovers are together.   755
But lovers who don't see each other
or arrange to meet, except from year to year,
never have enough of that sweet labor
of being close and observing each other.
As for Eufemie, she is driven wild,   760
seeing each day what she desires
and being deprived of her desire.
She desires him to know
that she would have no other lover but him,
but she doesn't have the courage   765
to tell him that she's in love with him.
Shall I say that she is happy,
when she does absolutely nothing
with regard to her heart's desire
excpet love him and not dare to say so?   770
If she finds happiness in loving,
she finds such bitterness in suffering
that I dare not call this happiness.
If she's getting any out of it, it's not much!
In the grip of sorrow,   775
thinking only of love,

37

Gemist, fremist et dist: "Caitive!
Jo ne sui morte, ne bien vive.
Par Deu, ai mainte gent sane[e],
Al daërrain sui engane[e]:   780
Car or sai tres bien par verté
Que par Cador ai l'enferté.
Trestolt l'ai par cest damoisiel.
Jel vi ersoir si gent, si biel,
Sovint moi de son vasselage,   785
Si senti plus grief mon malage.

Amors m'a mis en noncaloir,
Ars ne engiens n'i puet valoir.
Jo doins as altres medecine,
Mais moi ne valt une fordine   790
Quanque jo sai dire et canter.
Mar vi onques icest anter!
Mar fust li serpens ainc peüs!
Mar fust li venins ainc veüs,
Dont Cador fu si atornés!   795
Li mals en est sor moi tornés.
Ainmi! lasse!" dist Eufemie.
"Jo cuit qu'il a allors amie.
S'il n'eüst kiuls de feme prendre
Jo i peüsce alques atendre.   800
S'il n'eüst de feme esliçon—
Cho soit a la maleÿçon—
Li rois de droit ne me falroit.
Ne sai que rover me valdroit,
Car cho n'estroit* pas honestés   805
Por cho qu'il a avant les dés;
Car s'il me violt, avoir me puet,
U se cho non, ne li estuet.
E! Dex! com a chi grant anui!
S'il violt, n'arai ja part en lui/   810
Et il m'a, voir, sans parçonier.
Lasse! Jo vi sa façon ier.
Il ert plus bials que n'est la rose.
Ne fis jo moult estrange coze
Et n'eu jo moult le sens mari   815
Quant jo si tenpre le guari!
Car j'euc vials ains bone oquoison
D'aler sovent en la maison.

38

she moans and shudders and says, "Wretched me!
I am neither dead nor alive.
My God, I have cured many a man,
but I have been badly repaid by the last one.   780
For now I know the truth very well:
I caught this disease from Cador.
This young man is highly contagious.
I saw him last night, so gracious, so handsome;
I remembered his brave deed,   785
and felt my malady grow worse.

Love has made me incapable of action.
Neither my learning nor my native intelligence can help me.
I prescribe medicine to others,
but all my fancy accomplishments   790
aren't helping me one bit.
Damn this whole relationship!
damn that dragon (whoever raised him!),
damn the cursed venom
that made Cador so sick!   795
The curse has come upon me.
Oh my! alas!" said Eufemie.
"I think he has another love.
If he didn't have his choice of a wife,
I might have some slight hope.   800
If he couldn't have the wife of his choice—
damn that, too—
the king wouldn't fail to do me justice.
I don't know what good asking would do.
That wouldn't be fair,   805
for he has first throw of the dice.
If he wants me, he can have me,
and if not, he doesn't have to.
God, what an awful situation!
If it's his wish, I'll have no part of him,   810
but he can, if he wants, take all of me.
Alas! I saw the way he looked yesterday.
He was lovelier than a rose.
Wasn't that a crazy thing to do,
wasn't I completely out of my mind   815
to cure him so fast?
I had ample opportunity
to visit him frequently.

39

Que il langui! Mais moi que calle,
Mais qu'il guarisse et qu'il valle,   820
Por tolte ma male aventure
Qu'il sofrist longes tel ardure?"*
C'ert un petit devant le jor.
De paine traire n'a sejor.
Nue s'estent desos le lambre;   825
Et Cadors ert en l'altre cambre.
Ne puet la nuit repos avoir,
Ne son pooir ne puet savoir,
Car s'il son pooir vials seüst,
Qu'il Eufemie avoir peüst,   830
De grant dolor fust alegiés,
Et ses travals fust abregiés.
Et s'Eufemie resust* certe
Qu'il tel paine a por li sofierte,
El li feroit jo cuit dangier.   835
Mais ne* set pas qu'ains le mengier
Li volra dire sa destrece,
Com Amors le castie et blece.

Ançois que l'aube soit veüe,
S'en est la mescine meüe.   840
Viers son ami s'en violt aler,
Mais as degrés al devaler
Revient en soi meïsmes toute.
L'aler avant crient et redoute,
Blasme son cuer et sel castie   845
Et dist: "Quelle m'avés bastie!
Fel cuers, tres donc que vos creï,
Honors ne biens ne me tehi,
Mais moult grans hontes et fors blasmes,
Cuers, car me viols [tu] que tu asmes!   850
Veuls me tu avoir parhonie?
Folie m'est trop enbonie
Quant de ma cambre m'en issi
Por home a ceste hore enissi.
De honte ai aficiet mon sain.   855
Bien pert que j'ai ronpu mon frain.
Cuers, jo t'acorcerai les resnes.
Ja fus tu ja plus durs que cesnes,/
Or te lasse si amolir,
Tolte m'onoir me viols tolir.   860

40

So he would have been sick a little longer! Why should I have
    cared,
as long as he eventually recovered his health,   820
if he suffered such torment longer,
considering all my misery?"
It was a little before daybreak.
She had had no respite from her pain.
She lay naked in her ornate room,   825
and Cador was in the chamber below.
He had had no rest that night, either,
nor did he know his power;
for if he had only known
that he could have Eufemie,   830
his great sorrow would have been assuaged,
and his sufferings shortened.
And if Eufemie had known for certain
that he was suffering such pain for her,
she would have granted him all he desired, I'm sure.   835
He didn't know that before breakfast
she would tell him of her distress,*
how Love was tormenting and wounding her.

It was still before dawn
when the girl made her move.   840
She was on her way to her beloved,
but halfway down the stairs
she came to her senses.
She dreaded and feared the thought of advancing.
She blamed her heart and chastised it, saying,   845
"You really got me into a mess,
traitorous heart! Ever since I trusted you,
you have brought me nothing good or honorable,
only tremendous shame and dishonor,
heart, for you want to make my decisions for me.   850
Do you want me to be completely dishonored?
I was overcome by madness
when I left my room
at such an hour for the sake of a man.
I have transfixed my own breast with shame.   855
I'm obviously completely out of control.
Heart, I'm going to rein you in tightly.
You always used to be harder than oak,
now you've gone completely soft;
you want to strip me of all my honor.   860

41

Viuls cuers fait home aler a rage.
Miols valt hals cuers en bas parage
Que ne fait home estre balli
D'un grant roiame a cuer falli.
Viuls cuers, cho me fais tu de gré."   865
Atant se ciet sor le degré.
.ii. fois se pasme en un tenant.
Et quant puet parler, maintenant
Apiele Cador et si nome.
En tols ses mos est cil la some.   870
Cador languist, se n'i puet estre,
Et l'un et l'autre Amors adestre.
S'il voelent garison avoir
Dont covient il par estavoir
Et lui garir par la mescine   875
Et li avoir par lui mecine.
U cascuns d'als son per garra,
U la mecine n'i parra.

Li jors apert et Eufemie
Saut sus que ne s'atarja mie.   880
Vient en la cambre a son ami.
Dist li: "Amis, parlés, haymmi!"
Dire li dut: "Parlés a moi,"
Mais l'Amors li fist tel anoi
Que dire dut: "Parlés a mi,"   885
Se li a dit: "Parlés, haymmi!"
"Parlés a mi" dire li dut,
Mais "haymmi!" sor le cuer li jut.
Si tost com ele ot dit "amis,"
En la clauze "haymmi!" a mis.   890
"A mi" dut dire, et "haymmi!" dist,
Por la dolor qui en li gist.
Grant esperance li a fait
Que li a dit "haymmi!" a trait,
Car el l'ot ains "ami" nomé.   895
Or cuide avoir tolt asomé.
Cist doi mot "haymmi!" et "amis"
Li ont moult grant confort tramis.
Cis mos "amis" mostre l'amor,
Cis mos "haymmi!" fait le clamor.   900
Or a Cadors joie a voloir,
Qu'Amors le painne et fait doloir.
Cis mos "amis" fait esperer

42

A vile heart makes a man go mad.
A noble heart in one of low rank
is worth more than if a man is master
of a great kingdom and has a faulty heart.
Vile heart, you are doing this on purpose."   865
Then she sat down on the steps
and fainted twice in a row,
and when she was able to speak again,
she called Cador by name.
He was the substance of all her speech.   870
But Cador was languishing, so he couldn't be there.
Love has both of them in hand.
If they want to be cured,
then it will be necessary
for him to be cured by the girl,   875
and for her to take her medicine from him.
Either each of them will cure the other,
or there will be no curing.

Day breaks, and Eufemie
delays no longer. She jumps to her feet,   880
comes into her lover's room
and says to him, "Ami, speak, ah me!"*
She should have said, "Speak to me,"
but Love has tricked her:
she should have said, "Speak to me,"   885
but she says, "Speak, ah me."
"Speak to me," she should have said,
but "ah me!" is in her heart.
As soon as she said, "ami,"
Love put "ah me!" into the sentence.   890
She should have said "to me" and she said "ah me,"
because of the terrible sorrow within her.
She gives him a great deal of hope
when she clearly says "ah me!" —
for thus she calls him "ami."   895
Now he thinks he has figured the whole thing out.
These two utterances, "ah me" and "ami,"
have brought him great comfort.
The word "ami" is evidence of love,
the words "ah me" say it loud and clear.   900
Now Cador has joy to his liking,
after Love has given him pain and grief.
The word ami gives Cador cause to hope

43

Cador qu'or pora averer
Cho qu'il plus convoite et desirre. 905
"Aimmi!" demostre le martyre, /
Le paine d'amor qu'a sofierte
Mais que li parole est coverte,
Car ja soit cho qu'ami le claimme
N'est pas provance qu'ele l'ainme, 910
Car tels hom est "amis" clamés
Ki de fin cuer n'est pas amés.
Por cho est Cador en dotance,
Por quant sin a grant esperance
Quant l'apiele "ami" u li "amie." 915
Or savés qu'il nel laira mie
Ne parolt ensi qu'ele l'oie, —
Car tres bien l'a mis en la voie, —
Et dist: "Dolce, li vostre plainte
M'a grant dolor el cuer enpainte. 920
La vostre grans bontés m'ensengne
Se vos plagniés que jo me plagne.
Se vos plagniés, bien le sarai,
Se mal avrés, le mal avrai.
De vostre joie doi joïr, 925
Car vostre sens me fait joïr,
Aler, et parler, et veïr,
Et en tols sens me fait tehir.
Se nule cose avés averse,
Ma vie doi mener enverse: 930
Plorer de *v*ostre aversité,
Rire en *v*ostre prosperité.
Tolt mon pooir vos doi voloir
Se mal avés, bien doi doloir.
Car si fesistes vos del mien, 935
Del mal me mesistes el bien."
"Cho est li voirs," dist Eufemie,
"Qu'esté vos ai en liu de mie.
Del venim vos ai fait delivre,
Dont vos envenima la guivre. 940
Et jo m'en sui si enivree,
Ja n'en cuic estre delivree.
L'enfertés est sor moi venue
Que entor vos me sui tenue.
Si siolt malages* sovent faire: 945
Ki a malade gent repaire,
Moult li va bien s'il n'a sa part.

44

that he will now be able to attain
what he covets and desires most.   905
"Ah me" is proof of martyrdom,
the pain of love that she has suffered—
except that the word is ambiguous,
for the fact that she calls him "ami"
is no proof that she loves him.   910
A man may be called "ami"
and not be loved with a noble heart.
That is why Cador is uncertain,
however much hope it gives him
when they call each other "ami(e)."   915
Now you know that he will not fail
to speak so that she can hear him—
for she has very much put him on the right track—
and he says, "Sweetheart, your lament
has filled my heart with great sorrow.   920
Your great goodness is an example to me.
If you complain, then I will, too;
if you are afflicted, then I will be, too.
If you suffer, I will bear that pain.
I will rejoice in your joy,   925
for everything about you fills me with joy—
the way you look and walk and talk—
it elevates me in every way.
If you encounter adversity,
I will have to change my life accordingly: 930
I want to weep at your adversities,
delight in your prosperity,
I want to devote myself completely to you.
If you are hurt, I owe it to you to suffer,
for that's the way you were with me;   935
you gave me good for bad."
"That's the truth," said Eufemie.
"I served you as physician,
I saved you from the venom
with which the dragon poisoned you.   940
And from that I became so delirious
I don't think I can be cured.
I caught the disease
from being around you.
It's often that way with illness: 945
he who keeps sick people company
will be very lucky not to share the illness.

Jo n'i sui pas venue a tart.
Mais que que soit de m'enferté,
Acreäntés me par verté, 950
Por cho qu'adonques vive soie
Et qu'enfertés ne vos deloie,
Quel mois devant a moi vendrés
Et que vos, amis, me prendrés*/
En gueredon de mon service. 955
Bials amis, s'onors vos justice
Et le francise vos castie,
Si bone le vos ai bastie,
Se valors vos a en destrece
Et se gentils cuers vos adrece, 960
Dont ferés vos que dit vos ai.
Et jo certes cortois vos sai,
Et bien ensegniet, et moult sage—
Mais ch'onors mue trop corage.
Bials dols amis, ne vos en poise: 965
Mes cuers ne porrist en richoize.
Com la richoise plus engragne,
Tant frit plus malvais hom et gragne;
Com plus a vils cuers plus empire.
Amis, jo l'ai bien oï dire 970
Del serpent que vos ocesistes—
Dont vos grant hardement fesistes—
Que li rois fist tele bonté
Qu'il vos a otroié conté
Et feme a prendre avoic a cois 975
A an, a posan u a mois."
Et Cador li respont en oire:
"Ma damoisiele, c'est la voire;
Et li rois m'en a fait fiance
Et bien me tenra covena[n]ce 980
D'une conté, de feme a quois.
Mais el roiame n'en a trois
Dont la mellor presisse mie
S'une m'en faut, bele Eufemie."
Biele Eufemie, cho est l'une 985
A cui li cuers Cador s'aüne!
De l'une est Eufemie gloze,
Mais que sor li prendre ne l'oze,
Qu'en li n'en a pas tant d'ozer
Qu'ele sor li l'oze glozer. 990
Doute qu'il ait dit altrement

46

It didn't take me long to catch it.
But whatever illness I contracted,
swear to me by all that's true,   950
in order to keep me alive,
and you from being sick,
that this very month you will come to me
and take me, beloved,
as a reward for my services.   955
Sweet love, if honor governs your actions,
and noble character keeps you in check,
if what I propose appeals to you,
if manly virtue constrains you,
and a noble heart guides you,   960
you will do what I have told you.
And truly, I know you to be courteous,
well-bred and very wise—
unless 'honor changes a man' too much.*
Dear sweet friend, don't worry;   965
my heart cannot be corrupted by wealth.
As riches breed more riches,
a wicked man burns more and grinds his teeth;
the worse his heart, the worse he gets.
My love, I have heard   970
with regard to the dragon you killed
(a most courageous deed)
that the king gave you a fine reward;
that he granted you a county
and whomever you wish for a wife,   975
in a year, next year, or next month."
And Cador replied at once,
"Mademoiselle, that is so.
The king swore an oath to me,
and he will certainly keep his pledge   980
of the land and a wife of my choice.
But I wouldn't take the best
of the top three in the kingdom
if one were denied me, belle Eufemie."
Belle Eufemie, she's the "one"   985
who is the choice of Cador's heart.
Eufemie is the gloss of "one."
But she doesn't dare take it as a reference to herself;
there's not enough daring in her
to gloss it as referring to herself.   990
She thinks he has said something else,

47

Et respondi isnielement:
"Sire, estes vos de tel dangier?"
"Nai jo, mais cuers ne puet cangier.
Franche puciele debonaire,   995
Vos me jabés, sel poés faire,
Qu'a mon vivant vos doi servisce.
Jo parlerai par amendise.
Vos parlés de mon mariäge:
Ne vos en poist, amie sage,   1000
Que jel vos di tolt a larron.
Altressi tost prendrés baron, /
Con jo, amie, feme a per.
Mais ne me puet pas escaper
Qu'a vos noces ne vus adestre,   1005
Quar se jo vif g'i volrai estre.
Li rois vos fist pieça le don
Por moi guarir en gueredon
Qu'a vostre kius prendrés mari
Si tost com vus m'avrés guari.   1010
Or avrés vus vostre voloir,
Et moi covenra, las! doloir
De grant enferté ki me vient."
"Cis mals coment, sire, vos tient?"
"Biele, j'ai calt et froit ensanble.   1015
Ne puis garir, si com moi samble;
Si grans cals ne puet vaintre mie
Le froit que j'ai, bele Eufemie.
Li frois ne puet avoir valor
Ki puisse vaintre ma calor.   1020
Anbedoi sunt ivel en force;
Li uns enviers l'altre s'esforce,
Ne puet l'uns l'altre sormonter.
Oïstes vos ainc mais conter
De calt, de froit, qui sunt contrarie,   1025
Que en un cors peüscent faire?
S'en moi peüst valoir Nature,
Ja voir si estrange aventure
A mon las cors n'en avenist;
L'uns viers l'altre ne se tenist.   1030
Mais jo sui tols desnaturés
Et si cuic estre enfaiturés.
Jo voel mangier et si ne puis;
Tant de nature en moi ne truis
Que puissce mon mengier joïr,   1035

48

and replies quickly,
"Sir, are you saying this lightly?"
"No, my heart can never change.
Gentle, noble girl,   995
your words mock me, and you have the right,
for I owe you service for my life.
I will speak to make amends.
You have mentioned my marriage;
don't be offended, wise friend,   1000
if I speak so as to obscure the meaning.
You shall take a noble husband
precisely when I take a wife who is my peer.
But it will not be possible
for me not to be beside you at your wedding,   1005
for if I am alive, I will be there.
A while ago, the king granted you,
as a reward for curing me,
the husband of your choice,
as soon as you had cured me.   1010
Now you shall have your wish,
and I, alas, will have to suffer
from this terrible sickness that comes over me."
"Sir, what are the symptoms of this disease?"
"Dearest, I am hot and cold at once.   1015
It seems to me I can't be cured.
There is no heat hot enough to conquer
the cold I feel, belle Eufemie.
There is no cold that has the strength
to overcome my heat.   1020
Both are equal in strength;
one contends with the other;
neither can overcome the other.
Have you ever heard tell
what the opposition of heat and cold   1025
can do inside one body?
If Nature could assert her strength in me,
this strange state of affairs
could not occur in my weary body;
the one would not struggle with the other.   1030
But I am totally dis-natured;
I think I am bewitched.
I want to eat and yet I can't;
I can't find enough nature in me
to be able to enjoy my food,   1035

Ne men las cors avoec norir.
Quant jo somel dont m'esperis
Si griément por poi ne peris."
"Bials dols amis," dist la meschine,
"Nos convenroit une mechine, 1040
Car nos avons une enferté.
Mais or me dites verité.
Coment cis mals est apielés?
Se vos savés nel me celés."
"Bele, jo sui de jovene eé 1045
Mais que j'ai oï maint sené
Ki dient que cil ki se painnent
En amer u en amors mainnent
En sont al loing moult adamé
S'il aiment et ne sunt amé. / 1050
Mais s'il doi sunt qui s'entr'acuellent,
Por cho qu'il andoi bien se vuellent,
Puis que verté vos doi jehir,
D'un* bazier pueënt plus tehir
Que n'aient en un an pené, 1055
Car cho me dient li sené."
"Amis, or m'avés vos aprise:
Or sai qu'Amors m'a en justisce.
S'estre puis d'un baisier sanee
Dont sui jo certes enganee 1060
Se mes dols amis ne me baise,
Se jo par tant puis estre a ase."
"Quele, Eufemie! A Deu pleüst
Cascuns de nos çaiens eüst
Cho qu'il plus covoite et desirre, 1065
Et dont li ozast son bon dire!"
"Amis, que valt a soshaidier?
Sohais ne puet nul home aidier!
Jo ne vi onques par sohait
Plus tost venir u biel u lait. 1070
Mais or me dites, bials amis,
N'est voirs que li rois nos a mis
A nostre kius de mariäge,
Moi por garir vostre malage,
Et vos por le serpent ocirre? 1075
Or poriens nos nostre b*u*en dire
Tolt coiement, chi a larron,
Quel feme amés, jo quel baron.
Car en faisons chi l'afiänce

50

not to speak of nourishing my weary body.
When I sleep, I wake up in such pain
that I am nearly perishing."
"Dear, sweet friend," said the girl,
"we really need some medicine,   1040
for we both have the same disease.
But now tell me, truly,
what is the name of this malady?
If you know, don't keep it from me."
"Lovely one, I am still quite young,   1045
but I have heard many older men say
that those who suffer
the bitter pangs of love
are greatly harmed in the long run
if they love and are not loved in return.   1050
But if there are two who are in accord,
so that each loves the other,
since I'm supposed to tell you the truth,
they can benefit more from one kiss
than they have suffered in a year —   1055
that's what experienced men have said to me."
"Friend, now that you have told me that,
I shall let you know that Love has captured me.
If I can be cured by a kiss,
then I am certainly being cheated   1060
if my sweet friend doesn't kiss me,
when I can be cured at such a price."
"What, Eufemie! may God grant
that each of us here may have
what he most wishes and desires,   1065
and may he dare to name that wish."
"Friend, what good does wishing do?
Wishing never helped anyone.
I never saw anything, good or bad,
come to pass sooner through wishing it.   1070
But tell me now, dear love,
isn't it true that the king
has given us a choice of spouses,
me for curing your illness,
you for killing the dragon?   1075
Now we can make our wishes known
in secret and in private —
what woman you love, and I, what man.
Why don't we swear an oath right here and now

Del bien celer, et l'aliänce   1080
Que nel dites, se n'est par moi,
Ne jo, se par vos non, par foi.
Primes dirés et puis dirai,
Que ja de rien n'en mentirai.
Vos estes hom, ains devés dire,   1085
Se devés ains de moi eslire."
"Tolt si l'otroi," Cador le dist,
"Or l'afions, car cho i gist,
Que nos dirons trestolt nostre estre."
Li uns prent l'autre par la destre,   1090
Et escalfent si del tenir
Qu'il ne se pueënt abstenir
Ne mecent les boces ensanble.
Sans dire font, si com moi sanble,
De fine amor moult bone ensegne,   1095
Car li baisiers bien lor ensegne,/
Et li qu'il trait paine et martire,
Et lui qu'ele l'aime et desire,
Car n'est pas baisier de conpere,
De mere a fil, de fil a pere: 1100
Ainz est baisiers de tel savor
Que bien savore fine amor.
Et se vus verté m'en querés,
Ja par moi sage n'en serés
Se dunques baisierent sovent,   1105
Se cho fu uns baisiers, u .c.
Mais j'os bien verté aficier,
Tolt sans mentir et sans trecier,
Qu'anchois que de baisier cessassent,
Ne qu'il onques un mot sonasscent, —   1110
Peüst on une liue aler.
Bon keu ot al mangier saler:
N'i ot ne peu ne trop de sel,
Ne ne savore point de mel.
Car si l'amer lor savorast,   1115
Ja nus d'als tant ne demorast.
Tant com li savors est plus dolce
Del baisier ki lor cuer atolce,
Tant croist lor amors plus adés.
Et por cho qu'il sont ore a és   1120
De cho qu'il onques plus desirent
Et il de lor bon se consirent,
Si est doblee lor dolors.

to hide it well, and make a pact   1080
that you won't say it except to me,
nor I, upon my faith, except to you.
First you tell and then I will,
and I won't lie about anything.
You're the man, so you go first;   1085
you should choose before I do."
"I agree to all this," Cador said to her.
"Now let's swear, since things are so,
to speak our minds right now."
Each takes the other by the hand—   1090
they are so carried away by this
that they cannot prevent themselves
from putting their mouths together.
It seems to me that, without speaking,
they are giving a fine demonstration of courtly love,   1095
for kissing teaches them both a good lesson,
both her who causes him pain and torment,
and him whom she loves and desires.
For this is not a comradely kiss
of mother to son, of son to father;   1100
no, it is a kiss of such savor
that it savors much of courtly love.
And if you want to know the truth,
you'll never hear it from me—
whether they kissed often then,   1105
or whether it was one kiss or one hundred.
But I will venture to confirm this much,
without any lying or cheating:
before they stopped kissing
and before a single word was spoken,   1110
you could have traveled a mile.
A good chef had seasoned the dish:
there wasn't too much or too little salt,
nor did it taste bad to them at all,
for if it had tasted bitter to either of them,   1115
they wouldn't have stayed at table so long.
Just as the savor of the kiss
that touched their hearts grew sweeter,
just so their love grew after that.
And because they are now so close to obtaining   1120
what they have most desired,
and yet are deprived of what they want,
their pain is also doubled.

Moult mue et cange lor colors.
Bone sanblance en puis mostrer: 1125
Ki faim a dont n'oze goster
De cel mangier qu'il tient as mainz,
De tant l'agoisse plus li fainz.
El baisier dont ont lor voloir
Gist moult de cho quis fait doloir,   1130
Ki les tormente, et qui les paine.
Mais si sont lié de cele estraine
Qu'il claimment bien la painne cuite
Por lor baisier ki lor delite.
Li baisiers forment les avance,   1135
Si les met plus en esperance.
Si ont tolt mis en bel deport,
D'esperance ont fait contrefort,
Por cho qu'or cuident averer
Lor bien qu'il pueënt esperer,   1140
Ne pueënt le mal consentir.
Cel saciés vos tolt sans mentir: /
Longement baisent et acolent;
Quant pueënt parler, si parrolent.
Il l'aparole, ele respont,   1145
Et lor error illuec deffunt.
"Amie, jo sui vostre amis.
Li vostre cors le mien a mis
Moult longement en grant batalle."
"Amis, cho saciés vos sans falle,   1150
Qu'ai[n]si sui jo l[a] vostre amie
Et qu'el mont fors [vos] nen a mie
Qui ma dolor puist estancier,
Ma santé rendre, n'avancier."

Il n'ont mais entr'als nule error;   1155
Ainz sevent ore la verror,
Qu'il est amis et ele amie.
N'i a cel d'als qui ja laist mie
Ne voist son don al roi rover,
Car or le volront esprover   1160
Com lor ami al grant besoing.
Tols ont les cols cargiés de soing
Qu'il ne truisent le roi estable,
Ne sa parolle veritable.
Car ki bien aime n'est sans dote,   1165
Ne ne puet tenir droite rote,

54

Their color changes profoundly.
I can give you a good analogy for this: 1125
he who is hungry and dares not taste
of the food he has in his hands
is all the more tormented by hunger.
From the kiss they both desired
comes much of their sorrow,   1130
their torment and their pain.
But they are so delighted by this gift
that they would call it an even exchange: their pain
for this kissing that fills them with such delight.
The kissing has furthered their cause considerably;   1135
it gives them greater hope.
They have given themselves over to delight;
they have fortified themselves with hope.
Since now they think they can attain
happiness, now that they can hope for the good,   1140
they cannot feel the pain.
And this I'll tell you truly:
they kissed and hugged a long time,
and when they were able to speak, they spoke.
He spoke to her, and she replied,   1145
and any misunderstandings vanished on the spot.
"Beloved, I am your lover.
Your own sweet self has vanquished me
after a long and mighty battle."
"Beloved, I want you to know   1150
that I love you truly,
and that their is no one else in the whole world
who could assuage my grief,
restore me to health, promote my well-being."

There is no longer any misunderstanding between them;   1155
from now on they know the truth,
that they are friends and lovers.
Now they are both more eager than ever
to demand their reward of the king.
Now they want to test him   1160
as their friend in time of great need.
Both are burdened with the fear
that the king will prove false,
and his word unreliable.
A person deeply in love is filled with doubt   1165
and cannot keep things straight.

Ne cho qu'il set ne puet savoir.
Bone provance en puis avoir:
Escriziés moi ens en le cire
Letres que om bien puisse lire.   1170
Faites le cire dont remetre.
Enne perist donques la lettre?
Oïl, par Deu! par le calor.
Nient plus n'a cuers d'amant valor
De bien retenir s[a] mimorie   1175
Que cire encontre fu victorie
De retenir la lettre escrite.
Qu'angoisse d'amor n'est petite,
Car cho qu'est voirs cho fait mescroire,
Et tenir fause coze a voire;   1180
Et met por poi en esperance.
Amans est por nient en dotance.
Or saciés que cil sunt en painne
Et que griés tormens les demainne,
Qu'il ont le baisier trovet tel   1185
Qu'il n'i a trop ne peu de sel.
Si en sunt moult en grant batalle
Que al sorplus ne facent falle. /
Dont devisent que il iront
Al roi, et lor bon li diront.   1190
Donques rebaisent altre fois:
Tant sunt il en gregnor destrois.
Ne puëënt de baizier retraire
Quant esperance lor fait faire,
Qui lor promet sans demorer   1195
Plus que baisiers puist savorer.
Et par itant li baisiers fine,
Congié ont pris, l'uns l'autre encline.

Cador remaint, cele s'en torne,
Et il et ele bien s'atorne.   1200
Que valt alongier trop se rime?
Andoi vienent a ore prime
Al roi por rover lor promesse.
Encor n'avoit oïe messe.
Ne parloient pas a laron,   1205
Ainz les oïrent .c. baron
Ki o le roi la messe atendent.
Li home i sunt qu'a lui apendent.
Cador li pros parla devant

56

He doesn't know what he knows.
I'll give you a good example of this:
just write clearly and legibly
on a piece of wax;   1170
then melt the wax.
Don't the letters vanish?
Of course, by God! because of the heat!
The heart of a lover is no more able
to retain its memory   1175
than a piece of wax its victory
over the written letter.
Love's anguish is no trifling matter,
for that which is true is not believed,
while false things are taken to be true.   1180
A lover hopes with scant cause,
and doubts for very little reason.
Now I must tell you they are suffering,
and grievous torments are their lot,
because they found their kiss so well-seasoned—   1185
neither too much nor too little salt.
They are in agony for fear
of missing the next course.
Therefore, they agree to go to the king
and tell him of their desire.   1190
And so they kiss once more.
This only worsens their distress:
they can't stop kissing
because it gives them such hopes
and promises   1195
of soon savoring more than kisses,
and that is why the kissing ceases.
They bowed to each other, and took their leave.

Cador remained, she returned to her room,
and both took pains with their attire.   1200
Why prolong the suspense?
They both came at a very early hour
to ask the king to fulfill his promise.
He had not yet heard mass.
They did not speak privately;   1205
on the contrary, they were heard by a hundred barons
who were waiting to attend the king at mass.
All his vassals were gathered there.
Valiant Cador spoke first

Et dist al roi: "Le don demant   1210
Qu'a celui promesistes, sire,
Qui le serpent iroit ocire.
Jo l'ocis: chi n'a cel nel sache
De quanque en a en ceste plache."
"Et vos avrés," li rois li dist,   1215
Vostre demant, car cho i gist.
Jo vos donrai une conté
Et feme de moult grant bonté.
Il n'i a nule sans calenge,
Se vos volés, qui ne vus prenge.   1220
C'est par raison, si com moi samble."
"C'est moult," cho dient tuit ensamble.
"Et bien ait sire qui cho done
Et ki les siens si abandone."
Atant si parla la puchiele,   1225
En cui joie d'amors reviele,
Et est tolte d'itel faiture
Com la sot miols faire Nature.
Dés l'ortel trosqu'ens en la face
N'a sor li rien qu'a blasmer face.   1230
Et dist al roi par avenant:
"Sire, tenés moi covenant
De vostre parent qu'ai guari
Dont jo vos vi moult esmari. /
Or ai ma painne despendue   1235
Et la vie li ai rendue."
Li rois li dist: "Ma bele amie,
Por vos ne mentirai jo mie.
Mentir a roi n'est mie gius.
Baron avrés a v[ost]re kius.   1240
Uns sans calenge m'en trovés:
Quels que il soit, sil me rovés.
Amie, ne vus esmaiés:
Ja n'iert si haus que nel aiés,
Soit cuens, u dus, u castelains."   1245
"Ne vos ruis, sire, plus ne mains,"
Cho li respondi la puchiele.
Li rois ses barons en apiele
A un consel moult bielement,
Et cil i vont isnielement.   1250
Cador remaint et la mescine,
Sor cui li consals pent et cline.
Remés sunt andoi en la place.

and said to the king, "I request the reward   1210
that you promised, Sire.
to the one who killed the dragon.
I killed it: who is there of all those gathered here
who doesn't know that?"
"And you shall," the king said to him,   1215
have your reward, as is right.
I will give you a county
and a wife of high degree.
There is none free to marry
who will not accept you if you wish.   1220
This is reasonable, it seems to me."
"That's a lot!" said all his men together.
"Good fortune to a lord who gives so freely
and is so liberal with his possessions!"
And now the girl speaks,   1225
in whom *joi d'amors* is revealed.*
She is absolutely of the highest quality
that Nature could produce.
She had no defect in her person,
from her toes to her head.   1230
She spoke to the king as was fitting:
"Sire, keep your promise to me
for having cured your nephew,
about whom you were so distressed.
I took great pains with him   1235
and saved his life."
The king answered her, "My lovely friend,
I will never lie to you.
A king must never lie.
You shall have the lord of your choice.   1240
Just find me one who is free:
whoever it is, ask him of me.
Friend, don't hesitate;
none is so highly placed that you can't have him,
be he count or duke or keeper of castle."   1245
"I ask of you, Sire, no more and no less."
Thus the girl answered him.
The king summoned his barons
to a formal council,
and they assembled quickly,   1250
leaving Cador and the girl,
who were the reason for the council.
Both remained there.

Nus d'als ne set preu que il face:
Criement cil consals ne lor nuise,   1255
Et li rois okison ne truise
De lor proiere deporter.
Mais ne lor esteüst doter:
S'il seüssent la covenance,
Il fuscent tuit lors fors d'errance.   1260
Li rois parole. Oiés qu'a dit.
"Segnor, entendés me .i. petit.
Jo ne vus quiier un point celer:
De le feme et del baceler
Cador voel faire aliëment.   1265
Si estevroit castiëment
Al consel descovrir tel home
Ki lor seüst mostrer la some,
Die lor qu'il sunt d'un eäge,
D'une bialté, de halt parage,   1270
Et quant eäges les ivuelle,
Et bialtés, n'estroit pas mervelle
S'andoi quesisent l'aparel
Qu'il en amor fuscent parel.

Segnor, jo voel que Cador ait   1275
Iceste mescine entresait.
Jes voel ensamble marier
Tolt sans respit, sans detrier,
Por cho qu'andoi le vollent faire,
U, se non, nen puis a cief traire,   1280
Se jo ne me voel desmentir,
Ainz me doinst Dex la mort sentir./
Nes voel mener oltre raison,
Ne querre viers els oquison
Qu'il n'aient lor plain anbedoi.   1285
Ferai lor bien que faire doi.
Mais il puet a tel feme tendre,
Et ele a tel baron entendre,
Qu'il m'en covenra moult pener
Ains que les puisse a cief mener: 1290
Et tols jors le m'estera faire.
Segnor, et por iceste afaire,
S'il s'acordassent ore ensamble,
C'estroit moult bien, si com moi samble.
Si lor donroie l'an .m. livres,   1295
Car j'en seroie donc delivres:

60

Neither was sure what would happen:
they were afraid that this council might harm their cause
and that the king might find some way   1255
to deny their request.
But they had nothing to worry about:
if they had known the king's intention,
they would have stopped worrying.   1260
The king was speaking. Listen to what he said:
"Lords, hear me out.
I do not wish to conceal from you
that I want to make an alliance
between Cador and the maiden.   1265
It would be a good thing
if there were someone at this council
who could explain the advantages to them,
tell them that they are similar in age,
beauty and high lineage,   1270
and since they are equal in youth
and beauty, it would not be surprising,
since both are seeking their like,
that they might be alike in love.

Lords, I want Cador   1275
to have this girl immediately.
I want to marry them
without any delay or hesitation —
that is, if they are willing.
If they are not, I cannot accomplish this,   1280
unless I want to prove myself a liar —
I would rather God struck me dead.
I don't want to put unreasonable pressure on them,
nor do I seek anything for them
except that both should have their due.   1285
I will do what is best for them, as I ought.
But he might choose such a woman
and she such a man
that I might have to work very hard
to convince them,   1290
and yet I would have to do my duty.
Lords, with regard to the matter before us,
if they were to reach an agreement at this time,
it would be a very good idea, it seems to me,
to give them a thousand pounds a year,   1295
I would grant them this myself,

61

Et la tiere de Cornüälle
Apriés la mort Renalt sans falle.
Ceste est sa fille, il est ses pere,
N'ont plus d'enfans, il ne la mere."   1300
Cho dient tuit: "Bien dist li rois.
N'est pas irouis, a fuer d'Irois:
Anchois a dit com hom loials.
Li siens covens est bien roials,
Car il ne menti ainc a home   1305
U voir dut dire, c'est la some.
A lui se doit on bien froter,
Car chi puet on grant bien noter."

Li cuens de Cestre a lui s'atrait
Et dist li bielement a trait: 1310
"Sire, jo nel vos quier celer
D'Eufemie et del baceler.
Jovente et folie les tensent.
Cuident voirs soit quanque il pensent.
Il cuident plus en .i. mois faire   1315
Qu'en lor vivant puissent atraire.
Alcuns i voist qui cors les tiegne
Et del bien monstrer li soviegne:
S'il ne font vostre volenté
N'aront la lor pas a plenté."   1320
Cho dist li rois: "Bials dols amis,
De ma part i serés tramis.
Alés i: jo vos i envoi.
A cest besoing mellor n'i voi
Ki miols les sace amoloier,   1325
Se vos les veés foloier."
Li cuens li dist: "Moult volentiers:
Et vos estés chi dementiers."
Atant s'en vait viers les amans
Et prie moult que Sains Amans/   1330
Meiche entr'als si grant amor
Que on n'en oie mais clamor.
Mais [ne] li esteüst proier,
Qu'il s'en lairont bien amoier.
Se sa proiere fust si voire   1335
Tols jors, et il m'en volsist croire,
Ne fineroit de proier donques;
Car il ne cuident veïr onques
Eure ne tans c'on les espouse.

and the territory of Cornwall
upon the death of Renald, without fail.
She is his daughter, he is her father;
she is her parents' only child."   1300
They all said, "The king speaks well.
He is no crazy Irishman;
he has spoken like an honest man.
His plan is most royal.
He has never lied to anyone   1305
when he was supposed to tell the truth, that's a fact.
One should really pay careful attention to him,
for one can learn an important lesson from him."

The count of Chester approached the king
and spoke courteously and with deliberation: 1310
"Sire, I do not wish to conceal
my opinion of Eufemie and the young man.
They are both prey to youth and folly.
They think whatever they think is true.
They think they can do more in a month   1315
than they could accomplish in a lifetime.
They need someone to set them straight
and show them where their interests lie:
if they do not do your will,
they are only cheating themselves."   1320
The king said, "Dear, good friend,
you shall be sent on my behalf.
Go to it! You shall be my envoy.
I can't think of anyone more suitable,
or who could persuade them better,   1325
if you see that they are being foolish."
The count said, "I'd be delighted!
You just wait here in the meantime."
So then he went to the lovers,
praying fervently that Saint Amant   1330
would cause the greatest love ever heard of
to spring up between the two.
But he really didn't have to pray;
they will easily be persuaded.
If I could convince him that all his prayers   1335
would always be so efficacious,
he would spend all his time praying.
For they didn't think they would ever see
the day when they'd be married.

63

Et l'uns et l'autres le golouse,   1340
Et prendent moult a mervellier
Que li rois a a consellier.
Dient que vile et mainte joie
Va par consel a male voie.
Cador a dit: "Que c'est tolt nient!   1345
Se on droiture ne nos tient,
Amie, j'en ferai mervelle,
Car mes corages me conselle
Que en essil o vos m'en voise,
Tolt a laron, sans faire noise."   1350
Ele respont: "Tel n'oï onques!
Bials amis, mervelliés vus donques
S'essil sofrés por vostre amie,
Or voi qu'es homes nen a mie
Si grans cuers com g'i ai creü.   1355
Amis, or ai jo bien veü
Et sai de fi et sui certaine
Que del mal dont ne sui pas sainne
Que vos estes en grant fretel.
Mais jo certes ne m'esmervel   1360
S'en bos vois o vus u en lande,
Car Amors le rueve et conmande
Que cascuns doie assés savoir*
Cho qu'aime s'il le puet avoir
Certes qu'a cho cil qui bien ainme,   1365
S'il sor icho quiert plus et claimme,
Il nen est pas bien fins amans.
Haymmi! bials sire Sains Amans,
Se jo avoie mon ami
En un esscil ensamble o mi,   1370
Del sorplus voir ne me calroit!
Et tols li mons que me valroit,
Se cho que j'aim me fasoit falle?
Petit u nient, se Dex me valle!
Se cho que j'amer puis me faut,   1375
Cho que jo n'aim petit me valt.
Ki onques n'a cho qu'il desire
Que li valt quanque il luite et tire?/
Bials dols amis, se jo vos ai,
Assés avrai." "Se jo vos ai?   1380
O vos, amie, vos m'avés,
Tolt de fiänce le savés
Et qui vostre amor me tolroit

But both of them were longing for it,   1340
and they began to wonder a lot
about what was happening at the king's council.
They said that charters and many a cause for joy
come to a bad end at councils.
Cador said, "It doesn't matter   1345
if they don't deal fairly with us, love,
I'll give them a surprise,
for my innermost being counsels me
to seek exile with you,
in all secrecy, without making a noise."   1350
She replied, "I've never heard of such a thing!
Dear love, it would certainly be amazing
for you to suffer exile for your beloved!
Now I see that men's hearts
aren't as great as I had thought.   1355
Beloved, now it's clear to me,
I've seen for certain,
that you are profoundly disturbed
by that illness from which I suffer, too.
As for me, I certainly wouldn't think it strange   1360
to wander with you in forest or field,
for Love so orders and commands
that each should know well
that if he can have the one he loves,
if the lover has his beloved   1365
and seeks and demands more than this,
he is surely not a noble lover.
Ah me, good Sir Saint Amant!
Truly, if I had my beloved
in exile with me,   1370
I wouldn't ask for anything more.
And what would the whole world matter
if I didn't have the one I love?
Little or nothing, so help me God!
If what I love is missing,   1375
what I don't love doesn't matter much to me.
What good are all the efforts and struggles
of one who never has what he wants?
Dear sweet love, if I have you,
I will have enough." "'If I have you?'   1380
Beloved, you have me with you,
you know it, completely and utterly,
and whoever deprived me of your love

De tolt le mont ne me solroit,
Car altre riens ne me delite: 1385
Com le clameroie dont cuite?
Vie n'est el que deliter.
Ki vie tolt puet se acuiter?
Acuiter? nenil, par ma destre!"
Atant si vint li cuens de Cestre.   1390
Voit les parler et consellier
Priveëment et orellier;
Et lor parole si despendre
Que li uns l'autre puet entendre
Encor oïssent il bien dur.   1395
Car il ont trovet ja moult sur
De celer lor penser adés:
Por cho parolent prés a prés.

Li cuens de Cestre est moult voiseus:
Ainc nen oïstes mains noiseus.   1400
Voit les cluignier et lor esgart:
Dés or n'a il mais nul regart
Qu'il n'ait trestolt lor vol ſeü.
Fait quanses qu'il ne l'ait veü.*
Estosse. "Eheu!" fait il, qu'il voient,   1405
Car cortois est, si violt qu'il l'oient:
Ne violt d'als faire pas lonc conte
Si sutilment qu'en n'aiente honte,
Qu'il ert en amor asociés,
Si ot esté moult asociés.   1410
Set bien qu'en amor a vergoigne.
Cador l'entent, de li s'eslogne.
Muent andoi moult tost color
Com cil qui ont al cuer dolor.
Cho que viermel fu en la face   1415
Devint assés plus pers que glace.
Le pers remue en color blance
Plus que n'est nois desor la brance:
Et quel verté que on roiogne,*
Por cho qu'il ont si grant vergogne,   1420
Si vient del blanc colors vermelle.
Et jo si ai moult grant mervelle
S'ainc fu en tierre tainturieres,
S'il onques fu nus painturieres,
Ki seüst si tost un drap taindre,   1425
Ki peüst tant tost un fust paindre/

66

could not recompense me with all the world.
Nothing else delights me: 1385
how could I say we were quits?
Delight is the essence of life.
Can one who deprives me of life be acquitted?
Acquitted? No! upon my oath!"
And then the count of Chester arrived. 1390
He saw them talking and taking counsel
privately and whispering
and speaking in such low voices
that they could hear each other,
but not without great difficulty, 1395
for they have taken every care
to conceal their thoughts until now:
that is why they were standing so close while talking.

The count of Chester was very prudent;
you never heard of anyone less rash. 1400
He saw their lowered eyes, their looks:
he didn't need a second glance,
he saw at once what they wanted,
but he acted as if he hadn't noticed.
He coughed. "Ahem," he said, so they would see him, 1405
for he was courteous, he wanted them to hear him.
He didn't want to observe them for a long time
unobserved, so that they would feel ashamed,
for he knew much about love;
he had had much experience with love. 1410
He knew very well that lovers are easily shamed.
Cador heard him and moved away from her.
They both changed color rapidly,
like those whose hearts are filled with sorrow.
He whose face was crimson 1415
became much bluer than ice.
The blue changed to a white
whiter than snow upon the branch.
However one tonsures the truth,
they were so embarrassed 1420
that from white they turned to crimson again.
And I would be very surprised
if there were dyers in the land
or if ever there were painters
who could dye cloth so quickly 1425
or paint a beam so speedily

Tantes colors en si poi d'eure
Com li vergoigne a fait ambeure,
Primes vermel, puis piers, puis blanc;
Et sunt puis plus vermel de sanc.   1430
Or sachiés que sans grant dolor
N'ont pas mué si tost color.

Li cuens i vint. Dist: "Dex vus salt!
Ciertes, mes consals ne vus falt."
Puis a parlé com hom senés.   1435
Dist: "Jo me sui por vos penés."
"Vos, sire, a cui?" "Enviers le roi."
"Viers lui, bials sire, et vos, de quoi?"
"Cador, ne m'alés fausnoiant.
Or le dirai chi, vostre oiant: 1440
Que vos amés biele Eufemie,
Et ele voir ne vos het mie
Jo m'en sui bien aperceüs,
Encor m'en soie jo teüs.
Il me sovient que j'amai ja,   1445
Si seu bon gré qui m'en aida.
Or vos ai jo moult bien aidié.
Se vos l'eüsciés soshaidié,
S'estroit il bien, se Dex me valle!
Car vostre iert tolte Cornuälle   1450
Apriés le mort Renalt le conte.
Or est il bien que jo vos conte:
Cesti* devroit estre la terre,
Mais n'i a droit qu'ele puist estre,
Car cho savés par les .ii. contes   1455
Ki s'entr'ocisent, cho fu hontes,
Par l'oquoison des .ii. jumieles
Perdirent femes et puchieles
Lor droit de tiere calengier.
Or violt li rois cesti engier,   1460
Et vos avoec, de la conté.
Ene vos fait il grant bonté?"

Il oënt que li cuens de Cestre
Voit et entent trestolt lor estre.
Dient: "Se nos le seüsciens,   1465
Que nos avoir le peüsciens,
Et la conté et l'ireté,
Dont diriens nos par verité

68

with so many colors in so short a time
as shame has done with the two of them,
first red, then blue, then white,
and then more red than blood.   1430
You should know that without great suffering
they wouldn't have changed color so fast.

The count approached them. He said, "God greet you.
You certainly don't need my advice."
Then he spoke like the politician he was.   1435
"I have gone to a lot of trouble for you."
"You have, sir? With respect to whom?" "The king."
"The king, good sir? And what about?"
"Cador, don't play games with me.
I'll say it right to your face: 1440
you love belle Eufemie,
and she obviously doesn't hate you.
I've seen it quite clearly all along,
but I have kept it quiet until now.
I remembered that I have been in love,   1445
and I was grateful to him who helped.
Now I have helped you a great deal;
if you had asked me to help you,
it wouldn't have turned out better, so help me God!
for all Cornwall will be yours   1450
at the death of Count Renald.
Now it would be a good idea to explain:
the land should have been this lady's,
but she no longer has a right to it.
For, as you know, because of the two counts   1455
who killed each other so disgracefully
on account of the twin maidens,
women and girls have lost the right
to lay claim to land.
Now the king wants to bestow the land   1460
on this lady and you.
Isn't he doing you a tremendous favor?"

They could hear that the count of Chester
saw and understood their situation very well.
They said, "If we knew   1465
that we could have
both county and inheritance,
then we would indeed say

69

Que vos avriiés fait por nos."
"Par Deu! plus ai jo fait por vos,/   1470
Car j'ai le roi tant losengié
Que vos serés sempres engié
De tiere ki valt l'an .m. livres.
Li rois en violt estre delivres.
Offiert l'a ja, voiant sa gent."   1475
"Chi a," font il," bel offre et gent."
"Jo cuit qu'il vos esposera."
Il respondent: "Car fusce ja!"
Fait il: "De par le Creator,
Avés vos donc trestolt l'ator?"   1480
"Oïl, par Deu, trop en avons."
Li cuens sorrist et dist: "Alons!"
Et cil: "En voies!" ki ont haste.*
Li cuens fait sanblant qu'il ait laste.
Dist lor: "Alés plus bielement,   1485
Car trop alés isnielement."
Cho fait il por auls tariier,
Qu'il desirent le mariier
Tant nequedent qu'il les amainne
Al roi, et dist: "Sire, a grant painne   1490
M'ont [il] otroié la requeste;
Por quant merciiés lé de ceste,
Car il l'ont fait por vostre amor,
Trestolt sans noise et sans clamor."
Cho dist li rois: "Jes en merci,   1495
Et se nus d'aus rien i pert chi,
Dont me raés une corone."
La ot le jor mainte persone.

Li rois a dit, voiant trestols:
"Cador, vos n'estes mie estols,   1500
Ne vos, biele Eufemie, estolte,
Quant ma requeste faites tolte.
Par an .m. livres en avrés
Et quanque vos sos ciel savrés
Que li cuens Renals tint de moi."   1505
Il en merchient moult le roi.
Ançois que tierce fust sonee
Fu bele Eufemie donee.
Cador li preus l'a affiee,
Puis l'en ont al mostier menee.   1510
Ses esposa uns arcevesques.

that you have done much for us."
"By God, I did even more for you: 1470
I handled the king so smoothly
that you will have in perpetuity
land worth a thousand marks a year.
The king will award this to you;
he has already promised in the presence of his men."   1475
"This is a fine and noble offer," they said.
"I think he will have the two of you wed."
They replied, "If only we were already!"
He said, "By the Creator,
are you ready to do it right now?"   1480
"Yes, by God, we are more than ready!"
The count smiled and said, "Let's go!"
And they, in a rush, said, "Let's hit the road!"
The count pretended to be weary.
He said to them, "A little more decorum!   1485
You're moving much too fast!"
He did it to tease them
for wanting to get married.
But nevertheless, he brought them to the king
and said, "Sire, it took a lot   1490
to get them to agree to my request,
yet you should thank them for it,
because they did it out of love for you,
without any fuss or protest."
The king said, "I do thank them,   1495
and if either of them loses anything by this,
may I be tonsured and made monk!"

There were many people present that day.
The king said in the presence of everyone,
"Cador, you are no fool,   1500
and neither are you, belle Eufemie,
for fulfilling my request.
You shall have a thousand pounds a year,
and anything under the sun you can think of
that Count Renald holds in fief from me."   1505
They thanked the king very much for that.
Before tierce was sounded,
belle Eufemie was given away;
valiant Cador became her fiance.
Then they were taken to the cathedral,   1510
where an archbishop married them.

71

Assés i ot abés et vesques,
Et dus et barons et princiers.
Li rois kis ama et tint ciers
Fait noces faire mervelloses,   1515
Poi mains des soies precioses.
Or a Cador li preus s'amie.
Demander ne lor estuet mie/
S'a voloir ont delit adés
Tres puis que il sunt mis a es.   1520
Ki longement a consirré
De cho que plus a desirré
Ja nel plaindrai s'il en consire.
Li rois fait metre .i. brief en cire
Sil tramet dant Renalt le conte.   1525
Or oiés que la lettre conte:
"Al bon Renalt de Cornuälle
Mande li rois qu'il vivie et valle.
Vostre fille ai Cador donee
Et grant riçoise abandonee.   1530
Par an lor ai doné .m. livres.
Bials sire cuens, j'en sui delivres.
Se vos volés, venés por li,
U vos le lassciés entor mi.
Forment l'a chiere la roïne   1535
Car ainc n'acointa tel meschine."
Li cuens entent ceste noviele.
Sachiés de fit moult li est biele.
S'a fait de gent grant assamblee,
Qu'aler n'i violt pas a emblee.   1540
.d. enmainne o soi de pris,
Tels com les a esslis et pris
En la tiere de Cornuälle.
Vint il al sieme jor sans falle
La u rois Ebains tient sa cort.   1545
Grans gens point contre lui et cort,
Car il ert hom sans vilonie,
Larges, cortois, sains felonie:
Et tels gens ert adonc amee.
Mais or est Faintise entamee*   1550
Et Vilonie est aforee.
Lozenge a le bouce doree;
Et Verités de corte est rese
Si qu'ele n'i valt une frese.
Et Amors et Valors mendie.   1555

72

Plenty of abbots and bishops were there,
and dukes and barons and princes.
The king, who loved them and cherished them,
had a marvelous nuptial feast arranged,   1515
only slightly less splendid than his own.
Now the valiant Cador has his beloved.
They didn't have to ask any longer;
they could take their pleasure to their hearts' content,
now that they were placed in such proximity.   1520
Whoever has long been deprived
of what he has most desired—
I won't pity him if he doesn't help himself to it!
The king had a letter sealed
and sent to Count Renald.   1525
This is what the letter said:
"To good Count Renald of Cornwall
the King sends greetings: may he live long and prosper!
I have given your daughter to Cador
and granted them a large fortune.   1530
I have given them a thousand pounds a year.
Good Sir Count, I have granted it.
Come to fetch your daughter, if you wish,
or leave her with us, if you so desire,
for the Queen is very fond of her;   1535
she has never known such a charming girl."
When the count received this news,
it was very good news to him indeed.
He summoned a large number of men—
he didn't want this trip to be a secret.   1540
He took five hundred worthy men,
chosen and selected
from the land of Cornwall.
On the seventh day he reached the place
where King Evan was holding court.   1545
Many people hastened to meet him,
for he was a man of great nobility.
generous, courteous and without treachery,
and such men were cherished in those days.
But now Deception is silver-plated,   1550
and Baseness has a high market value;
Flattery has a gilded mouth,
and Truth is shaved so close
it's not worth a strawberry,
while Love and Virtue go a-begging.   1555

73

Ne sai mais, las! que jo en die.
Honors ne valt mais une tille.
De Honte ont fait lor ciere fille.
Il ne le voelent marier,
Por rover ne por tarier,   1560
Mais retenir veïr en voel.*
Qu'en puis jo donc, se jo m'en duel?
Hontes a trop esté a cort:
A cascun més trote et acort.
En li a mais vielle puciele,   1565
Il n'a en tiere damoisiele/
Se tant se fust a cort tenue
Com Hontes est, ne fust kenue,
Vils a veïr et a savoir.
Et Honte voelent tolt avoir: 1570
Honte ont et Honte les maintient,
O cui vivre .m. mars sont nient.
Miols doi dire morir que vivre
Car Hontes est mors, kis enivre.
Tans seroit mais de lasscier Honte.   1575
Or voel repairier a mon conte.

Li cuens ne se tint mie a lent.
Il vient al roi, mercie l'ent
De l'onor que sa fille a faite.
Acorde soi; et puis afaite   1580
A cascun ki del sien li rueve.
Ki bien i quiert francise i trueve.
Cador l'oneure moult et ainme.
De lui desos Deu se reclaime,
Devient ses fils, et cil ses pere.   1585
"Or voel," cho dist li cuens, "qu'il pere
Que pris vos estes a prodome."
Al roi l'enmainne, c'est la some,
Si l'a illueques ravestu
De quanque il tient par un festu,   1590
Poruec que sa fille a oir viegne;
Se sans oir muert, icil le tiegne
Ki doit tenir. Les .m. livrees
Ait Cador, com li a livrees.
Cil l'en mercie de l'estrainne.   1595
Li cuens prent congié, sis enmainne
Cador et sa fille Eufemie.
De sejor n'i ot parlé mie,

74

Alas, I don't know what more to say.
Honor isn't worth a piece of string.
They have made Shame their dear daughter;
they don't want to find a husband for her,
however much they are asked and nagged.   1560
But I can't stand to keep looking at it!
What good can my grief possibly do?
Shame has been received at court for far too long;
she is at everyone's beck and call.
She'll always be an old maid.   1565
There's no damsel in the world
who wouldn't be all shriveled up
if she'd been around as long as Shame,
vile to know and see.
But they all want Shame;   1570
Shame they have and by Shame they are sustained,
for whom a thousand marks to live on are as nothing.
I should say die rather than live,
for Shame is death to him who yields to her.
But now it's time to leave Shame;   1575
I want to return to my story.

The count didn't hesitate.
He came to the king and thanked him
for the honor he had done his daughter.
He gave his consent, and then gave freely   1580
of all his possessions to anyone who asked him.
Whoever sought generosity found it there.
Cador honored and loved him greatly;
he prayed to God to protect him;
they became like father and son.   1585
"Now," said the count, "I want you to see
that you are in the hands of a worthy father."
In short, he took Cador to the king
and invested him then and there
with whatever he held in fief,   1590
provided his daughter should have an heir.
If she died without an heir, it should go
to the rightful claimant. The thousand pounds
were given to Cador, as had been arranged.
Cador thanked him for his generosity.   1595
The count took leave; with him he took
Cador and his daughter Eufemie.
They never spoke of staying;

75

Si vinrent en lor tiere arriere.
Tant vont par sente et par carriere   1600
Qu'al sieme jor sans falle [i] sunt.
Cil del païs grant fieste i funt,
Ainc mais ne vit nus hom gregnor.
De Cador fait li cuens segnor
Del tolt, sauve sa feëlté.   1605
Entr'als nen ot ainc cruelté,
Ne male amor, ne felonie.
Nus hom n'i vit ainc vilonie.
Cador le tient cier com son pere,
La contesse ainme com sa mere.   1610
Mais la vie Renalt fu poie.
Apriés la fieste et cele joie
Ne vesqui c'un an et un jor.
Car de nos gens n'i a c'um tor:
Que que nus engigne u açaigne,   1615
U il voelle, u il n'adagne,
Morir l'estuet, et nos tretolt,
Foibles et fors, humeles, estolt.
Tolt alsi fist Renals li buens.
Or a Cador grant dol li cuens.   1620
Tolte la gens de la contree
S'est illuec al cors encontree:
Et la plainte qu'il funt commune
Nen est fors solement cest'une:
"Li mors Renalt, ki nos a mort,   1625
Or nos acostume et amort
A dolozer, a dol mener,
Tant com vivrons et a pener.
Quant vos ne poés vivre o nos,
Ne nos morir ensanble o vos,   1630
Tel compagnie vos tenrons
Qu'a nostre vivant dol menrons."
Pleure Eufemie, et plaint sa mere
Son baron, et ceste son pere,
Quant Cador le conforte et dist   1635
Que plaindre apriés mort valt petit.
Ne voelle mais trop mener joie,
Ne plaindre trop por quanque il oie,
Ne por joie trop esjoïr,
Por rien trop mener dol, n'oïr.   1640
Cador le castie et conforte:
"Quant li cors est fors de la porte

76

they returned home to their lands.
They traveled so fast by street and way   1600
that they arrived on the seventh day.
The local people prepared a magnificent feast,
no one has ever seen a greater one.
The count made Cador overlord of all,
without asking his oath of fealty.   1605
There never was any discord between them,
or bad faith or treachery.
No one ever saw the slightest trace of base conduct.
Cador held the count as dear as his own father;
he loved the countess like a mother.   1610
But Count Renald didn't live much longer.
After the feasting and this joy
he lived only a year and a day.
It's the same for all of us:
whatever a man's clever schemes or plots,*   1615
whether he wants to or doesn't deign to,
he has to die—and so do we all,
strong or weak, proud or humble,
and that is what Renald the Good did.
Cador mourned the count profoundly.   1620
All the people in the land
gathered around the body,
and the common lament they raised
was always one and the same:
"Renald's death has killed us,   1625
it will change our way of life
to one of mourning and suffering
and bereavement for as long as we live.
Since you cannot live among us,
and we cannot die with you,   1630
we will keep you company
by living a life of mourning."
Eufemie wept, her mother grieved,
one for her lord, one for her father.
Cador comforted her and said   1635
that grief after death is of little use.
One should never rejoice to excess
or grieve too much for any reason.
One should not rejoice too much from joy
or grieve too much, whatever the news.   1640
Cador chided and comforted her,
"When the body is out the door

77

Et enfoïs et enterrés,
El sarcu mis et enserrés,
Si est li diols apetiziés." 1645
Cador a fait com hom voisiés,
Que anchois que li cuens morust,
Que folors n'i entrecorust,
En tols les castials mist ses gardes,
Tels gens ki ne sunt pas coärdes. 1650

Chi le lairons del mort ester.
N'i fait pas trop bon arester:
Ki vis est o les vis se tiegne.
Deu, se lui plaist, des mors soviegne.
Huimais orrés conte aviver, 1655
Sans noise faire et estriver.
De Cador, de s'engendreüre
Comence chi tels aventure
C'ainques n'oïstes tele en livre.
Si com l'estorie le nos livre, 1660
Qu'en latin escrite lizons,
En romans si le vos disons. /
Jo ne di pas que n'i ajoigne
Avoic le voir sovent mençoigne
Por le conte miols acesmer: 1665
Mais se jel puis a droit esmer
N'i metrai rien qui m'uevre enpire
Ne del voir nen iert mos a dire
Car la verté ne doi taisir.
Avint si par le Deu plaisir 1670
Que Eufemie ot conceü.
Quant li cuens l'a aperceü,
Si prie Deu moult, par sa grasce,
Que de cel fruit haitië le face,
Si com par lui vint a semence, 1675
Par pechié qu'aient fait ne mence:
Mais soit l'enfantemens salvables,
Et l'enfes ait menbres raisnables,
Que rien n'i ait mespris Nature
Quant molla cel fruit en figure; 1680
Et quant la dame en iert delivre
Qu'ele ait santé, l'enfes puist vivre.
A une part la dame enmainne.
Parole moult de cele estrainne
Dont Dex lor a fait demostrance: 1685

78

and in the ground and covered with earth
and sealed in the tomb,
then it's time for sorrow to diminish."   1645
Cador acted like a prudent man:
as soon as the count died,
to prevent any rash behavior,
he stationed his guards in all the castles,
the kind of men who are not cowards.   1650

Let's stop talking of death now;
it's not such a good idea to dwell on it.
The live are better off among the living;
let it please God to be mindful of the dead.
From now on you shall hear a lively tale,   1655
without any further fuss or ado.
Of Cador and his offspring
begins such a tale of adventure
as you never heard of in any book.
Just as it was written   1660
in the Latin version we read,
we will tell it to you in French.
I'm not saying that there isn't
a good deal of fiction mingled with truth,
in order to improve the tale,   1665
but if I am any judge of things,
I'm not putting in anything that will spoil the work,
nor will there be any less truth in it,
for truth should not be silenced.
It so happened that it pleased God   1670
to have Eufemie conceive a child.
When the count was told of this,
he prayed fervently that God in his mercy
might make this fruit healthy
and let it ripen as if it were His,   1675
and not let it be defective from parents' sin,
but let the pregnancy progress safely,
and let the child have proper limbs,
and let Nature have neglected nothing
when she molded this fruit into human shape;   1680
and when the lady is delivered of it,
let her be well and let the child live.
He took the lady aside
and discussed this gift
with which God had favored them.   1685

79

"Devant le colp ai grant dotance,
Biele, que nostre engendreüre
Tort a femiele porteüre,
Se Dex tant done que il nasce;
Que li rois Ebayns pas ne lassce 1690
Que femes aient iretage
A son vivant, por le damage
Des .ii. contes par les jumieles,
Sin ont moult perdu les femieles."

"Bials sire ciers," cho dist la dame, 1695
"En moi, cho savés, n'a nul blasme
Quels qu'il soit, masles u femiele;
Mais Dex qui crie home et apiele
Otroit que lie en soit la mere
Et soit a plaizir de son pere." 1700
"Ma dolce amie," dist li cuens,
"Jhesus li pius, li vrais, li buens,
Il fist Adan, cho est la voire,
Et Evain de sa coste en oire.
Es vos l'entensiön reposte 1705
Por quoi il le fist de sa coste,
Qu'ensi fuscent d'une voellance
Com il sunt fait d'une sustance,
Andoi eüscent un voloir,
A l'esjoïr, et al doloir. / 1710
Entr'ome et feme a grant commune,
Car d'als .ii. est la sustance une,
Et adonques meësmement
Quant il i a esposement,
Car el saintisme sacrement 1715
De nostre Noviel Testament
Met on entr'als tele aliänce,
Cho sachiés vos tolt a fïance,
C'uns sans et une cars devienent:
Sor als est puis s'il ne se tienent. 1720
Biele, quant nostre cars est une,
Soit nostre volentés commune.
Le sanc avons [nos] als commun,
Or aiens le voloir commun."
La dame li repont: "Bials sire, 1725
Ja rien que vostres cuers desire
N'orés par moi estre escondie."
"Entendés moi, suer, dolce amie,

80

"My dear, I am deeply concerned
about the possibility that the child we have engendered
might turn out to be female
(if God allows it to be born),
and that King Evan may not allow   1690
women to inherit
as long as he lives, because of the damage done
to two counts by twin girls,
through which females have lost so much."

"Dear, sweet Sire," said the lady,   1695
"I am not to blame, you know,
whether the child is male or female.
God who created and who watches over mankind
has decreed that the mother should be happy
and the father pleased with any child."   1700
"My sweet love," said the count,
"Jesus the pious, true, and good
created Adam, this we know to be true,
and right away created Eve from his rib.
And here is the hidden reason   1705
why he made her from his rib:
so that they would be of one mind,
as they are made of one substance.
Both should be of one mind,
united in joy and sorrow.   1710
There is great unity between man and woman,
because the two are of one substance.
And it is the same
when they are married,
for, with the most holy sacrament   1715
of our New Testament,
such an alliance is made between them
that you should know for certain
they become one flesh and blood.
It is upon their heads if they don't hold to this thereafter.   1720
Since, my sweet, our flesh is one,
let our will be one as well.
Since our blood is one,
let us be of one mind."
The lady replied to him, "Sweet lord,   1725
nothing that your heart desires
will I refuse you."
"Hear me, sister, sweet friend:

81

Quant vos ventres vos akioldra
(Cho iert adonc quant Dex voldra)   1730
A vo delivrer n'avra mie
Fors une feme, dolce amie.
—Ne le me tornés mie a blasme—
N'i avrés c'une sole dame.
Feme fu un per d'Engletiere   1735
Ki morut l'autrier d'une guere,
Et la dame en remest enchante.
Apriés sa mort cha vint a m'ante.
D'enfant se delivra l'altrier:
Par non l'apiela on Galtier.   1740
Ne vesqui mais tant solement
.viii. jors puis le baptisement.
La dame si est ma cosine
Et somes trestolt d'une orine.
Cesti seule vos voel livrer   1745
Quant cho vendra al delivrer.
Lequel qu'aiés, masle u femiele,
Par la dame me mandés, biele,
Que un bel fil avés eü,
Oiant trestols qu'il soit seü.   1750
Car se nos avons une fille
N'avra al montant d'une tille
De quanque nos sos ciel avons,
Se nos l'afaire ne menons
Si cointement par coverture   1755
Que on n'en sace l'aventure.
Faisons le com un fil norir,
De priés garder et bien covrir,/
Si le porons* del nostre engier.
Nus nel pora ja calengier."   1760
Cho respont la contesse encontre:
"Dex me doinst, sire, mal encontre,
Se jo nel fac moult volentiers."
La dame mande endementiers,
Et cele i vient isnielement   1765
Et est rechute bielement.
Li cuens se cozinain enmainne
O lui en sa cambre demainne,
Se li demostre tolt l'affaire
Si qu'ele entent bien que doit faire.   1770
Li cuens li fait bele promesse
Et moult li promet la contesse.

when it is time for you to give birth
(which will happen in God's time),   1730
you shall have only one woman
to deliver you, sweet love —
please do not blame me for this —
you shall have only one lady.
She was the wife of a peer of England   1735
who died a while ago in a war,
leaving the lady pregnant.
After his death, she came to my aunt's
and was shortly delivered of a child
who was given the name of Walther.   1740
He lived only a week
after being baptized.
The lady is my cousin;
we are very closely related.
I will bring you this one woman alone   1745
when it is time for the baby to be delivered.
Whichever you have, male or female,
you shall have the lady announce to me,
sweet, that you have had a fine son;
let it be announced in the presence of all.   1750
For if we have a daughter,
she won't get a single shred
of our earthly possessions,
unless we arrange things so
cleverly and secretly   1755
that nobody finds out what we're up to.
We will raise her as a boy,
watch her closely and keep her covered up.
Thus we will be able to make her our heir;
no one will be able to challenge it."   1760
To this the countess replied,
"May God see fit to punish me,
if I do not do this most willingly."
Then they sent for the lady;
she came right away   1765
and was most cordially received.
The king conducted his cousin
to his private chambers
and there explained the whole situation to her,
so that she understood perfectly well what to do.   1770
The count promised her many things;
the countess promised her a great deal.

Cele dist qu'el le servira,
Venra entor li et ira.
La dame plus et plus apoise   1775
Et de son mal le conte poise.
L'enfes l'angoissce, et point, et broce.
Li jors del agezir aproce.
Vos savés qu'a moi nient ne monte
C'on mecce en rime ne en conte   1780
Come la dame fu penee
A l'enfanter et demenee.
Mais tant dirai, ele enfanta,
Et ot enfant, tant en pena.
Moult fu la contesse adolee   1785
Car l'enfertés li est colee
El cuer, es os, es niers, es vainnes,
Car moult a eü de grans painnes.
La dame ert cozine al segnor.
Onques n'ot mais traval gregnor,   1790
Car seule fu sans compagnesse
Al delivrer de la contesse.
Et on vos a sovent retrait
Que mal a ki malade trait.

Or voel a l'enfant repairier   1795
Et demostrer et esclairier
Liquels cho fu, masle u femiele.
Segnor, cho fu une puchiele.
Nature i mostre tolte s'uevre.
Se jo le vus di et descuevre   1800
Quels l'uevre fu, ne vos anuit,
Car vos devés bien estre aduit,
Se vos volés savoir un conte,
D'entendre et oïr cho que monte.
Nature qui moult grant force a   1805
Vint a l'enfant, si s'esforça. /
Dist: "Or voel faire ouvre forcible."
Tolt si com cil qui prent un crible,
U tamis, u un buletiel,
Quant faire violt blanc pain e biel,   1810
Et quant la farine i a mise
Dunt crible, u bulette, u tamise,
Et torne le flor d'une part,
Et le gros terchuel en depart,

84

The lady said she would serve her;
she would act as go-between.
The countess grew heavy with child;   1775
the count was distressed by her discomfort.
The child pressed upon her and kicked her and jabbed her.
The day of her confinement grew near.
You know that I have no special interest
in telling in prose or verse   1780
how the lady suffered torment
and how her body was contorted in childbirth.
But I will say this: she went into labor
and had the baby, however much pain it cost her.
The countess was in agony.   1785
The spasms coursed through her heart
and bones and nerves and veins.
Hre contractions were prolonged and very painful.
The lady who was the lord's cousin
never had a more difficult task,   1790
for she was alone, without anyone to help her,
throughout the countess's delivery.
And, as has often been said,
ill-used is the one who treats the ill.

Now let us turn to the child   1795
and clear things up and reveal
whether it was a boy or a girl.
My lords, it was a girl!
She was a triumph of Nature's art.
If I tell you all about   1800
this handiwork, don't be annoyed,
for you ought to be well informed,
if you ask to hear a story,
in order to understand what it's really about.
Nature, who has great powers,   1805
came to the child and took hold of it
and said, "Now I'm going to create a masterpiece."
Just like the one who takes a sieve
or sifter or colander
when he wants to make beautiful white bread,   1810
and sifts the flour through
the sifter, sieve or colander,
and puts the extra-fine flour on one side
and the coarse bran on the other,

Et fait adonc un entreclos   1815
Entre le fleur blance et le gros,
Si qu'o le fleur n'a nule palle,
Ne busce nule, ne escalle,
Ne entre tolt l'autre monciel
De fleur vallant un botonciel,   1820
Et de la fleur fait ses gastials,
Et del tercuel torte a porciels,
Tolt si com cis fait sans dotance
Que chi ai mis en la sanblance,
Si fait Nature, c'est la some,   1825
Quante faire violt un vallant home
Que voelle ovrer par majestyre.
Premierement prent sa matyre.
Avant tolte ouvre si l'esmie,
Et moult l'espurge, et esniie;   1830
Et quant l'a moult bien esmiié
Si oste del gros le delié.
De cel delié si fait sans falle
Les buens, et del gros la frapalle.
Mais se il avient que Nature   1835
Soit corocie, u que n'ait cure
C'un poi del gros al delié viegne
Et al mollier avoec se tiegne,
Cil gros se trait al cuer en oire.
Et se ne me volés or croire   1840
Vos le poés par vos prover.
Ne poés vos sovent trover
Vil cuer et povre, et riche cors
Kist sarpelliere par defors?
Li cors n'est mais fors sarpelliere,   1845
Encor soit de la terre chiere;
Mais li cuers ne valt une alie
K'*est* fais de grosse et de delie.*
Et s[e] un poi de chiere terre
Se melle avoec la grosse et serre   1850
Dont Nature fait le bas home,
Al cuer se trait, c'en est la some.
Et par cho vient que halt corage
Ont mainte gent de bas parage. /
Si com maint noble sont sollié,   1855
De lor vils cuers entoëllié,
Si sunt li bas de grant affaire
A cel pooir qu'il pueent faire;

and carefully keeps   1815
the extra-fine flour separate from the coarse,
so that the fine flour has no straw
or chaff or husks in it,
and the other little heap
doesn't have the least little bit of fine flour,   1820
and makes fine cakes of the flour
and loaves for the pigs out of the bran —
just like this, without a doubt,
like the one we have depicted here,
does Nature, to be brief,   1825
proceed when she wants to make a noble human being
that she wants to be a masterpiece.
She first prepares her raw material.
Before starting to work, she breaks it up
and purifies it and cleans it,   1830
and when she has broken it into little pieces,
she separates the fine from the coarse.
She always makes quality folk from
the refined clay, and riff-raff from the coarse.
But if it happens that Nature   1835
is in a bad mood and isn't careful,
so that a little of the coarse gets mixed in with the fine
and is retained in the molding,
this coarse matter attacks the heart right away.
And if you don't care to believe me,   1840
you can prove it for yourself.
Don't you often find
a poor, vile heart with a rich body,
which is nothing but sackcloth on the outside?
The body is mere sackcloth,   1845
even if it's made from the finest clay,
and the heart made of coarse mixed with fine
isn't worth a crab-apple.
But if a bit of fine clay
is mingled and sticks with the coarse stuff   1850
out of which Nature makes the low-born,
it works upon the heart, in truth.
And that is why lofty character
may be found in many of low station,
just as many nobles are sullied,   1855
dragged down by the vileness of their hearts,
while there are men of low degree but noble character
who do the very best they can,

87

Et plain de moult grant honesté
Sunt, et seront, et ont esté. 1860

De cho le lairai ore atant.
Repairier voel a cel enfant
Dont jo vus ai fait mentiön.
Nature i mist s'ententiön.
Li matere est et biele et pure. 1865
Ainc de mellor n'ovra Nature.
Biele est, sel fait encor plus bele,
Car faire en volra sa puciele.
Cho dist Nature l'engignose
Ki en s'ovraigne est mervellose: 1870
"Ainc mais nen endurai a prendre
Ceste matere, ne despendre:
Or la prendrai houes ma mescine.
Tant com la materre est plus fine
Covient il plus l'uevre afiner, 1875
Bien commencier et miols finer.
La matere ai moult estuïe,
Si a[i] estei moult anuïe
De grosse ouvre, et de vilainne.
Or voel a cesti mettre painne. 1880
En li sole, car bel me sanble,
Metrai plus de bialté ensanble
Que n'aient ore .m. de celes
Qui en cest monde sont plus beles.
Alcune fois doit paroir m'uevre." 1885
A son secré va, si descuevre.
Molles i a bien .m. milliers,
Que cho li est moult grans mestiers,
Car s'ele n'eüst forme c'une,
La samblance estroit si commune 1890
De tolte gent, c'on ne savroit
Quoi, ne quel non, cascuns avroit.
Mais Nature garda si bien
En s'uevre n'a a blasmer rien.
Ele a formes grans et petites, 1895
Laides, contrefaites, parfites,
Car si sunt faites tolte gent,
Grant et petit, et biel, et gent,
Tant mainte forme i a diverse.
Et Nature en a une aërse. 1900

and are full of integrity;
are, were, and always will be.   1860

I'm going to drop this subject now;
I want to get back to that infant
whom I mentioned to you before.
Nature puts forth her noblest efforts.
The clay is beautiful and pure.   1865
Nature never made anything better.*
The child is beautiful; Nature is making her more beautiful
    still,
for she wants her to be her own little girl.
Thus speaks ingenious Nature,
whose works are marvelous: 1870
"I will no longer hesitate to take
this clay and use it:
I will use it now to make my girl.
The finer the material,
the more fitting it is to do fine work,   1875
to begin well and finish better.
I have been very sparing with good material,
but now I am quite bored
with crude work and vulgarity.
Now I want to take pains with this one.   1880
In her alone—for I wish it to be so—
I shall assemble more beauty
than a thousand of the most beautiful girls
in the whole world now possess.
Once in a while I must show what I can do."   1885
She goes to her coffer and opens it up.
She has at least a million molds there,
and she has very great need of them,
for if she had only one form,
everyone would look so much alike   1890
that no one would ever be able to tell
who was who or what their name was.
But Nature takes such care
that there is nothing to fault in her work.
She has forms both big and little,   1895
ugly, misshapen, and perfect,
for thus all people are fashioned,
big and little, handsome and fine,
she has so many different forms.
But one mold she has kept aside;   1900

Ainc mais user ne l'endura.
Nature quanque a fait jura
Qu'or a d'ovrer moult bon talent.
Prist cele forme, porta l'ent,
Va cele part a entençon   1905
U doit ovrer, comence en son:
Biel cief fait, bloie kievelure
Ki luisent cler par nuit obscure.
La kavelure recercelle;
De la greve dusque a l'orelle   1910
Com une ligne droit descent
Sique ses poins ne se desment.
La kavelure al cief li serre:
Ja n'estevra la greve querre,
Ne al pinier ne al trecier,   1915
Car Nature iert al redrecier.
Les orelles li fait petites
Nature, ki les a escrites,
Les sorcils bruns et bien seöir,
Nul hom ne puet si bials veöir.   1920

Cho dist Nature: "Jo m'en duel
Se riens i falt." Dont part l'entruel
De son polcier si bielement,
Et dont li fait isnielement
Plain volt, et face bien retraite,   1925
Et la color si bien refaite.
Cho dist Nature: "C'iert ma fille."
Atant la face li bresille,
Et com plus croistra la puciele,
Et li colors en la masciele.   1930
La bouce escrist, fait l'overture
Petite, et levres a mesure,
Sor le menton les dens serrés.
Ja nul si bel volt ne verrés.
Apriés li fait col blanc et lonc,   1935
Voltice espaule par selonc,
Et les bras li fait si tres drois,
Les mains petites, lons les dois,
Le pis bien fait, graisles les flans,
Miols faite ne vit sers ne frans.   1940
Et les hances si fait voltices,
Les cuisses moles et faitices.
Les janbes droites fist Nature,

90

she has never used it yet.
Nature swears by all she has made
that she really feels like getting to work now.
She takes that mold and carries it out
and goes to where she intends to work   1905
and begins right at the top.
She fashions a beautiful head, blond hair—
the kind that shines brightly in the dark night.
The head of hair curls around;
from the part to the ear   1910
it falls evenly,
Nature's hand is so steady.
She attaches the hair to the head:
you won't have to look for the part,
whether you comb it or braid it,   1915
for Nature will set it perfectly straight.
Nature designed and drew
a pair of little ears,
made eyebrows, brown and very neat;
no one has ever seen such beautiful ones.   1920

Then Nature says, "I would be sorry
if anything were lacking." Then with her thumb
she forms the space between the two eyes beautifully,
and quickly makes
the whole face, and traces a well-turned visage   1925
and colors it most beautifully.
Nature says, "This will be my girl!"
The more she applies color to the face,
the more the girl's beauty will be enhanced.,
and the color on her cheeks deepened.   1930
She designs the mouth, makes the opening small,
and forms the lips to match,
places the teeth well and forms the chin—
you will never see a more beautiful face.
And then she makes a long white neck,   1935
and forms the curve of the shoulders along with it.
And she makes the arms very straight,
the hands small, the fingers long,
the bosom well-turned, slender sides;
neither serf nor freeman ever saw better.   1940
And she makes the hips rounded,
the thighs soft and shapely.
Nature makes the legs straight,

Et piés, et ortals a mesure.
Que vos feroie huimais alonge?   1945
Vos le tenrés puet s'estre a songe.
Ainc belizors voir ne vesqui
De li el monde, ne nasqui,
Al plus droit que jo puis esmer.
En li n'a niënt a blasmer/   1950
Fors solement qu'ele est trop biele,
Que tant en a en la puciele
Qu'a .m. peüst assés savoir,
Se tant en peüscent avoir
Et de bialté et de faiture.   1955
Ainc n'ovra mais si bien Nature
A rien ki morir doive vivre.
Bele Eufemie en est delivre.
De l'angoisse est resalenee,
Que sa fille est si biele nee.   1960
La grans angoisce l'atenrist,
Mais cele bialtés amenrist
Sa grant angoisse et s'enfertés.
Si con ç'avint dirai vertés.
Cele qui fu o la contesse   1965
Cui li cuens ot fait la promesse,
Et fu sa cozine germaine,
Al conte vait noncier l'estraine.
Vient en la sale tolt riant,
Oiant tols les barons criant: 1970
"Faites vos liet, bials sire cuens!
Jhesus li pius, li vrais, li buens,
Un moult bel fil vos a tramis.
Or avés vos moult plus d'amis."

Tolte la cors est esjoïe   1975
Por la noviele c'ont oïe.
N'i ot ainc mais joie gregnor.
Li cuens mercie cel Segnor
Par cui il pluet, et vente, et halle,
Lequel qu'il ait, femiele u malle;   1980
Mais volentiers, se Deu pleüst,
Presist le fil se il l'eüst.
Si en est en moult grant error,
Car il n'en set pas la verror.
O l'error se melle esperance,   1985
Et o l'espoir se melle errance.

92

and feet and toes in proportion.
Why should I go on like this?   1945
You'll probably think it's all a dream.
But never, in truth lived a more beautiful creature
in this world, nor was anything more lovely ever born.
As near as I can estimate,
there is absolutely nothing wrong with this girl—   1950
except that she's too beautiful.
For there is so much beauty in her
that it would be plenty for a thousand,
if they could share
such beauty and workmanship.   1955
Nature will never work so well
on any mortal being again.
Belle Eufemie was delivered of this child.
Her anguish was somewhat assuaged
because her daughter was born so beautiful.   1960
She was weak from her terrible ordeal,
but this beauty attenuated
her great pain and weakness.
Now I will tell you truly what happened next:
the woman who was with the countess—   1965
the one the count had promised so much
and who was his first cousin—
went to announce the news to the count.
She came into the room all smiles,
and cried out in the presence of all the barons,   1970
"Rejoice, good Sir Count!
Jesus the pious, the true, the good
has granted you a most beautiful son—
a fine addition to the family."

The entire court rejoiced   1975
when they heard the news;
there never was greater rejoicing.
The count gave thanks to the Lord
who brings rain and wind and scorching heat
for whichever it was, male or female.   1980
But he would gladly, if it pleased God,
have taken a son if given one.
He was in a state of tremendous uncertainty,
for he didn't know the truth.
With uncertainty, hope was mingled,   1985
and with hope, uncertainty.

La lie chiere de la dame
Ki en riant nonça la fame
L'errance de son cuer deboute;
Mais par lui mesme i est la doute,   1990
Qu'il rova porter la noviele,
Que qu'il eüst, malle u femiele,
Qu'il eüst un bel fil eüt.
Desire qu'ait le voir seüt.
La sale est de chevaliers plaine: 1995
Grans est la joie c'on i mainne.
Uns bedials crie c'om s'acoise:
"Ma dame n'a mestier de noise!"/
Cil voidierent errant la cort,
Et li cuens en la cambre acort   2000
Por l'estre savoir et enquere.
L'uis de la cambre apriés lui serre.
Li voloirs qu'a del voir savoir
Tolt qu'il ne puet vergoigne avoir
Qu'al lit ne voist de l'acolcie.   2005
De sa main destre l'a tocie,
Et cele en a moult grant vergoigne.
Li cuens porquant ne s'en eslogne,
Ainz dist: "Comment est, biele amie?"
Cele respont qu'el n'avra mie   2010
Angoisse que ne puist porter
Tolt por son segnor conforter.
"Biele, de vostre engendreüre
Voldroie savoir l'aventure,
Lequel cho est, malle u femiele,   2015
Oïr en voel certe noviele."
"Se vos, bials sire, nel savés,
Jo vos di c'une fille avés.
S'est la plus biele creäture
C'ainc en cest mont fesist Nature."   2020
Atant sa fille li ensaigne.
Li cuens le voit, et si le saine.
Puis dist: "Li Sires ki te fist,
Et en tel figure te mist,
Te doinst cho que desir veïr,   2025
Et croistre te face et tehir,
Et a ta mere doinst santé."
Li cuens s'en a forment vanté,
Qu'il ne donroit mie une tille

The cheerful demeanor of the lady
who smilingly announced the news
opposed the doubt in his heart,
but he himself had caused this doubt   1990
when he asked her to announce
that he had a fine son
whether it was a boy or a girl.
He wanted to know the truth.
The hall was full of knights;   1995
everyone was celebrating wildly.
An official called for them to be quiet:
"My lady has no need of noise!"
They emptied out the hall and scattered.
The count rushed to the bedchamber   2000
to find out how things really stood.
He locked the door of the bedchamber behind him.
His desire to know the truth
took away any feeling of shame
which would have kept him from approaching a woman in
     childbed.   2005
He took her hand in his;
she was very embarrassed at this,
but the count did not go away.
He said, "How are you, dearest love?"
She said there would never be   2010
pain too great for her to endure
for the sake of her lord's well-being.
"Sweet love, I wanted to know how things turned out,
whether you gave birth
to a boy or a girl,   2015
I would like to know for certain."
"If you don't know, dear lord,
I will tell you that you have a daughter.
She is the most beautiful creature
ever placed in this world by Nature."   2020
Then she showed him his daughter.
The count saw her and blessed her.
Then he said, "May the lord who created you
and gave you such a lovely form
grant you whatever you desire   2025
and make you grow and flourish,
and grant good health to your mother.
The count swore up and down
that he wouldn't give a trifle

De solte a un fil de sa fille,   2030
Car ainc ne vit si biele cose.
Color i voit de lis, de rose.
Se Deux en done l'aventure
Qu'il en puist faire coverture,
Donques a il quanque il desire.   2035
A la contesse prent a dire:
"Consel nos convenra aquierre
Que nos oirs ne perge sa tierre.
Je le voel, biele, desguiser,
Si com m'oïstes deviser.   2040
Faire en voel malle de femiele.
Or en pensés, amie biele,
Car nos ne poö[n]s pas savoir
Se jamais poriens malle avoir.
Nos n'en somes pas aseür,   2045
Et se nos l'avons par eür/
Cesti ferons desvaleter.
Nus ne nos en pora reter
De traïson, de felonie,
De malvaistié, de vilonie.   2050
Et se nos falons a oir malle,
Ceste ira al vent et al halle,
A la froidure et a la bize.
Moult bone garde i avra mize.
Devant le ferai estalcier,   2055
Fendre ses dras, braies calcier.
Et ceste dame i metra painne,
Ki est ma cozine germainne.
Devenra por m'amor norice.
Se jo sui manans ele iert riche.   2060
Mar avra ja de honte soig
S'or me secort a cest besoing.
Sel faisons ore baptizier
Et nostre dolte apetizier,
Car se de baptesme a l'eür   2065
Nos en seromes plus seür.
Sel faisons apieler Scilense
El non de Sainte Paciensce,
Por cho que silensce tolt ance.
Que Jhesus Cris par sa poissance   2070
Le nos doinst celer et taisir,
Ensi com lui est a plaizir!

to exchange his girl for a boy, 2030
for he had never seen such a beautiful thing.
She was the color of lilies and roses.
If God gives him the chance
to conceal her sex,
he will have everything he wants. 2035
He said to the countess,
"We ought to devise a plan
to keep our heir from losing her lands.
Dearest, I want to disguise her,
as you heard me say before. 2040
I want to make a male of a female.
Think about it, dearest love,
for there is no way we can know
if we will ever have a son.
We can't be sure of it, 2045
and if we do have one, by any chance,
we'll turn this one back into a girl.
That way, no one can accuse us
of treason or felony,
of wickedness or villainy. 2050
But if we don't have a male heir,
this girl-child will wander in wind and scorching sun,
in freezing cold and autumn breeze.
We will watch over her very carefully.
We will have her hair cut short in front, 2055
have her wear garments split at the sides and dress her in
    breeches,
and the lady who is my first cousin
will take care of everything.
She will be nursemaid out of loyalty to me.
If I prosper, she shall be rich. 2060
She will never have to worry about being poor or abandoned
if she helps me now with this task.
Now let us have the baby baptized,
and then we can relax a little.
For if we are lucky with the baptism, 2065
we will be in a much stronger position.
We shall call her Silence,
after Saint Patience,
for silence relieves anxiety.
May Jesus Christ through his power 2070
keep her hidden and silent for us,
according to his pleasure.

Mellor consel trover n'i puis.
Il iert només Scilenscius;
Et s'il avient par aventure   2075
Al descovrir de sa nature
Nos muerons cest -us en -a,
S'avra a non Scilencia.
Se nos li tolons dont cest -us
Nos li donrons natural us,   2080
Car cis -us est contre nature,
Mais l'altres seroit par nature."
Dunt dist la contesse et la dame:
"En quanque dit avez n'a blasme,
Se l'enfes fust crestienés."   2085
Dont vient li cuens ki est senés.
Un drap li loie entor les rains
Imesmes de ses bieles mains,
Que li prestres par aventure
Nen aparçoivie sa nature.   2090
Si dira on al capelain,
Ançois qu'il i mecce sa main,
Que il en haste le baptize,
Car la vie li apetize, /
Et que l'enfant poroit tuer   2095
Ki le drap volroit remuer.
El conte ot bien cointe home et sage;
De soi meïsme a fait message.
Le capelain vias apiele,
Se l'amainne en la capiele,   2100
Se li a dit: "Mes fils se muert."
Et li priestres ses puins detuert.
Li cuens li dist: "Ne monte rien,
Vos diols ne fait ne mal ne bien.
N'avra por cho ne bien ne mel.   2105
Mais aprestés l'aigue et le sel."
Et il dist a son clerc: "Diva!
Va ent poruec!" Et cil i va,
Prent aigue en un vassiel de lanbre
Et sel a pris en une canbre   2110
Ki voisine ert a la capiele.
Li cuens sa cozinain apiele
Et ele vient atolt l'enfant
Oltre ses bras son cief pendant.
Com s'il deüst morir li loche,   2115
Car la dame de gret l'ahoce,

98

I can't think of a better plan.
He will be called Silentius.
And if by any chance   2075
his real nature is discovered,
we shall change this -us to -a,
and she'll be called Silentia.
If we deprive her of this -us,
we'll be observing natural usage,   2080
for this -us is contrary to nature,
but the other would be natural."
The countess and the lady both said,
"Everything you say is true,
if the child were to be christened thus."   2085
Then the clever count came
and put a cloth around the child's hips
with his own hands,
so that the priest might not
accidentally perceive her nature.   2090
The chaplain will be told,
before he lays a hand on the child,
that he must baptize it in haste,
because its life is ebbing fast,
and the child might die   2095
if its wrap were removed.
The count was truly a clever man;
he brought the message in person.
He called the chaplain right away,
and led him to the chapel   2100
and said to him, "My son is dying."
The priest wrung his hands.
The count said, "That's no help.
Your grief can do no good nor harm;
he'll neither be harmed nor helped by it.   2105
Prepare the water and salt instead."
The priest said to his clerk, "Hey, hurry!
Get moving!" And the clerk went
and took water from a marble vessel
and salt from a chamber   2110
next to the chapel.
The count summoned his cousin
and she came holding the infant
with its head dangling from the crook of her arm,
drooping as if the child were dying,   2115
for the lady was letting it wobble on purpose,

99

Ki ert voisose, et moult recuite,
Si est de barat tres bien duite.
Dist lor: "L'enfes a poi de vie.
Hastés vos tost, ainz qu'il devie."   2120
Li capelains ki grant haste a
Baptizié l'a en .i. hanap,
Dont ot envolepé ses rains,
Car crient ne muire entre ses mains.
Quel gret qu'*ai*ent nature et li us   2125
S'est apielés Scilentius.

[P]artolt tresvole la noviele
Que l'enfes muert: ne lor fu biele,
Car il orent bien oï dire
Que moult l'ot fait bel nostre Sire.   2130
Por cho si en font gregnor plainte.
La ot mainte gent de dol tainte.
Dient qu'il ert et gens et bials;
Ja s'il fust lais, bochus, mesials,
Si tost la vie ne rendist.   2135
Mais cho est bien voirs que l'on dist:
Li buen, li biel el siecle muerent,
Li lait, li malvais i demeurent. /
Es vos por nient gens esmaris.
L'enfes, qui mal n'ot, est guaris.   2140
Il n'est garis qu'il n'ot nul mal.
En la tiere ot un senescal.
O la contesse estoit norris,
Parens Renalt, kist ja porris.
Cil amoit plus bele Eufemie   2145
Qu'il ne fasoit sa fille mie.
En un bos mest, devers la mer.
Li cuens le prent forment amer,
Qu'il en ot oï grans biens dire,
Et que moult loials est li sire.   2150
Et dist: "Dame, jel manderai,
Et l'enfant li commanderai.
Une maison li ferai faire
El bos, soltive et solitaire.
O l'enfant iert iceste dame,   2155
S'en face si qu'ele n'ait blasme,
Et nul n'i voist et nus n'i viegne,
N'a le maison rote ne tiegne,
Un enfant i ait qui le sierve,

which was very clever of her indeed.
She was quick to learn deception.
She said to them, "The child is barely alive.
Hurry up, all of you, before it dies."   2120
The chaplain, who was in a tremendous hurry,
baptized the child in the piece of cloth
which was wrapped about its hips,
for he was afraid it would die in his arms.
However nature and custom may have felt about it,   2125
the child was named Silentius.

The news spread rapidly everywhere
that the child was dying. No one was pleased,
for the had heard it said
that our Lord had made the child very beautiful.   2130
That only increased their lamentation.
Many people were pale with sorrow;
they said that he was graceful and beautiful,
and that if he had been ugly, hunchbacked or leprous
he wouldn't be dying so young.   2135
And what they say is certainly true:
the good and the beautiful die young in this world;
the wicked and ugly remain alive.
But here you have people upset for nothing,
for the child who wasn't sick was cured.   2140
Actually, he wasn't cured because he wasn't sick.
There was a seneschal in the land
who had been raised with the countess
and was a close relation of Renald, who lay moldering.
He loved belle Eufemie   2145
even more than his own daughter.
He lived in a forest near the sea.
The count had taken a great liking to him,
for he had heard many good things about him,
and the man was very loyal.   2150
He said, "Lady. I will send for him
and entrust the child to him.
I will have him build a house
in the woods, isolated and solitary.
This lady shall be there with the child.   2155
This way, she will have no problems:
there'll be no coming and going,
there'll be no household staff,
only a child to serve her,

O petit sens, ki rien n'entierve,   2160
Ne ne face conoistre l'uevre;
Et nequedent tols jors se cuevre.
L'aiue avra forment petite
Por le covrir, mais le merite
Iert graindre, voir d'une sesmainne,   2165
Que ne soit grans d'un an la painne.
Li seneschaus li face avoir
Quanqu'il onques porra savoir
Que ele avoir voelle et commande.
Et se la fole gens demande   2170
Porqu'ele est o l'enfant si seule,
On dira que n'a soig de peule,
Qu'ele a de l'enfant norir honte
Por cho qu'ele est parente a conte."

La dame estoit al deviser   2175
Ki l'enfant devoit desirrer,
Et dist lor bien segurement
Et si lor jure durement
Qu'ele fera tel coverture
En cele soie noreture   2180
Que tolte gent en decevra,
Que nus le voir n'aparcevra,
Ne ja n'en oront mentiön
Desque avra tele ente[n]tiön,
Qu'il sache bien conoistre l'uevre   2185
Por que on le coile si et cuevre./
Dont ont le senescal mandé.
Il vient quant il l'unt commandé.
Receüs est par grant amor,
Sans noise faire, et sans clamor.   2190
Il mostrent donques tolte l'uevre
Et prient moult que bien le cuevre,
Qu'il en soit gardé qu'il norissce,
Que vraie noviele n'en isce.
Li seneschals donques lor jure   2195
Quanque il puet et asseüre,
Se l'enfes plus d'amis n'eüst
Ne mais lui seul, et Deu pleüst,
Qu'il celeroit la verité
Por rendre a l'enfant l'ireté.   2200
Li cuens meïsmes dont l'encline
Et la contesse sa cozine.

one too young to understand anything 2160
or betray the secret,
and yet she will have to be constantly on her guard.
She will have very little help
in keeping things hidden, but the benefit
will be greater in one week 2165
than if one took pains for a year.
The seneschal will see that the lady
has whatever she wishes and commands
whenever he hears of any need.
And if foolish people ask 2170
why she stays so isolated with the child,
we will say she doesn't want anyone around.
that she is ashamed to be nursemaid
because she is of noble birth."

The lady who was to mis-raise the child 2175
was in agreement with the plan,
and she assured them absolutely
and swore a solemn oath to them
that she would do such an excellent job
of concealing things, in her role as nursemaid, 2180
that everyone would be deceived;
no one would find out the truth,
nor would they ever hear any mention of it.
Since the lady was of this mind,
they then summoned the seneschal, 2185
so that he would be well acquainted with the plan,
and know why they were concealing the child.
As soon as they summoned him, he came
and was received as an intimate friend,
without fanfare and public spectacle. 2190
They told him everything,
and begged him to conceal it,
and keep his role of guardian secret,
so that the truth would not get out.
The seneschal swore to them 2195
the most solemn oaths possible and assured them
that even if it were God's will
that the child should have no other friend but him alone,
he would conceal the truth
in order to secure the child's inheritance. 2200
The count himself bowed low to him,
as did the countess to his cousin.

Moult funt de doner, de promeitre
A la dame por en grant mettre
Qu'ele nen ait pas en porvil   2205
De norir lor fille por fil.
Et jo certes n'i voi nul blasme
Se grant loier donent la dame,
Car de mescine avront vallet,
Et de lor fille un oir mallet.   2210
Congiet ont pris moult bonement,
Si s'entrebaisent dolcement.
Li seneschals met se el retor
Car tels fais n'a point de sejor.
La dame otolt l'enfant enmainne.   2215
Or monte l'engiens et la painne
Al senescal de celer l'uevre.
Vient en maison et si se cuevre
Viers privés, viers estrange gent.
Un ostel a fait bel et gent   2220
En la forest joste la cort.
Cuidiés que moult biel ne s'atort?
Oïl! et l'ostels est de bos,
De mur, de plaseïs enclos.
Li senescals, ki que l'en ferme   2225
I fait metre une moult fort ferme,
Qu'il savra tres bien son françois,
Quels que il soit, tres bien ançois
Que il le pié dedens i mete.
Moult est li cors et biele et nete.   2230
Met i .ii. bones fermeüres,
.ii. vierals, et fors serreüres.
Clés i a mises trosqu'a quatre,
Que nus vilains n'i puist enbatre. /
Les .ii. retient et les .ii. balle   2235
Celi qui de l'enfant est balle,
Que il i ait d'entrer pooir,
Et ele en issce a son voloir.
La dame et l'enfant i a mis.
De tols biens lor i a tramis   2240
A grant fuison et a plenté;
Et un enfant a volenté
Ke soolté* li tiegne itant.
[Il] ne lor fa/t ne tant ne quant.
N'i met pas home qui le serve   2245
Qui l'estre de l'enfant enterve,

104

They gave many gifts and promises
to the lady to secure her good will,
so that she would not disdain   2205
to raise their girl as a boy.
And I certainly see nothing wrong
with rewarding the lady handsomely,
for they will be getting a boy for a girl,
a little male heir instead of a daughter.   2210
They took affectionate leave of one another
and embraced most tenderly.
The seneschal hastened to return,
for such matters admit of no delay.
He took the lady and the child.   2215
Now it was up to the senschal to conceal
the matter by clever planning and hard work.
He went home and kept things secret
from everyone, both familiars and strangers.
He constructed a charming lodging   2220
in the forest near his estate.
Do you think he did a good job?
Indeed he did! And he enclosed the lodging
with woods and walls and palisades.
However one might blame him for it,   2225
the seneschal had a strong gate built,
so that he could identify a man
very well, whoever it might be,
long before he could set foot inside.
It was large and thick and well-fashioned.   2230
He put two good bars across it,
two bolts and strong locks.
He locked it with four keys,
so that no villain could force his way in.
He kept two and gave the other two   2235
to the lady in charge of the child,
so that he could enter
and she could leave at her will.
He installed the lady and child there.
He supplied them with all kinds of good things,   2240
plentifully and abundantly,
and a child to serve her,
to keep her company.
They were lacking for absolutely nothing.
He didn't appoint a man to serve them,   2245
because he might discover the child's true nature,

Qu'il ne fesist par aventure
Demostrement de sa nature.
Li seneschals atant s'en vait
Et la dame lie s'en fait   2250
Quant prise s'est a si prodome.
Or vos ai jo dite la some,
L'oquison de ceste aventure,
Com cis ouevrent contre Nature,
Ki l'enfant ont si desvoié   2255
Com jo vos ai chi devisié.

Quant Nature s'est aperçute
Qu'il l'ont enganee et deçute,
Que s'uevre li ont bestornee
De si come l'ot atornee,   2260
Cuidiés que forment ne s'en duelle,
Et que grant mal ne lor en voelle
De cangier sa fille por fil,
Et que ne l'ait moult en porvil?
Oïl! cho sachiés entresait!   2265
"Il ont en mon desdaing cho fait
Quanses que miols valt Noreture
Que face m'uevre!" dist Nature.
"Par Deu! par Deu! or monte bien!
Il n'a en tiere nule rien,   2270
Ki par nature ait a durer,
Ki puist al loing desnaturer.
Le cuer ai plus froit que glaçon
Por maltalent de ma façon
Que Noreture me desguise.   2275
Gregnor bialté i euc assise
Qu'on ne peüst en .m. trover.
Mon pooir i vol esprover.
Or m'est torné a g[ra]nt dolor.
Meësmement por sa color,   2280
Por cho que fis en son visage
Del blanc al vermel mariäge,/
Jo fis l'un l'altre variier,
Por tolt le monde tariier.
Del blanc i mis a grant mervelle   2285
Qu'ele ne fust pas trop vermelle.
Vermel i mis de grant valor
Li blans n'i trasist en palor.
Et or en ont fait un oir malle

106

or the child might accidentally
do something to reveal its sex.
The seneschal took his leave,
and the lady, happy, realized   2250
how much she owed to this good man.
Now I have told you everything:
how this strange turn of events came to pass,
and how these people worked contrary to nature
and turned the child from her proper path,   2255
as I have just finished telling you.

When Nature realized
that they had tricked and deceived her
by turning her work into the opposite
of what she had turned out,   2260
you can imagine how disturbed she was
and how much she wanted revenge upon them
for changing her daughter into a son,
and how much she despised their plan.
Oh yes! You can be sure of that right now!   2265
"They have insulted me," said Nature,
"by acting as if the work of Nurture
were superior to mine!
By God, by God! We'll see about that!
There is nothing on this earth   2270
created by Nature
that can be dis-natured in the long run.
My heart feels colder than ice,
I am so furious about the way
Nurture is disguising my creation.   2275
I put more beauty into her
than could be found in a thousand.
I wanted to prove my prowess with her.
Now they have ruined that for me.
It's the same with her complexion—   2280
when I painted her face,
I married white with red,
mixed them in such proportions
as to excite the envy of everyone.
I put in a good amount of white,   2285
so that she wouldn't be too red,
and put in a large quantity of red,
so that she wouldn't be too pale.
And now they have made a male heir of her,

Ki ira al vent et al halle,   2290
Com se cho fust une grosse ouevre.
Se jo a loing ne le descuevre,
Dont puet plus certes Noreture
Que jo ne puissce," dist Nature.
Segnor, par Deu, Nature a droit!   2295
Car nus hom tel pooir n'aroit
Qu'il peüst vaintre et engignier
Nature al loig, ne forlignier.
Jo sai tres bien, par Noreture
Fait mains hom bien contre Nature   2300
U por efforcement de gent,
U faire ne l'oze altrement.
Et ki fait bien par estavoir
Ne por crieme de pis avoir,
Cho n'est pas naturals faintize,   2305
Ainz est paors qui le justize.
Et quant il est fors de la crieme,
Cuidiés *que sis** cuers ne l'enprieme?
Oïl! car il li dist et conte
Que miols valent .m. mars a honte   2310
C'un denier mains a grant honor.
Miols valt li graindres del menor.
Nos veomes maint home enbatre
Un an, u .ii., u .iii., u quatre
En bon us tolt par noreture   2315
Mal gré u non sa vil nature:
Et puis apriés si s'en repent,
De son bienfaire se reprent*
Et s'achieve sa felonie,
Ki le renbat en vilonie.   2320
Car li nature vils l'enerre,
Et li cuers de la grosse terre
Ki tient sor lui la segnorie
Et solle la parmenterie.
Et mains cuers de gentil nature   2325
Empire moult par noreture,
Et a grant honte si [a]hert,
Qu'a moult grant painne puis le pert.
Car gentils cuers, s'il acostume
La malvaistié et l'amertume,/   2330
Se il s'enprent a enivrer,
Envis s'en puet si delivrer,
Com li malvais del bien retraire.

who will go out in the wind and scorching sun,   2290
as if he were of crude workmanship.
If I don't unmask her in the long run,
Nurture's power will be proven
stronger than mine," said Nature.
Lords, by God, Nature is right!   2295
No man has the power, in the long run,
that he can vanquish and outwit
Nature, or betray heredity.
I know very well that many a man acts contrary to his nature,
does the right thing because of nurture,   2300
whether somebody forces him to,
or whether he doesn't dare to do otherwise.
But a man who does the right thing out of necessity,
or for fear of coming off badly —
this is not natural restraint;   2305
it is fear that keeps him straight.
And when he is not governed by fear,
don't you think his heart will put its stamp on him?
Yes! for it will tell him
that a thousand ill-gotten marks   2310
are worth more than a denier less earned honorably,
that more is worth more than less.
We have seen many a man do the right thing
for one, two, three or four years,
only because of nurture,   2315
whatever his vile nature wants,
and then afterwards repent of it,
go back on his fine behavior;
thus his wicked nature wins out
by plunging him back into villainy.   2320
For his vile nature has paid a deposit on him,
and his heart of coarse clay
holds sway over him
and soils his fine apparel.
And many a heart of noble nature   2325
becomes much worse through nurture
and hardens itself to very shameful ways,
so that it has a hard time shedding them later.
For if a noble heart becomes accustomed
to wickedness and bitterness,   2330
once it has begun to be poisoned by them,
it can only be saved with great difficulty,
the way bad can be drawn out of good.

Prover le puis par cest affaire
C'uns petis hanas plains de fiel   2335
Honiroit plus un mui de miel
C'uns muis de miel n'amenderoit
Un lot de fiel, ki l'i metroit.
En un poi de vil noreture
Empire plus bone nature   2340
Que longhe aprisons de bienfaire
Puist amender cuer de pute aire.
Ichi a certes trop a dire,
Mais mes cuers tent a ma matyre;
A parler de l'enfant goloze,   2345
Que Nature plaint et dolose.
De maltalent fremist et groce,
Viers Noreture se coroce.
Mais ne li valt pas une tille:
Silence n'iert a an mais fille.   2350
Dire vos puis seürement
Que l'enfes croist moult durement
Plus en l'an c'uns altres en trois.
Onques d'enfant norri en bois
Ne vos pot on si grans biens dire.   2355
Por cho que tels est li matyre,
Si ai m'entente plus penee,
La rime assise, et miols menee.

Quant li enfes pot dras user,
Por se nature refuser   2360
L'ont tres bien vestu a fuer d'ome
A sa mesure, c'est la some.
Li senescals i vait et vient,
L'enfant et cele dame tient
El bos moult honorablement.   2365
Et si l'a fait sensablement
Car l'enfant fist letres aprendre
Si tost com il i pot entendre.
Car por icho le violt destraindre
Et faire entor ostel remaindre,   2370
Qu'en tel liu le portaist enfance
U li enfes par ignorance
Descovrist as gens sa nature,
Se fust falsee Noreture.
Al doctriner n'a que la dame: 2375
Si bien le fait que n'i a blasme,

I can prove it by this example:
a little tumbler-full of gall   2335
would harm a measure of honey
more than a measure of honey
could improve a quart of gall, if you poured it in.
A little bad nurture
harms a good nature more   2340
than lengthy instruction in doing good
can mend a heart intrinsically evil.
There is certainly much to say about this,
but my heart belongs to my subject matter.
I yearn to speak of the child   2345
that Nature was mourning and grieving over.
She scolded and shook with anger;
she was furious with Nurture.
But it didn't help a bit:
Silence wasn't any more of a girl in a year.   2350
I can tell you one thing for certain—
the child grew more sturdily in a year
than others do in three.
No one could ever give a better account
of any child ever raised in the woods.*   2355
Since that is the way the story goes,
I have redoubled my efforts,
ordered and improved my rhyming.

When the child was of an age to wear clothing,
in order to deny her nature,   2360
they took care to dress her in male clothing
made to her measure.
The seneschal came and went,
cared for the child and the lady
most honorably in the woods.   2365
He did this very sensibly:
he had the child learn his letters
as soon as he was capable of it,
for he wanted to restrain him by this means
and make him stay inside the lodging   2370
rather than spend his childhood somewhere
where, not knowing any better,
he might reveal his nature to people,
thus contradicting nurture.
There was none but the lady to teach him.   2375
She did it well, beyond reproach.

111

C'ainc ne veïstes tel norice.
L'enfant estruist et si l'enthice/
De bones mors de faire honor
Et al gregnor et al menor.   2380
Moult bien le doctrine et ensegne.
Li enfes pas ne la desdegne,
Ainz est moult liés de l'apresure
Car cho li fait bone nature.
Li enfes est de tel orine   2385
Que il meïsmes se doctrine.
Ceste vos est sovent retraite
Que bons oisials par lui s'afaite.
Et cis par soi meïsme aprent
Moult plus qu'a son eé n'apent.   2390
Enfans ot donc ens el països*
De la tiere et d'allors naïs
E[t] cis a cestui s'aparelle;
Mais nus a cest ne s'aparelle,
Ne de bonté, ne de science.   2395
Itant vos dirai de Silence:
Tant com il est plus bials de tols,
Tant est il plus vallans et prols
Que il ne soient tolt ensanble.
Or vos ai dit cho que m'en sanble.   2400

Li senescals a tolt conté
Al pere et mere sa bonté.
Dist lor qu'il a par Deu tel grasce.
Cuidiés que haitiés ne les face?
Oïl! onques si lié ne furent   2405
Quant la verté en aparçurent!
Li senescals la les enmainne
Et l'enfes plus et plus se painne
De faire bien, quant il le loent.
Mais li malvais, quant il cho oent   2410
Que on les prise, dont s'orguellent
Et grant folie en auls acuellent,
Que il ne valent une pie.
L'orgiols lor valt une pepie;
Torgent les cols, cho sachiés vos.   2415
Con di me tu? Qui somes nos?
Segnor, de moult legier empire
Ki tent a malvaistié et tyre,
Si com jo puis a droit esmer.

112

You never saw such a devoted nurse.
She instructed him, taught him principles
of good conduct, to honor
both great and humble.   2380
She taught and instructed him very well.
The child was not ungrateful;
he was very glad of such learning —
that was the effect of his good nature.
The child's innate qualities were such   2385
that he taught himself.
You have often been told
that a good falcon trains himself,
and this child learned more by himself
than anyone else his age.   2390
There were children in the country,
both foreign-born and native,
and they were all alike,
but none was like this one
in goodness or in learning.   2395
I will tell you this much about Silence:
just as he was the most beautiful of all,
he was more valiant and noble
than all the others put together.
Now I have told you how I see it.   2400

The seneschal told the father and mother
all about the child's good qualities;
he told them his gifts were due to God's grace.
Don't you think that made them happy?
Indeed, they had never been so glad   2405
as when they were able to see for themselves that it was true.
The senschal brought them there,
and the child took more pains
to do well when they praised him.
But the wicked, when they hear   2410
that they are being praised,
become so full of vanity and folly
that they are not worth a magpie.
Pride is like pip to them —
it strangles them, as you well know.   2415
"What are you saying? Who do you think we are?"
Lords, he who tends and is drawn to wickedness
becomes worse for no reason at all,
as far as I can rightly judge.

113

Ne por loer ne por blasmer   2420
Ne se puet malvais hom retraire
De cho que cuers li loe a faire;
Et por cho di jo que Nature
Signorist desor Noreture.
Ki en ses vils fais s'abonist   2425
Et voit et set qu'il se honist,/
Se il se honist si de gré,
Dont le tienc jo a forsené.
Et se ses vils cuers li fait faire
Qu'il ne s'en puissce pas retraire,   2430
Dont est il sers et ses cuers sire,
Espi! quant tels cuers le maistyre.
Li cuens a son enfant veü,
De grant sens a aparceü
Qu'il est de tel discreciön.   2435
Deu prie et fait afflictiön
Que lui de son enfant sovigne,
Qu'en cele longes le maintigne.

Quant l'enfes est de tel doctrine
Qu'il entent bien qu'il est mescine,   2440
Ses pere l'a mis a raison,
Se li demostre l'oquoison
Por que on le coile si et cuevre.
"Se li rois Ebayns seüst l'uevre
Que nos de vos, bials fils, menons,   2445
De quanque nos sos ciel avons
Estroit li vostre pars petite;
Car li rois, bials fils, desirite
Toltes les femes d'Engletiere,
Tolt par l'oquoison d'une guerre   2450
De .ii. contes ki en morurent
Par .ii. jumieles ki dunt furent.
Bials dols ciers fils, n'est pas por nos
Cho que faisons, ainz est por vos.
Tolte l'oquoison, fils savés.   2455
Si chier come l'onor avés,
Si vos covrés viers tolte gent."
Et cil respont moult dolcement,
Briément, al fuer de sage enfant:
"Ne vos cremés, ne tant ne quant,   2460
Car, se Deu plaist, bien le ferai,
Viers tolte gent me coverrai."

114

Neither praise nor blame 2420
can restrain an evil man
from what his heart counseld him to do.
And thus I say that Nature
is superior to Nurture.
If a man persists in doing wrong, 2425
and sees and knows that he is dishonoring himslef,
if he thus dishonors himself on purpose,
I hold him to be a madman.
But if his vile heart forces him to do it,
so that he cannot stop doing it, 2430
he is the servant and his heart the lord.
See what happens when such a heart is master!
The count, observing his child,
felt a great sense of satisfaction
that he was so well behaved. 2435
He prostrated himself and prayed to God
to be mindful of his child
and to preserve his sense of discretion.

When the child was old enough
to understand he was a girl, 2440
his father sat down to reason with him
and explain the circumstances
which had led them to conceal his identity this way.
"If, dear son, King Evan knew
what we are doing with you, 2445
your share of our earthly possessions
would be very small indeed.
For the king, dear son, disinherited
all the women of England
on account of the death of two counts 2450
in a battle they fought
over twin heiresses they had married.
Dear sweet precious son, we are not doing this
for ourselves, but for you.
Now, son, you know the whole situation. 2455
As you cherish honor,
you will continue to conceal yourself from everyone."
And he replied very sweetly,
briefly, as befits a well-bred child,
"Don't worry the least little bit. 2460
So help me God, I will do it.
I will conceal myself from everyone."

Moult le castie biel li pere
Et alsi fait sovent la mere,
Li senescals et la norice. 2465
De faire bien cascuns l'entice.
Il est de tel entendement
Qu'il croit bien lor castiement.
Li senescals por essaucier
Et por aprendre a chevalcier 2470
Le mainne en bos et en rivieres
Ki sunt el païs bien plenieres.
Sel mainne plus sovent el halle
Par cho quel violt faire plus malle. /
Il a us d'ome tant usé 2475
Et cel de feme refusé
Que poi en falt que il n'est malles:
Quanque on en voit est trestolt malles.
El a en tine que ferine:
Il est desos les dras mescine. 2480
Li senescals sor tolte rien
Es premiers ans le garda bien.
Com plus croist l'enfes en grandece,
Tant amenrist plus sa destrece.
Quant on n'i puet folie ataindre 2485
Por quoi le devroit on destraindre?
Cho qu'il crient sa droiture perdre
Le fait plus a savoir aherdre.
Ses cuers meïsmes bien l'escole
Al deguerpir maniere fole. 2490
Por cho a il lassor assés
Et quant il ot .xi. ans passés
N'i a un seul de lui plus maistre.
Quant il joent a le palaistre,
A bohorder, n'a l'escremir, 2495
Il seus fait tols ses pers fremir.

[S]ilences forment s'enasprist,
Car ses corages li aprist
K*e si* fesist par couverture.
Apriés .xii. ans si vint Nature 2500
Ki le blasme forment et coze.
Dist li: "Chi a estrange coze,
Ki te deduis al fuer de malle,
Et vas si al vent et al halle,
Car une speciäl forme ai 2505

116

The father gave him much good advice,
as did the mother often,
and the seneschal and the nurse;   2465
they all urged him to be good.
He was receptive to their teaching
and heeded their admonitions well.
In order to build up his endurance
and teach him to ride, the seneschal   2470
took him through woods and streams,
which were plentiful in the countryside.
He took him out often in the scorching heat,
in order to make a man of him.
He was so used to men's usage   2475
and had so rejected women's ways
that little was lacking for him to be a man.
Whatever one could see was certainly male!
But there's more to this than meets the eye—*
the he's a she beneath the clothes.   2480
The seneschal watched the child closely
during his early years,
but the older he grew,
the easier that seneschal's task became.
When one could find no folly in him,   2485
what was the use of restraining him?
What they thought would cause him to be unsteady
only caused him to adhere more closely to discretion.
His heart itself schooled him
to eschew foolish behavior.   2490
Because of this, he was given a good deal of freedom.
And by the time he was in his twelfth year,
none was his master any more.
When they practiced wrestling,
jousting or skirmishing,   2495
he alone made all his peers tremble.

Silence was deeply disturbed about this,
for her conscience told her
that she was practicing deception by doing this.
In her twelfth year, Nature appeared,   2500
grumbling and complaining and blaming her.
She said to her, "This is a fine state of affairs,
you conducting yourself like a man,
running about in the wind and scorching sun
when I used a special mold for you,   2505

117

Dont a mes .ii. mains te formai.
Et la bialtet qu'ai tant celé[e]
Ai tolte en toi amoncelee.
.m. gens me tienent por escarse
Por la bialté, dont tu iés farse;   2510
Car jo ai de .m. gens retraite
La bialté, dont tu iés refaite.
.m. femes a en ceste vie
Ki de toi ont moult grant envie
Por le bialté qu'eles i voient,   2515
Car puet scel estre eles i croient
Tel cose qu'en toi nen a mie.
Et tels est ore moult t'amie/
Qui te haroit de tolt le cuer,
Se il de toi savoit le fuer,   2520
Qu'el s'en tenroit a malballie
Que s'esperance estroit fallie.
Tu me fais, certes, grant laidure
Quant tu maintiens tel noreture.
Ne dois pas en bos converser,   2525
Lancier, ne traire, ne berser.
Tol toi de chi!" cho dist Nature.
"Va en la cambre a la costure,
Cho violt de nature li us.
Tu nen es pas Scilentius!"   2530
Et cil respont: "Tel n'oï onques!
Silencius! qui sui jo donques?
Silencius ai non, jo cui,
U jo sui altres que ne fui.
Mais cho sai jo bien, par ma destre,   2535
Que jo ne puis pas altres estre!
Donques sui jo Scilentius,
Cho m'est avis, u jo sui nus."
Dont se porpense en lui meïsme
Que Nature li fait sofime: 2540
Por cho que l'-us est encontre us
N'a pas a non Scilentius.
Aler en violt a la costure
Si com li a rové Nature,
Car por fief, ne por iretage,   2545
Ne doit mener us si salvage.

Atant i sorvint Noreture
Et voit que parole a Nature.

118

when I created you with my own hands,
when I heaped all the beauty I had stored up
upon you alone!
There are a thousand people who think I'm stingy
because of the beauty I stuffed you with,   2510
for I extracted the beauty of a thousand
to create your lovely appearance!
And there are a thousand women in this world
who are madly in love with you
because of the beauty they see in you—   2515
you don't suppose they think something's there
that was never part of your equipment at all?
There are those who love you now
who would hate you with all their hearts
if they knew what you really are!   2520
They would consider themselves misused,
having their hopes so cruelly dashed.
It's a very nasty thing you're doing to me,
leading this sort of life.
You have no business going off into the forest,   2525
jousting, hunting, shooting off arrows.
Desist from all of this!" said Nature.
"Go to a chamber and learn to sew!
That's what Nature's usage wants of you!
You are not Silentius!"   2530
and he replied, "I never heard that before!
Not Silentius? Who am I then?
Silentius is my name, I think,
or I am other than who I was.
But this I know well, upon my oath,   2535
that I cannot be anybody else!
Therefore, I am Silentius,
as I see it, or I am no one."
But then she convinced herself
that Nature's spurious argument was plausible: 2540
that because the -us was contrary to usage,
her name was not Silentius.
She wanted to go and learn to sew,
just as Nature demanded of her;
she should not cultivate such savage ways   2545
for fief or inheritance.

But then Nurture arrived on the scene
and saw that he was talking to Nature

Di li: "Que fais tu, diva, chi?"
Cil dist: "Nature tence a mi.   2550
Et si n'est pas, par foi, a tort
Qu'ele m'acostume et amort
A tel us ki est droitureus,
Car cis us n'es pas natureus.
Ainc feme, voir, de mon parage,   2555
Ne mena mais si fait usage,
Ne jo plus longhes nel menrai:
A us de feme me tenrai.
Jo ne voel pas moi estalcier,
Fendre mes dras, braies calcier,   2560
Ne mais vivre a fuer de garçon,
Prendre mon coivre, et mon arçon.
Avint adonques mais a nule?
Nenil! adunc quant jo m'afule
Por moi de tel giu a retraire   2565
Com vallet suelent encor faire, /
Dont dient tuit mi compagnon:
'Cis avra moult le cuer felon
Se il vit longhes entressait.'
Mais ne sevent com moi estait.   2570
Se me desful par aventure
Dont ai paor de ma nature.
Conjoie moult diversement.
En cort aloie conversant,
Tolt cho metrai ariere dos   2575
Et viverai dont a repos.
Cis Dameldex qui me fist naistre
Me puet bien governer et paistre:
Queles! ja n'ai jo oï conté*
Qu'il est plains de si grant bonté   2580
Et done a tolte creäture
Sofisalment lonc sa nature?
Fu ainc mais feme si tanee
De vil barat, ne enganee
Que cho fesist par covoitise?   2585
Nel puis savoir en nule guise."

Quant Noreture cho oï
Cuidiés qu'ele s'en esjoï?
Nenil! anchois fremist et groce.
Enviers Nature se coroce   2590
Et si l'esgarde surement.

120

and said to him, "Hey! What are you doing here?"
He said, "Nature is scolding me,   2550
and she's right, in fact,
to get me accustomed
to appropriate habits,
for this behavior is unnatural.
Truly, no woman of my lineage   2555
ever behaved in such a way,
nor wil I do so any longer!
I will keep to women's ways.
I won't cut my hair short any more,
wear slit garments and breeches   2560
and live like a boy
with bow and quiver.
Did anything like this ever happen to anyone?
Never! Now, when I get dressed,
and don't participate   2565
in the kinds of games that boys are used to,
all my companions jeer,
'This one will be a terrible coward,
if he lives that long!'
But they don't know how it is with me.   2570
Whenever I happen to get undressed,
I am afraid my sex will be discovered.
My idea of fun is very different.
I have been spending my time at court,
but I will put all this behind me   2575
and live very quietly from now on.
The good Lord who created me
will be my shepherd and my guide.
Haven't I heard it said
that in his great goodness   2580
he dispenses of his bounty to each creature
according to its nature?
Was any female ever so tormented
or deceived by such vile fraud
as to do what I did out of greed?   2585
I certainly never heard of one!"

When Nurture heard this,
do you think she was overjoyed?
Hardly! on the contrary, she quivered and scolded.
She was furious with Nature.   2590
She looked her straight in the eye

121

Puis li a dit moult durement:
"Lassciés ester ma noreçon,
Nature, a la maleÿçon.
Jo l'ai tolte desnaturee.   2595
N'avra ja voir o vus duree.
Se ne lassciés icest anter
Bien vos porés al loig vanter
Se jo ne fac par noreture
.m. gens ovrer contre nature.   2600
Jo noris tres bien, c'est la some,
D'un noble enfant un malvais home.
Jo te desferai tolt ton conte.
Nature, envoies o *ta* honte."
Quant Nature s'en fu alee   2605
Et o le roce a devalee
U Noreture ot si tencié,
Es vos l'estor recommencié
Seur Scilence: car la Raisons
Li monstre, et dist les oquoisons   2610
Que poi li valt mains de la mort
Se il s'acostume et amort
A deguerpir sa noreture
Por faire cho que violt Nature./
"Croi mon consel, amis Silence,   2615
Et aies en toi abstinence.
Fai de ton cuer une ferté.
S'a lui te prent, de la verté,
Nature, qui t'angoisce adés,
Ja n'ieres mais vallés apriés.   2620
Tolt perdrés cheval et carete.
Ne cuidiés pas li rois vos mete
En l'onor, por estre parjure,
S'il aperçoit vostre nature."

Raisons ja od li tant esté,   2625
Se li a tant admonesté
Que Silences a bien veü
Que fol consel avoit creü
Quant onques pensa desuser
Son bon viel us et refuser,   2630
Por us de feme maintenir.
Donques li prent a sovenir
Des jus c'on siolt es cambres faire
Dont a oï sovent retraire,

and said most severely,
"Nature, leave my nursling alone,
or I will put a curse on you!
I have completely dis-natured her.   2595
She will always resist you.
If you don't stop haunting her,
you'll have small reason for vanity left,
if I make a thousand people
work against their nature through nurture.   2600
I have succeeded very well
in turning a noble child into a defective male.
I will undo all your work.
Nature, begone in disgrace!"
When Nature had gone away   2605
and descended from the rock
where Nurture had attacked her so,
the battle for Silence began again,
as you shall hear, for Reason
stated her case, citing examples   2610
as to why, if she abandoned her nurture
to take up the habits of nature,
it would be almost as bad
as killing herself.
"Believe what I say, friend Silence,   2615
and forbear!
Fortify your heart,
for if Nature, who is now pressing you so hard,
takes it from you, believe me,
you will never train for knighthood afterwards.   2620
You will lose your horse and chariot.
Do not think the king will go back on his word
and acknowledge you as rightful heir,
when he finds out your true nature."

Reason stayed with him for so long   2625
and admonished him so severely
that Silence understood very well
he had listened to bad advice
ever to think of doing away
with his good old ways   2630
to take up female habits.
Then he began to consider
the pastimes of a woman's chamber—
which he had often heard about—

Et poise dont en son corage   2635
Tolt l'us de feme a son usage,
Et voit que miols valt li us d'ome
Que l'us de feme, c'est la some.
"Voire," fait il, "a la male eure
Irai desos, quant sui deseure.   2640
Deseure sui, s'irai desos?
Or sui jo moult vallans et pros.
Nel sui, par foi, ains sui honis
Quant as femes voel estre onis.
Gel pensai por moi aäsier.   2645
Trop dure boche ai por baisier,
Et trop rois bras por acoler.
On me poroit tost afoler
Al giu c'on fait desos gordine,
Car vallés sui et nient mescine.   2650
Ne voel perdre ma grant honor,
Ne la voel cangier a menor.
Ne voel mon pere desmentir,
Ainz me doinst Dex la mort sentir.
Por quanque puet faire Nature   2655
Ja n'en ferai descoverture."

Si est li voirs, cho dist l'estorie
Ki de Silence fait memorie,
C'onques ne fu tels abstinence
Com poés oïr de Silence.   2660
Jo ne di pas qu'il ne pe[n]sast
Diversement, et ne tensast/
Diverse cogitatiön
Com enfant de tel natiön,
Meësmement enfant si tendre.   2665
Ki doit a tel usage entendre.
Et cuers s'est une creäture
Mervelles d'estrange nature:
Qu'il pense voir moult largement,
Torne et retorne trop sovent   2670
Les larges pensers que requelt
Dont motes foie[e]s se due[l]t.
Et por cho di jo de Scilence
Qu'i ert de moult grant abstinence,
Que ses pensers le tormentoit   2675
Et il le sentoit et sofroit.

124

and weighed in his heart of hearts   2635
all female customs against his current way of life,
and saw, in short, that a man's life
was much better than that of a woman.
"Indeed," he said, "it would be too bad
to step down when I'm on top.   2640
If I'm on top, why should I step down?
Now I am honored and valiant.
No I'm not, upon my word—I'm a disgrace
if I want to be one of the women.
I was trying to make life easy for myself,   2645
but I have a mouth too hard for kisses,
and arms too rough for embraces.
One could easily make a fool of me
in any game played under the covers,
for I'm a young man, not a girl.   2650
I don't want to lose my high position;
I don't want to exchange it for a lesser,
and I don't want to prove my father a liar.
I would rather have God strike me dead!
Whatever Nature may do,   2655
I will never betray the secret!"

If what the story that keeps alive
the memory of Silence tell us
is true, you never heard of such forbearance
as was to be found in Silence.   2660
I'm not saying that he didn't
go through periods of hesitation
and inner conflict,
as might be expected in a young person who came of such
      good stock,
but who was also a tender child   2665
who had to force herself to live that way.
And the human heart is a creature
that has a strange and peculiar nature:
it thinks a great deal,
turns the deep thoughts it harbors   2670
over and over again, far too often,
and causes itself a great deal of grief.
And that is why I say that Silence
showed such great forbearance,
for his thoughts tormented him,   2675
and he felt this and suffered from it.

Et tols jors ert pres a contraire
A cho que ses cuers voloit faire.
Et qui ouevre contre voloir
Soventes fois l'estuet doloir. 2680
Silences ot le cuer diviers.
Cho fu li dozimes iviers,
Li ans dozimes est entrés,
Des qu'il fu primes engenrés.
Bien ert cruels, s'ert bials et pros, 2685
Larges, cortois, amés de tols.
.ii. jors u .iii. mest o le pere,
Quant il voloit, et o la mere.

Oiés mervellose aventure
Si con nos conte l'escriture. 2690
En la tiere ot .ii. menestrels.
N'i ot eü onques mais tels.
Li uns ert li mioldres jogleres
Del mont, li altres ert harperes.
Avironee ont Engletiere, 2695
Grant avoir aquis en la tiere.
En Cornuälle sunt venu;
Del conte sunt bien retenu.
.viii. jors ont od lui despendus;
Bons loiers lor en fu rendus 2700
Si qu'al departir fu a gré.
Enviers la mer sunt puis alé
Car passer voelent en Bertagne.
Nuis les sosprent en une plagne
Dejoste une moult grant foriest 2705
U li més fu et encor est
U mest li senescals, li sire
De cui vos m'avés oï dire
Ki fil al conte norissoit.
Li maistre tors apparissoit,/ 2710
Sor tolt le bos une ruee,
Mais tant lor fait une nuee
Qu'il ne le pueent veïr preu,
Qu'il ert ja entre cien et leu.
Cil voient le bos espessir, 2715
Ne sevent u entrer n'isscir.
De cel païs ne sevent rien.
Dont dient: "Deu, Saint Juliien,
Trametés nos anuit tel oste

126

He was always ready to go against
what his heart wanted him to do,
and whoever works against his will
finds himself often in a state of unhappiness.   2680
Silence's heart was divided against itself.
It was the twelfth winter;
the twelfth year had begun
since he first came into being.
The winter was cruel; he was lovely and noble,   2685
generous, courteous, beloved by everyone.
He would spend two or three days with his father
whenever he wished, or with his mother.

Now you're going to hear something amazing!
As the manuscript tells us,   2690
there were two minstrels in the land,
the best you ever heard of.
One was the best jongleur in the world,
the other was a harpist.
They had made a tour of England   2695
and had been very successful there.
They came to Cornwall
and were well received by the count.
They spent a week at his court
and were well rewarded for it   2700
when it came time for them to leave.
Then they headed for the coast,
for they wanted to cross over to Brittany
Nightfall surprised them in a stretch of open country
next to a huge forest   2705
where the manor house was and still is
where the seneschal lived—
the lord I have been telling you about,
the one who was raising the count's son.
The main tower rose above the woods   2710
just a stone's throw away,
but the fog was so thick
they could hardly see it,
for it was already twilight.
They could see the forest growing denser,   2715
and they didn't know how to get in or out of it;
they didn't know the area at all.
They said, "God and Saint Julian,
just bring us this night a host

Nient ne nos doinst, nient ne nos oste,   2720
Ne nos tollent li male gent
Qu'avons aquis tant longement.
Salve nos, Dex, et nostre ator."
Dont voient umbroier la tor
Deseur le bos une ruee,   2725
Al descovrir d'une nuee.
En la forest estoit a destre,
Dont la voie estoit a senestre.
Si [se] metent en une sente,
Parvienent a la tor eënte.   2730
Que puet caloir quant il i sunt?
Altre demorance n'i funt.
Hucent en halt: "Ki est laiens?"
On lor a dit: "Gent a çaiens.
Ki estes vos et que querés?"   2735
Cil dient: "Ovrés, sel sarés."
Li portiers a le porte ovierte
Et cil l'oquison descovierte.
Dient: "Nos somes jogleör.
A chaiens nul herbergeör   2740
Ki nos herbergast ceste nuit?"
"Oïl! amis, si con jo cuit,
N'eüstes hostel mais si buen."
"Sals soit li sire, et tolt li suen!"
Cho respondent li menestrel.   2745
"A porte n'ot mais portier tel.
Par les serjans de la maizon
Puet on conoistre par raizon
Se prodom u non est li sire;
Que nos l'avons oï bien dire   2750
Que bons sire fait bons serjans
Trestolt sans batre de vergans.
Bon serjant refont bon segnor."
L'uissiers adestre le gregnor.
Quant lor chevals a assenés   2755
Les maistres a amont menés.
Le senescal i ont trové
Et por moult prodome esprové. /
Et quant cho vint apriés mengier
De lor mestier ne font dangier.   2760
Li uns viiele un lai berton,
Et li altres harpe Gueron.
Puis font une altre atempreüre

128

who won't rob us; we're not asking for pay— 2720
just don't let bad people take away
what has taken us so long to acquire.
Save us, oh Lord, and our belongings."
Then they saw the tower loom up
above the trees a stone's throw away, 2725
when the fog lifted for a moment.
It was to the right of the forest,
and to the left of the road.
They set out on a path
and came to the tower: it looked threatening, 2730
but what did they care, as long as they had found it?
They weren't about to hesitate.
They shouted from below, "Who's in there?"
The answer came, "The people inside!
Who are you and what do you want?" 2735
They answered, "Open up and we'll let you know!"
The porter opened the gate
and they explained their situation.
They said, "We are minstrels.
Is there no one inside 2740
who might offer us shelter for the night?"
"Yes, friends. there is! in my opinion,
you've never had such good lodgings."
"A blessing on the lord and all his men,"
the minstrels replied. 2745
"There never was such a porter at any gate.
By the officers of the household*
you may know for certain
whether the master is a decent man.
We have often heard it said 2750
that a good master makes a good officer
without beating him with sticks.
And good officers make good masters, in turn."
The porter shook hands with the leader.
When he had seen to the horses, 2755
he led their masters upstairs.
They found the seneschal there,
and they could tell he was a very good man.
So when they had finished their meal,
they were quick to practice their trade. 2760
One fiddled a Breton lai;*
the other harped "Gueron."
Then they chose a different rhythm

Et font des estrumens mesture.
Si font ensanble un lai Mabon—   2765
Celui tient on encor a bon—
S'en ist si dolce melodie
Qu'il n'i a cel quil bien ne die:
"Certes que Dex les amena!
Bien ait qui cha les adreça!"   2770
Mais ainz qu'il voient mais .ii. vespres,
Orront voir canter altres vespres
Dont plus dolans sera li sire
Que s'il veïst son fil ochire.

Li senescals mar les vit onques.   2775
Quant il ont assés joé, donques
S'en vait li senescals gesir.
Anuit perdra tolt son desir.
Li menestrel plus n'i demeurent.
Repozer vont, mestier en eurent,   2780
Car tolt sunt las de chevalcier.
Silences fu al descalcier:
N'i ot altre que lui la nuit.
Cui qu'il soit biel, ne cui qu'anuit,
Ne violt qu'altres sa main i mete   2785
Ne c'on sor lui ne s'entremete.
Colcié se sunt et cil les cuevre.
Moult fist benignement cele ouevre.
A cascun livre un orellier.
Cil prendent moult a mervellier   2790
D'enfant de son eé si tendre
Comment puet a service entendre.
Ainc enfes n'ot si grant francize
Ne ne fu de si grant servisce.
Demandent li: "Qui est tes pere?"   2795
"Uns vavasors, si est ma mere
Norrice a cel enfant gregnor
Ki est ainsnés fils al segnor."
Et cil li prendent dont a dire:
".ii. moult bials enfans a tes sire,   2800
Et si te fait gregnor honor
Que al plus grant, ne al menor.
Di nos, kieles, por quoi il fait,
Car nos savons tolt entressait,
Se ne fussces fils a princier   2805
Ja ne te tenist a si chier."/

and played their instruments together.
Together they played the "Lai Mabon" —   2765
this is still a popular piece.
They produced such sweet melodies
that there wasn't a one who didn't say,
"Surely, God has brought them here!
We wish him well who guided them to us!"   2770
But before two nights have passed,
they will sing a very different tune, believe me!
—one that will make the seneschal as sorry
as if he had seen his son get killed.

It's a pity for him that he ever laid eyes on them!   2775
After they had played a good deal,
the seneschal retired.
Tonight he will lose his heart's desire!
The minstrels didn't wait around.
They went to bed; they needed rest,   2780
for they were exhausted from the day's ride.
Silence was there to help them undress.
He was the only one there that night.
Whatever anyone thought of it,
he didn't want anyone else   2785
to lend a hand or intervene.
He helped them undress and saw to their bedcovers.
He accomplished these tasks most charmingly;
he brought each of them a pillow.
They were amazed that a child   2790
of such tender years
was able to be of such service;
they had never seen a child of such noble bearing,
nor one who was so accomplished at serving.
They asked him, "Who is your father?"   2795
"A vavassor; my mother
is nurse to an older child
who is the lord's elder son."
Then they said to him,
"Your lord has two beautiful children,   2800
but he does you greater honor
than to the elder or younger.
Can you tell us, please, why he does this?
for we could see at once
that he wouldn't hold you dearer   2805
if you were a prince's son."

"Oho!" fait l'enfes, "miols savés
Que vos ichi dit nen avés.
Li sages hom se rent plus fier
Sovent viers cho qu'il a plus chier.   2810
Et neporquant n'est pas fiertés,
Saciés de fit, ains est ciertés.
El seneschal a moult sage home,
N'a nul plus cointe trosqu'a Rome.
Ne violt ses fils bel sanblant faire,   2815
Ne folement sor lui atraire,
Faire vilains, ne orgellols.
Et jo si resui se fillols."
"Amis," font il, "quels que tu soies
N'iés pas vilains, ne ne foloies.   2820
Dex, ki te fist, porgart ta vie!"
"Segnor, et Dex vos beneïe!"

Silences vait en son lit donques,
Mais il n'i dormi la nuit onques.
Moult li remort sa consiënce.   2825
Ses cuers li dist: "Diva! Silence,
Ti drap qu'as vestut, et li halles,
Font croire as gens que tu iés malles.
Mais el a sos la vesteüre
Ki de tolt cho n'a mie cure.   2830
S'il avenoit del roi Ebayn
Que il morust hui u demain,
Feme raroit son iretage.
Et tu iés ore si salvage,
Ne sai a us de feme entendre.   2835
Alques t'esteveroit aprendre
Dont te seüsces contenir,
Car tolt cho puet bien avenir.
Et se coze est par aventure
Que si fais us longhes te dure,   2840
Bien sai, tu ieres chevaliers
Puet sc'estre coärs, u laniers,
Car ainc ne vi feme maniere
D'armes porter en tel maniere.
Tolt cho repuet avenir bien.   2845
Se ne ses donc alcune rien
Por tes conpagnons conforter,
Ne te volront pas deporter.
Car t'en vas vials en altre tierre

"Aha!" said the youth, "you know
better than what you've just said.
A wise man is often more severe
with the one he holds dearest.   2810
this isn't harshness, however;
you can be sure it's a sign of affection.
The seneschal is a very wise man,
the wisest one this side of Rome.
He doesn't want to be too gracious to his sons,   2815
or spoil them with too much attention,
and have them turn out bad-tempered or haughty.
As for me, I am his godchild."
"Friend," they said, "whoever you are,
you are no villain and no fool.   2820
May God who made you keep you safe."
"Lords, and may God bless you."

Then Silence went to bed,
but he didn't sleep a wink all night.
His conscience was bothering him a lot.   2825
His heart said, "Hey, Silence!
those clothes you're wearing and that sunburnt face
make people believe that you're a boy.
But what that boy has under his clothes
has nothing to do with being male!   2830
If it should happen that King Evan
died today or tomorrow,
women would inherit again,
and you are now so fierce
that you know nothing of women's arts.   2835
You really need to learn something
that would serve you in good stead,
for all that might come to pass!
And if it should turn out that
you have to keep up this pretense for a long time,   2840
you'll become a knight, as you well know,
and then maybe you'll be a terrible coward,
for I never saw a woman fit
to bear arms in such a manner.
All that may well happen.   2845
If you don't know a single way
to entertain your companions,
they won't want to spend their time with you.
Why don't you at least go abroad

Sens et savoir aprendre et quere.   2850
Entrues puet naistre tels noviele
Ki te sera puet sc'estre biele.
Que dira donc li cuens tes pere?
Que devenra donques ta mere?/
Que diront il quant le savront?   2855
Que puet caloir? Bien te ravront,
Par si que Dex l'ait destiné
Et que l'ait si determiné.
Avoec ces jogleörs iras.
Por cho que biel les serviras,   2860
Et que tu painne i voelles rendre,
Poras des estrumens aprendre.
Se lens iés en chevalerie
Si te valra la joglerie.
Et s'il avient que li rois muire,   2865
Es cambres t'en poras deduire.
Ta harpe et ta viële avras
En liu de cho que ne savras
Orfrois ne fresials manoier.
Si te porra mains anoier   2870
Se tu iés en un bastonage
Ke tu aies vials *el en gage*."*

Silences est en grant effroi
Qu'il cuide faire tel desroi
.ii. liues anchois qu'il ajorne.   2875
Sa sele met et bel s'atorne.
Moult par est bials ses caceörs.
Puis vait al lit des jogleörs
Et dist lor: "Segnor, dormés vos?"
"Amis," funt il, "par Deu, ne nos."   2880
"Segnor, g'irai el bois berser,
Mais s'il vus plaist a converser
Huimais ichi, tant vos dirai,
Por vostre amor pas n'i irai."
Et cil respondent comme sage: 2885
"Icho vus vient de bon corage.
Vostre offre amons nos durement,
Mais nos vus disons purement
Que por un grant avoir conquerre
Ne remanriens en ceste terre   2890
.ii. jors entiers a nostre voel.
Tart meüsmes de Tintaguel,

134

to gain some experience and acquire some expertise? 2850
In the meantime, you might hear
the kind of news that would make you happy.
What will your father the count say?
What will happen to your mother?
What will they say when they find out? 2855
What can it matter? They will have you back again
if that is God's will,
if that's the way it's meant to be.
You shall go with these jongleurs.
Provided you serve them well 2860
and are willing to work very hard,
you will learn how to play instruments.
If you are slow at chivalry,
minstrelsy will be of use to you.
And if the king should happen to die, 2865
you will be able to practice your art in a chamber;
you will have your harp and viele
to make up for the fact that you don't know
hoe to embroider a fringe or border.
You will be less bored 2870
in your captivity
if you at least have something to fall back on."

Silence is absolutley frantic,
for he plans to travel so fast
as to cover two leagues before daybreak. 2875
He equips himself well
and saddles his beautiful hunter.
Then he goes to the jongleurs' bed
and says to them, "Lords, are you still asleep?"
"Not us, friend," they say. 2880
"Lords," he says, "I am off to the forest to hunt.
But if you wish to remain
another day, I should like to say that
I'll stay here on your account."
And they reply like well-bred men, 2885
"This comes of your good character.
We are deeply moved by your offer,
but we will tell you quite simply
that we wouldn't willingly stay
two whole days in this land, 2890
even if we were offered a fortune.
We left Tintagel late yesterday

135

Ersoir, por venir a la mer:
Car nos poriens forment amer
Que nos fusciemes en Bertagne."   2895
"Segnor, et Dex vos doinst gaägne
Et vos escremissce de mort.
Li vens vus vient deviers le nort.
Se tost vus metés a la voie
Ains nuit i porrés estre a joie,   2900
Car li mers est ichi estroite.
Ki buen vent a et bien esploite, /
De primes trosqu'a miëdi
I puet tres bien estre de chi.
Trosque al port n'a solement   2905
Fors .x. liues escarsement."

Silences a itant s'en torne.
Ne cuidiés pas que mains sejorne:
D'une herbe qu'ens el bos a prise
Desconoist sa face et deguise.   2910
Ki bien l'esgarde viers le chiere
Bien sanble de povre riviere.
Al premier flot vient a la mer.
De tols les suens pense escaper.
Lieve se nef et puis i entre.   2915
Li jogleör vienent soëntre,
Font pris de passer, si entrerent.
Li maronier se desancrerent,
Lievent lor sigle, si s'en vont,
En Bertaigne venu en sunt.   2920

[A]nchois qu'il fuscent arivé
Ont de l'enfant moult estrivé.
Li uns a dit: "Dex, est cho il?"
Li altres dist: "Par foi! nenil!
Mal sanble la color celui   2925
A la color quist en cestui."
L'enfes ot tele ententiön
Qu'onques ne lor fist mentiön
Qui il fust ne que la fesist,
Ne que en Bertagne fesist,   2930
Qu'il ne desiscent a la gent.
Des nés isscent moult bielement.
Scilenses o çals s'acompagne,
Et quant il sunt a la campagne

in order to reach the sea,
for we would be very glad
to be in Brittany."   2895
"Lords, God prosper you
and shield you from death.
The wind is coming from the north.
If you set out right away,
you can reach your destination before nightfall,   2900
for the sea is very narrow at this point.
He who has good wind and makes good time
can easily be there
in half a day.
It is barely ten leagues   2905
from here to the port."

Then Silence went away.
But you mustn't think he was ready to leave yet:
first he stained and disguised his face
with a herb he found in the woods.   2910
Whoever looked at his complexion
would certainly think him of low station.
At first tide he reached the sea.
He wanted to escape from all his people.
The ship floated free and he went on board.   2915
The jongleurs arrived immediately after,
paid their passage and boarded the ship.
The sailors weighed anchor,
hoisted their sails and left;
they were on their way to Brittany.   2920

Before they arrived,
they talked a great deal about the youth.
One of them said, "Good lord, is that he?"
The other said, "Heavens, no. Certainly not.
This boy has a very bad complexion,   2925
compared to the other."
The youth intended
not to say a thing to them
about who he was or what he was doing there
or what he intended to do in Brittany,   2930
so they wouldn't tell anyone.
They disembarked without any complications.
Silence accompanied them,
and when they were in the countryside,

137

Demande lor u il iront.   2935
Cil dient qu'a Nantes giront
Se *il* le pueent esploitier.
"Pensés," fait l'enfes, "de qoitier:
Ki tempre puet ostel avoir
Al soper li torne a savoir."   2940
Trosques a Nantes sont venu.
Un home encontrent tolt kenu
Ki moult resamble bien prodome.
Cil lé herberja, c'est la some.
Usent lor vie a grant deduit.   2945
Silences siert tolte la nuit,/
Et cil prendent a mervellier
Et l'uns a l'autre a consellier.
"Si m'aït Dex, si com j'espoir,
C'est chi nostre vallés d'ersoir.   2950
Il est tols d'altretel servise,
Mais qu'il est trestols d'altre guise.
Et, par foit, c'est estrange cose:
Cil d'ersoir ot color de rose
Et cis ichi l'a si tré jausne,   2955
Com s'il fust tains d'ortie u d'aisne."

Silences les voit si doter,
Par eures l'un l'altre boter:
Et ot tres bien que c'est de lui.
"Segnor," fait il, "qu'est de celui   2960
Ki vos servi ersoir si bien?
Se jo i ai mespris de rien,
Une altre fois le ferai miols.
Jo ne sui mie moult trés viols.
Se vos *me* degniés rien aprendre,   2965
De bon cuer voel moult bien entendre.
Icil qui vos servi ersoir
Est miols apris que jo, espoir."
Sorrit, que cil l'ont bien veü,
Dont sevent qu'il sunt decheü   2970
Par la color qu'il a faitice.
Cil loe sa face traitice,
Et cis la color amortie.
Si pert la roze sor l'ortie,
Si pert la colors de nature: 2975
Blance et ver*m*elle est la mesture.
S'il est alcuns ki croire l'oze,

he asked them where they were going.   2935
They said they would spend the night in Nantes
if they could make good enough time.
"Let's try and make it fast," said the youth,
"for he who reaches the inn early
gets a savory supper."*   2940
They reached Nantes,
where they met an old gray-haired man
who seemed a very honest sort,
and he put them up, in short.
They had a most delightful time.   2945
Silence served them the entire evening.
They began to wonder
and consult on eanother:
"So help me God (I hope he will),
that is our valet from last night.   2950
He serves exactly the same way,
even though he looks completely different.
And indeed, it's strange:
the one last night had a rosy complexion,
while this one is all yellowish,   2955
as if he were stained with nettles or wine-dregs."

Silence saw them wondering
and nudging each other for hours
and could hear very well they were talking about him.
"Gentlemen," he said, "what's this talk   2960
of someone who served you so well last night?
If I have neglected anything,
I will do better next time.
I am still very young;
if you deign to teach me something,   2965
I will learn it with all good will.
The one who served you last night
was better trained than I am, I hope."
He smiled, and they looked closely at him
and realized they had been deceived   2970
by the color he had manufactured.
One praised his lovely face,
the other his fair complexion (under the deadening dye).
Thus the rose wins out over the nettle
and Nature's color becomes apparent.   2975
White and red are mingled:
if anyone dares to believe it,

Il passe anbeure et lis et roze.
Et quant li jogleör le sorent
Que cho fu il, grant joie en orent.   2980
Devisent dont que il ira
O als et si les servira:
Par tel covent l'aprenderont.
Afient dont qu'il l'atendront
Et voideront bien main la tierre,   2985
Que on nel viegne illuques querre.

Al seneschal voel revenir
Ki cel enfant devoit tenir.
Por cho qu'il siolt aler as chiens
Ne mespensa encore giens   2990
Desci que vint al anuitier.
Donc conmence en soi a luitier,
Et quant il voit que il demeure
Plus c'onques mais ne siolt nule eure,/
Set que li menestrel, ahyi!   2995
L'ont de son damoisiel traÿ.
Ki donc veïst larmies espandre,
Et ces cevials tirer et tandre,
Tordre ces puins, batre poitrines,
Plorer ces dames, ces mescines,   3000
Ronpent ces anials de ces mains
Al tordre qu'il funt, c'est del mains!
Car li sires et cele dame
Ki nori l'avoit dont se pasme.
La ot moult grant confondison.   3005
Quant revienent de pasmison,
.c. en sunt tramis par la tierre
Por celui cerkier et requierre.

Noviele atrote et si acort
Et vient moult tost corant a cort   3010
Que perdus est li damoisials
Ki ert si prols, si gens, si bials.
Et quant l'entent li cuens ses pere,
Et Eufemie, quist sa mere,
As cuers en ont tel dol, tel ire,   3015
C'on nel vos puet conter ne dire,
Non, certes, la centisme part:
Enaizes que lor cuers ne part.
Moult poi en falt que il ne crievent:

140

he outdoes both rose and lily.
And when the jongleurs knew
that it was he, they were overjoyed. 2980
They decided then that he would go
with them and serve them;
on these terms, they would instruct him.
They promised they would take care of him
and that they would leave the territory right away, 2985
so that no one would come and find him there.

Now I want to get back to the seneschal
who was in charge of the youth.
Because Silence was used to going off hunting,
the seneschal didn't think anything of it 2990
until it began to grow dark.
Then he began to worry.
And when he saw that the youth was staying out
later than and been his custom before,
he knew that the minstrels, alas! 2995
had robbed him of his young lord.
Then you could see tears shed
and pulling and tearing of hair
and wringing of hands and beating of breasts.
Ladies and girls wept loudly, 3000
they wrenched the rings from off their fingers
with the wringing they did; that's the least of it,
for the lord and lady
who had raised the youth fainted.
That caused great consternation. 3005
And when they recovered from their swoon.
they sent a hundred men throughout the land
to find Silence and bring him back.

The news traveled very fast,
and soon the entire court knew 3010
of the disappearance of the youth
who was so charming, handsome and brave.
And when his father, the count, heard the news,
and Eufemie, his mother,
their hearts were filled with such anguish 3015
that no one could possibly describe it;
no, not even one one-hundredth of it.
Their hearts were nearly breaking;
they were very close to death.

141

Sovent pasment, sovent relievent,   3020
Et li baron qui les sostienent
De pasmer moult envis s'astienent.
Por çals de pasmison retraire
Eskivent soi de noise faire:
Tant sunt il voir plus tormenté   3025
Et refragnent lor volenté.
Por cho c'on ait* al cuer eënte,
Quant on descuevre sa tormente,
Selonc cho c'on l'a de maniere,
U par demostrement de ciere,   3030
Quant on nen a de parler aase
U qu'eure soit que on le taise,
U par dire priveement
A conpagnon, u durement.
Quant il est lius de mener joie   3035
Apertement, si c'on bien l'oie,
U quant il est lius de parler
C'on voit sa coze devorer,
Moult grieve mains par certes l'uevre
Quant on le cuer si en descuevre,   3040
Com li afaires li requiert,
Et si con a le coze afiert. /
Mais cist nen osent faire noise
Que la contesse ne s'en voise,
Dont on ne puet coisir alainne,   3045
Et por le conte ki se painne:
Car par noisier un bien petit
Poroient rendre l'esperit.

Longe est et griés lor pasmisons—
Plus que nos, certes, ne disons—   3050
Et quant un poi sunt revenu,
Oiés com se sunt contenu.
En halt crient: "Bials fils Scilence,
Com nos kerkiés grief penitence!
Li diols qui por vos nos enivre   3055
Nos fait languir en liu de wivre.
Com plus verrons joie mener,
Tant nos convenra plus pener.
Mais com poriens nos pis avoir?
Certes, jo ne le pui savoir.   3060
Trestolt duel nos vienent ensemble
Quant nostre fils de nos s'en emble,

They kept on fainting and being revived,   3020
and the nobles who came to their asssistance
were scarcely able to keep from fainting themselves.
To keep the parents from swooning,
they refrained from giving vent to their grief;
by repressing their natural inclination,   3025
they only increased their own suffering, to be sure.
When one has an aching heart,
if one reveals one's anguish
by one's bearing
or facial expression,   3030
when one is not free to speak
or if it is appropriate to keep silent about the matter,
or by speaking confidentially or giving vent to grief
privately, with a close friend,
if the situation requires that one demonstrate joy   3035
openly, with loud rejoicing,
or if one has a chance to speak
when one's situation is truly desperate,
one certainly suffers far less
if one can open one's heart   3040
as the matter requires
and in a manner appropriate to the occasion.
But these people did not dare mourn openly
for fear of killing thre countess.
who was barely breathing,   3045
and the count, who was suffering terribly,
because the slightest bit of noise
might have killed them both.

They were prostrate with grief for a long time.
It was more painful than words can express.   3050
And when they had recovered a little,
this was their reaction:
they cried aloud, "Silence, our beautiful son!
What dreadful suffering you have caused us!
We are so tormented by grief   3055
that we are more dead than alive.
The more happiness we see,
the more we will suffer.
How could anything worse have befallen us?
(I certainly don't know the answer to that!)   3060
We are afflicted with all sorrows at once,
having our son run away from us.

143

Ki mireöirs estoit del mont,
Et de la mer trosqu'ens el font
Devriemes querre nostre preu.   3065
C'estroit noier et vivre peu.
Quant si grans dolors nos enivre,
Nos menres mals est petit vivre.
Moult par seromes esperdu,
Quant nostre joie avons perdu,   3070
Se convoitons vivre sans joie
Car nos noions quant il se noie.
Nostre [joie] est viers mer alee:
S'al fons ne fust adevalee
Qu'ele ne fust noïe tolte,   3075
Ja nen avriemes si grant dolte.
Mais por que iriemes nos dotant?
Nos mals ne vient pas degotant,
Mais a un fais sor nos chaï.
Por que seriemes esbahi?   3080
Car certes finement savons
Jamais n'avrons pis c'or avons.
De pis avoir n'avons dotance,
De miols avoir nule esperance.
Et nostre crieme et nostre espoir   3085
Avons nos perdu tres ersoir."
Trestols li païs plaint Scilence.
Cil ki est de povre abstinence
Ki ne se puet tenir de plor,
Icil ne fait la nul demor. /   3090
Loing en sus d'als s'en vait mucier,
Plorer son dol, plaindre et hucier.
Moult demainnent grant dol, por voir,
De cho qu'il ont perdu lor oir.

Segnor, oï avés la plainte.   3095
De teles funt cascun jor mainte.
Et si n'est fors joer et rire
A cho que l'on vos poroit dire;
Mais ki demainne trop le voire
As gens, l'en fait* sovent mescroire: 3100
Por cho ne voel jo pas trop dire.
Li senescals kin a grant ire
Nen oze pas a cort venir,
Qu'il ne set preu raison tenir
Que il a fait del fil al conte.   3105

He was the mirror of the world.
the best thing for us to do
would be to drown ourselves at the bottom of the sea, 3065
drown and end our lives.
When we are afflicted with such terrible suffering,
ending our lives would be the lesser evil.
We would be truly insane,
having lost the joy of our life, 3070
if we wanted to live without joy,
for we are drowned if he is.
Our joy went down to the sea.
If it were possible that he's not at the bottom of the sea,
if he weren't really drowned, 3075
we wouldn't feel such despair.
But how could we possibly doubt it?
Our misfortune doesn't come drop by drop,
it falls upon us all at once.
Why should we worry any more, 3080
when we know for certain
that the worst has already befallen us?
We have no fear of anything worse,
no hope of anything better:
last night we lost 3085
both fear and hope."
The entire country mourned Silence.
Those who had little self-control
and couldn't hold back their tears
left quickly. 3090
They went to hide themselves far from the parents
to moan, to grieve and wail aloud.
Truly, they mourned long and deeply
because they had lost their young lord.

Lords, now you have heard how they lamented. 3095
Every day there were fresh displays of grief.
And this is like play and laughter,
compared to what I could tell you.
But those who tell people too much
of the truth often destroy their credibility, 3100
and so I don't want to say too much.
The seneschal, who was dreadfully upset,
didn't dare to come to court,
because he hardly knew how to justify
what he had done with the count's son. 3105

Il n'en set preu venir a conte,
Tant que li cuens a lui le mande.
Voelle u non, se li conmande
Que il le verté li descuevre,
Tolt si com est alee l'uevre,   3110
Et cil nen oze mot celer.
Si ne fait fors renoveler
Et enaigrir lor dol, lor rage,
Quant cers les fait de lor damage.
Li cuens set que li jogleór   3115
Ont pris del mont le mireór.
Volés savoir que il lor fait?
I[l] fait banir par cel forfait
Les jogleörs tols de sa tiere,
Que rien n'i viegnent mais aquierre.   3120
S'on en puet un ballier u prendre,
Il le fera ardoir u pendre.
Ki en porra un atraper
Se de gré le lassce escaper,
On fera de lui altretel   3125
Com on feroit del menestrel.

Oï avés, cho est la some,
Que .m. gens muerent par .i. home:
Et par .ii. d'als, quant sunt falli,
Avient que .m. sunt malballi.   3130
Mais avis m'est, que c'on en die,
Que cist ne font a blasmer mie
Quel qu'ait li cuens damage u honte;
Car nel sevent pas fil a conte.
Ne sevent niënt de la voire: 3135
Qu'il jurast, nel peüscent croire,
Car il les siert si humlement.
Et se l'estorie ne me ment,/
Il a des estrumens apris,
Car moult grant traval i a mis,   3140
Qu'ains que li tiers ans fust passés
A il ses maistres tols passés,
Et moult grant avoir lor gaägne.
Por quant si ont moult grant engagne
Que nus d'als ne set que il face: 3145
Et por cho qu'il a gregnor grasce
Que il nen aient mais en cort,

146

He was scarcely able to give an account,
no matter how much the count asked for one.
Whether he wanted to or not, he was ordered
to disclose the truth,
exactly as it happened,   3110
and he didn't dare omit a word.
His explanation only renewed
their grief and made them more bitter and angry
by reaffirming their sense of loss.
The count knew that jongleurs   3115
had taken the mirror of the world.
Do you want to know what he did to them?
For this crime, he had all jongleurs
banished from his lands;
they were never to seek their fortune there again.   3120
Any who were seized or captured
would be burned or hanged.
Anyone who could have captured one,
but let him escape on purpose,
would suffer the same fate   3125
as the minstrel would have.

What you have heard all comes down to this:
a thousand people were doomed on account of one man;
because of two, whatever they might have done,
it happened that a thousand were persecuted.   3130
I don't care what anyone says; in my opinion,
those minstrels were not at all to blame
for whatever loss the count had suffered,
because they didn't know he was the count's son.
They didn't know a thing about it.   3135
And even if he had sworn it was true, they wouldn't have
    believed him,
because he served them so humbly.
And if we can believe the story,
he learned to play instruments so well,
he put such effort into it,   3140
that before the end of the third year
he had completely surpassed his masters,
and earned a great deal of money for them.
They were so humiliated by this
that they didn't know what to do.   3145
And because he found much greater favor at court
than they ever had,

147

Criement que l'enfes ne s'en tort
Et qu'o als mais estre ne voelle;
Et que il de cho s'en orguelle   3150
Qu'il seus set plus qu'il doi ne facent.
Cuidiés que granment ne l'en hacent?
Oïl, qu'il criement le damage.
Cuidiés qu'es cuers n'aient grant rage,
Que ne lor tort a moult grant honte   3155
Quant il sunt devant roi u conte,
Qu'il harpe et viiele a plaisir
Et c'on les fait por lui taisir?
Oïl! dont ont si grant anguissce
Nus ne se[t] que il faire puissce.   3160
Trestols li frons lor en degotte
C'on por un garçon les debotte.

Silences estoit ja si bials
N'ert pas garçons, mais damoisials.
Et estoit ja el quart esté   3165
Qu'il o ces maistres ot esté.
Grans est li diols qu'en fait li pere,
Tolt cil del païs, et la mere,
Car ainc nus n'i vient qui lor die,
Tant ait la tiere entor ordie: 3170
"J'ai veü vostre fil illuec:
Cho sachiés vos." Et neporuec
L'a fait li cuens bien sovent quere,
Tramis ses més de tierre en tierre.
Car cil a fait de son non cange,   3175
Si l'a mué por plus estrange.
A cort se fait nomer Malduit,
Car il se tient moult por mal duit,
Moult mal apris lonc sa nature.
Et sil refait par coverture.   3180
Il est forment de grant servisce,
Et si se paine en tolte guise
De çals servir a volenté.
Avoir porcace a grant plenté.
Por cho qu'ert bials, et si vallans,   3185
En son mestier si tres vallans,/
Ert il a cort tols jors li sire.
Porquant nel puet nus por voir dire,
Por nule honor c'on li fesist,
Que mains por cho s'entremesist   3190

148

they were afraid that the youth might change his mind
and not want to stay with them any longer;
that he might become vain   3150
because he alone could outdo the two of them.
Don't you think they hated him for this?
Yes, indeed, for they feared financial ruin.
And don't you think their hearts were filled with rage?
Can't you imagine how deeply ashamed they felt,   3155
when, in the presence of king or count,
he was asked to play harp or viele as much as he pleased,
and they were silenced so people could hear him?
Oh, yes, they felt such jealous rage
that neither of them knew what to do.   3160
Their foreheads dripped with sweat at the thought
that they were slighted because of a serving-boy.

Silence was already so handsome that he
was clearly no servant, but a young man of quality.
It was already the fourth summer   3165
that he had served these masters.
His father, his mother, and all his countrymen
continued to grieve deeply,
for none ever came to tell them,
however carefully they had combed the entire country,
"I saw your son in such-and-such a place;   3170
I thought I'd let you know." Nevertheless,
the count had him searched for again and again;
he sent his messengers from one country to another.
But the youth had changed his name   3175
to an even stranger one.
In public, he called himself Malduit,
because he thought himself very badly brought up,
very badly educated with regard to his nature,
and also to conceal his identity.   3180
He gave the very best of service
and exerted himself in every way
to do the minstrels' bidding and please them.
He earned a great deal of money.
Because he was handsome, gracious,   3185
and such an accomplished musician,
he was the center of attention wherever he went.
And yet, no one could truthfully say,
despite all the honors he may have received,
that he waited on the minstrels with any less care,   3190

149

De çals servir et descalcier,
Car ne se voloit essalcier.
Il les siert moult et biel et bien,
Mais ne li valt, voir, nule rien:
Car por servir, ne por bien faire,   3195
N'iert ja vencus cuers de pute aire.
Car li cuers cui francise adrece
N'iert ja vencus fors par destrece.
Li bontés a l'enfant acroist,
Li vilonie a çals aöist.   3200

Silences croist moult en francise,
Li jogleör en culvertise,
Tant com li buens tent a l'onor
Et malvais a le deshonor.
Oiés mervellose descorde!   3205
Se Dex, par cui li mons s'acorde,
N'aïe l'enfant qu'il escape,
Icil le prendront a le trape.
Por bien fait col* frait li rendront,
S'il pueënt, cho li atendront.   3210
Entr'als en vont moult devisant,
D'eures a altres mal disant,
Par l'enemi qui les tangone,
Ki les aömbre et avirone.

Un jor repairent de Gascoigne,   3215
Et vienent al duc de Borgoigne.
Moult biel et bien sunt retenu:
Puis sont as estrumens venu.
Silences i est plus eslis
Que il ne soient, et joïs,   3220
Qu'en lui ot moult bon menestrel.
Ens el palais n'ot ainques tel,
Si est moult bials, et bien senés,
Et si est granment plus penés
De faire bien et honesté   3225
Que li altre n'aient esté.
Et en cho gist moult de le grasce,
C'on loe tols jors, quoi qu'il fasce:
Paint d'acesmer sa volenté,
De faire honor, et a plenté   3230
Ait vials bials dis sor tolte rien,
Ki plus ne fait {cha ju} bien.*

serving them and taking their boots off.
He didn't want to give himself airs,
he served them well and efficiently—
but it certainly did him no good at all,
for fine service and good deeds   3195
never won foul heart,
while a noble heart
is won over by the mere sight of distress.
As the youth's goodness increased,
his masters' villainy grew.   3200

As Silence grew more and more admirable,
his masters became more and more deceitful,
just as a good man always tends toward honor,
and an evil one towards dishonor.
Now you'll hear of a terrible breach of trust.   3205
If God, from whom the world derives its order,
doesn't help the youth to escape,
they will catch him in their trap;
they will give him a broken neck for his trouble,*
that's what they'll do if they get the chance.   3210
They are plotting many things in secret;
they are thinking up one evil plan after another,
incited by the Enemy who goads them,
who has cast his dark shadow over them and has them in his power.

One day they left Gascony   3215
for the court of the Duke of Burgundy,
where they were very well received.
They proceeded to play their instruments.
Silence was more sought after
than they were, and enjoyed greater success,   3220
for he was a very fine minstrel.
The palace had never seen his like.
He was so handsome and accomplished,
and put much more effort into giving a fine performance,
put much more of himself into his art   3225
than the others ever did.
And these qualities were largely responsible for the
favor and praise he received whatever he did,
whether he strove to achieve greater self-discipline,
or to refine his performance, or whether he knew   3230
plenty of beautiful stories on any subject,
no one could outdo him {?}.

Ainz que li menestrel s'en isscent,
Congié ne qu'avoir le peüsscent, /
Li dus une grant fieste i tint.   3235
Icil ki l'a, plus le maintint.
Li menestrel i ont joé
Mais il i sont si desjoé
Que il n'osent un mot tentir,
Car li dus nes violt consentir,   3240
Ne mais Scilence solement.
Celui voelent oïr la gent:
Et cil en ont angoisse et honte,
Moult plus que ne vos di el conte.
Li diols lor est es cuers colés   3245
Que lor mestiers est refolés
Tolt par l'afaire d'un gloton,
Ki pas ne valoit un boton.
"N'a encor pas .iiii. ans d'assés,
Et or nos a ensi passés!"   3250
Font anbedui li menestrel.
"Kaieles! Ki vit mais itel?
Itels sordens* nos croist en lui
Ki nos fera encor anui.
Tel caiel norist l'om adiés   3255
Ki li cort a la janbe apriés.
Tels fait meïsmes le vergant
Dont on le bat. Nostre serjant
Avons desor nos fait segnor.
Nus hom n'ot mais honte gregnor   3260
Que nos avons ichi eü.
Nos somes plus que decheü.
U mainz savons que ja d'assés,
U cis vassals a tols passés
Les jogleörs de jogler bien.   3265
Car nus n'en sot ja viers nos rien.
Duree n'i puet nus avoir:
Cis a emblé nostre savoir.
Por voir, en son enmiodrement
Voi croistre nostre empirement.   3270
Nos savoirs monteplie en lui,
Et Dex, com j'en ai grant anui!
Il l'ont or tant proisié en cort.
Cuidiés vos or qu'il ne s'en tort?
Oïl, atolt nostre savoir: 3275
Si volra, partira l'avoir.

152

Before the minstrels left,
before they were granted permission to leave,
the duke gave a great feast.   3235
He showed even greater favor to Silence than before.
The minstrels began a concert there,
but they were so disconcerted
that they didn't dare say a word,
because the duke didn't want to hear them;   3240
he just wanted to hear Silence alone.
Everyone wanted to hear only him,
and the minstrels were enraged and humiliated at this,
much more than I am telling you.
Their hearts were pierced with grief   3245
that their craft was so disdained
all on account of some
no-good, no-talent nobody.
"He doesn't even have four years' experience
and he's outdone us like this!"   3250
both minstrels exclaimed.
"For heaven's sake! Who ever heard of such a thing?
He is about as welcome as a tooth-ache,
and as likely to continue giving us trouble.
It's like the dog   3255
that bites the leg of the man who feeds him.
It's like the one who cuts*
the stick that beats him—
we've created a master out of our servant.
No man has ever known greater shame   3260
than what we are experiencing now.
We are worse than outwitted:
either we're not as good as we used to be,
or this upstart is the best
jongleur that ever was.   3265
Nobody even came close to us before.
Things can't go on like this:
this upstart has stolen our artistry.
And the better he gets,
the worse things get for us.   3270
Our talents are multiplied in him.
God, this makes me sick!
To think how much they've praised him here at court!
Don't you think he's bound to turn on us now?
Of course! he has all our knowledge.   3275
If he wants to, he'll split the profits.

153

Nostre damages doblera,
Car nostre avoir enportera,
Et plus avoec: c'iert nostre grasce
Que en cort mais, u mestier fasce,   3280
N'iermes oï. Tant l'ont amé,
Trop iermes par lui adamé."/
"Mais se jo vo fiänce avoie,"
Cho dist li uns, "et jo savoie
Que vos men consel celissiés,   3285
Qu'a nului ne le desisiés,
Certes," fait il, "gel vos diroie."
"Tolés!" fait il, "gel jehiroie!
Nostre amistiés va degotant
Quant vos m'alés de rien dotant.   3290
Bials dols compaig, ne me dotés!"
"No[n] fac jo, voir! Or m'escoltés.
Ki par un mal puet abasscier,
Compaing, .d., doit lil lasscier?"
"Nenil! bials amis, par raison."   3295
"Jo prenc cestui a oquoison
De cest malvais garçon ochire,
Car ja s'il vit n'iermes sans ire.
Dites, conpaig, comment vos sanble!
Ferons nos iceste ouevre ensanble?"   3300

Li altres ert altels u pire,
Com hom cui l'enemis espire.
"Compaing," fait il, "par ces .ii. mains,
Jo n'en voel plus, jo n'en voel mains,
Ne en penser, ne en voloir.   3305
Li riens qui plus me fait doloir
Cho est qu'il dure tant en vie."
"Compaing, jon ai si grant envie
Que por poi que mes cuers ne crieve
C'on sor nos l'ensalce et eslieve,   3310
Et qu'il est a tols a plaizir,
Et c'on nos fait por lui taizir."
"Bials compaig," fait il, "mals fus m'arde
Se me donoie de cho garde
Qu'il seüst tant de la moitié,   3315
Ne qu'il eüst si esploitié.
Ne vos, compaig?" "Non de la dime!
Il l'a apris par lui meïsme,
U li malfet li ont apris

That will more than double our losses:
not only will he take away our earnings,
it will be our fate
never to be heard at any court   3280
where he has performed. He has become so popular
that he will rob us of all future profits."
"But if I felt I could trust you,"
one of them said, "and if I knew
that you would keep what I say a secret,   3285
and not tell anyone,
why, then I would certainly have something to tell you."
"Come on!" said the other. "You think I would tell?
Our friendship is really going down the drain
if you have begun to distrust me.   3290
Dear friend and companion, don't doubt me!"
"All right, I won't. Now listen to me:
if by one bad deed a man can avert
five hundred, old friend, should he refrain from it?"
"Not at all, dear friend; it stands to reason."   3295
"I'm just using this as an example
to justify killing this vile boy,
for we'll have nothing but trouble as long as he lives.
Tell me, comrade, what do you think?
Shall we do the job together?"   3300

The other was just as bad or worse,
like a man inspired by the devil.
"Friend," he said, "I swear by these two hands,
I want neither more nor less;
our thoughts and wishes are the same.   3305
What bothers me the most
is that he is still alive."
"Friend, I feel so eager to do it
that my heart is nearly bursting —
the way they raise him above us and praise him   3310
and the way they all favor him
and silence us so that he can perform."
"Friend," he said, "may Saint Anthony's fire* consume me
if I ever thought
he would learn even the half of what he has,   3315
or become so proficient.
What about you, friend?" "Certainly not!
He learned it all by himself,
or else some demons taught him

Ki en tel baldor l'ont ja mis. 3320
Enaizes voir que jo ne derve.
Or sagement, qu'il ne l'enterve!
Or l'aparlons plus bel qu'anchois:
Il sara moult bien son franchois
Se nos nel prendons a la trape. 3325
Sans caperon li ferons cape,
Car le cief perdra al trebuc.
Senpres prendrons congié al duc.
Por quoi iriens nos en Espagne,
Compaig, por golozer gaägne?/ 3330
Nostre [espoir] gist en lui ocire.
Parmi un bos est nostre pire,
Ki dure bien une jornee.
Nos i ferons la destornee.
Nos nos perdrons de gré sans falle 3335
En le plus espesse boscalle:
Et quant nos verrons nostre liu,
Nos li ferons .i. malvais giu."

Tolt cest affaire ont atiré
Et sont andoi si espiré 3340
Par l'enemi qui les enthice
A faire l'uevre de malice
Que pietés lor sanble dure,
Misericorde amere et sure,
Quant sans merite et sans deserte 3345
Voelent l'enfant livrer a perte.
Tant com il plus heënt l'enfant
Tant li mostrent plus bel sanblant.
Par decevable et par faintise
Voelent covrir lor covoitise. 3350
Cil jors lor sanbla durer trente.
Il usent moult a grant aënte.
Le soir vont al duc congié prendre,
Car il n'i voelent plus atendre:
Et li dus done a cascun d'eus 3355
Un marc d'argent, Silence .ii.
Envie les mort et tangone,
Por quant s'est lor, quanque on lor done.
A tols i ont dont pris congié.
Silences a le nuit songié 3360
Que chien le voelent depecier;
Et por cho qu'il crient le blecier,

to attain such excellence.   3320
It's really enough to drive a man crazy.
Now we'd better be careful, so he doesn't catch on!
Let's speak more kindly to him than we usually do.
He'll have to be very clever indeed
not to fall into our trap.   3325
We'll make him a cape without a hood,*
for he'll lose his head in our trap.
Let's take leave of the duke right away."
"Why should we bother to go to Spain,
friend, if we're eager to make a killing?   3330
Our profit lies in killing him here.
Our route takes us through a forest
that takes a whole day to get through.
We will make a detour there.
That's it: we'll pretend to get lost   3335
in the densest part of it.
And when we find a likely spot, we'll play a nasty trick on
    him."

Thus they plotted the whole thing.
Both of them were so inspired   3340
by the Devil, who kept urging them
to do this wicked deed,
that pity seemed hard to them
and mercy bitter and sour:
they wanted to murder the youth,   3345
who in no way deserved it.
The more they hated the youth,
the more they pretended to be nice.
They wanted to conceal their purpose
by means of deception and falsehood.   3350
That day seemed like a month to them,
it was so hard for them to get through it.
They took leave of the duke that evening,
for they could wait no longer.
The duke gave one mark of silver   3355
to each of them, and two to Silence.
They were tormented with jealousy,
despite that fact that all the money went to them.
Then they took leave of everyone.
During the night, Silence dreamt   3360
that wild dogs wanted to tear him apart.
And because he feared the pain,

Si est esperis de son somme
Ensi griément, cho est la some,
C'ainc puis ne dormi cele nuit.   3365
Volés oïr con s'a deduit?
Tolte nuit escolte et orelle,
Car de son songe a grant mervelle.

As jogleörs de l'altre part
Angoissce moult li cuers et art.   3370
Et c'est moult bone partissure
D'ome felon et plain d'ardure
Qu'il nen est mie daärains,
Anchois le conpre premerains,
Car ses fel[s] pensers le tormente   3375
Ains qu'il puist faire altre aënte.
Il est de ces tolt ensement
Qui sunt en maint porpensement /
Que cascuns d'als achiever puissce
Le mal dont il sunt en anguissce.   3380
Et cuidiés qu'a tols .iii. n'anuit
Qu'il ne pueënt dormir la nuit,
Li doi qui pensent le mal faire,
Li tiers de cho qu'il se crient traire?
Car il a songié hisdeus songe,   3385
Mais Dex li vertissce a mençoinge.
Tolt quoi se contient et escolte,
Et cil nen ont pas de cho dolte.
Cuident qu'il dormie com il siolt,
Com vallés qui reposer *violt*.   3390
Li uns dist: "Gel ferrai premiers,
Si croistra ma pars de deniers."
L'altres respont isnielement:
"Conpaing, parlés plus bielement,
Qu'il n'est pas lius de plaidoier.   3395
Nos iermes andoi moitiier
Et de l'avoir qu'il a aquis
Et del pechié, bials dols amis!
Mais or li disons qu'il s'atorne.
Faisons li croire qu'il ajorne.   3400
De nuit nos metons a la voie
Car tels fais n'a soig c'on le voie."

Silences entent et escolte.
Or n'est il pas de cho en dolte,

he awoke from his dream
in such a terrible state
that he slept no more that night.   3365
Shall I tell you what he did?
He listened to every sound the whole night through,
he was so disturbed by his dream.

As for the minstrels,
they were tormented and feverish.   3370
And it's only fair
that a man who is inflamed with evil desires
should pay in advance
rather than later:
his evil thoughts torment him   3375
even before he gets the chance to harm anyone.
And it's the same with these two
who are pondering
how they might be able to carry out
the wicked deed that is preying upon them.   3380
You can imagine how weary all three of them were
from not being able to sleep that night—
the two because of the evil they were planning,
and the third because of the evil he feared.
He has had a terrible dream;   3385
may God prevent it from coming true!
He remained motionless and listened,
and the others suspected nothing:
they thought he was asleep as usual,
like any youth who wants his rest.   3390
One said, "I'll strike the first blow;
that will increase my share of the money."
The other replied quickly,
"Take it easy, comrade;
this is no time to argue.   3395
The two of us will divide
his earnings
and the sin equally, my dear friend.
But now we'll tell him to get ready.
Let's make him believe it's near dawn.   3400
Let's get under way while it's still dark,
for such deeds are better done unseen."

Silence was listening and heard them.
There was now no doubt in his mind

Que li doi culviert desperé 3405
N'eüsscent son songe averé
Des chiens dont il avoit songié
S'il en eüscent le congié.*
Mais Dex ne le volt consentir.
Silences ne volt mot tentir, 3410
Ains gist tols cois et si orelle,
Si escolte cele mervelle.

Li jogleör plus ne sejornent.
Silence apielent, si s'atornent.
Dient li qu'il est piece a jors 3415
Et qu'il volroient estre allors.
"Levés!" font il. "Petit savés
Com grief* jornee a faire avés."
"Chi n'a" fait il, "mestier de gloze,
Car grief jornee est male coze, 3420
Et bien doit remanoir el mal
Ki de son gré se met el val."
Sa parole ont cil trestornee:
Dient que il ont grief jornee
Por cho que lor voie est pesans, 3425
Et lor jornee est longhe et grans. /
Si tornent le plus bel defors,
Mais malfés ont dedens les cors.
Que puet caloir, quant il ne crient?
Dex l'a bien guari, quil maintient. 3430
Dist lor: "Segnor, vos me dirés
Ains que jo mueuje, u vos irés,
Car aler poés en tel liu
U l'on me feroit malvais giu,
Se l'en m'i peüst atraper, 3435
Ains que jo peüsce escaper."

"Amis," font il, "ne vos cremés.
Nos amons vos, vus nos amés.
Quant dites qu'estes si haïs,
Cremons que ne soiés traïs. 3440
Se li malfaitor sont a destre,
Acuellons la voie a senestre.
Ses encontrons par aventure
Et faire nos voelent rancure,
Por nos meïsmes i serons. 3445

160

that these two desperados   3405
would, if given half a chance,
make his dream
of the two dogs come true.
But God won't allow it!
Silence didn't want to utter a word.   3410
Instead, he lay quietly and listened
to these strange goings-on.

The minstrels didn't wait any longer.
They called to Silence and began to get ready,
saying that it was near daybreak   3415
and they would like to be on their way.
"Get up!" they said. "Little do you know
what a hard journey you have to make."
"That needs no interpretation," said Silence.
"A hard journey is a dreadful indeed,   3420
and he richly deserves his evil fate
who deliberately puts himself at a disadvantage."
The minstrels turned his words around:
they said that they had a hard journey ahead
because the road was difficult,   3425
and that would make for a long and strenuous day's travel.
Thus they affected goodness,
while they were evil on the inside.
But what difference did that make, since Silence was
      unafraid?
God protected and watched over him.   3430
He said to them, "Gentlemen, before I make a move,
you must tell me where you are going,
because you could be headed for someplace
where someone might do me a bad turn
if they happened to catch me   3435
before I could escape."

"Friend," they said, "don't worry.
We are loyal to you, as you are to us.
When you say you feel threatened,
we, too, are afraid you might be in danger.   3440
If the criminals are on the right,
we will take the path to the left.
And if we should happen to encounter them,
and if they want to attack us,
we will all be there to help each other.   3445

161

S'il i fierent, nos i ferrons."
"Dirai vos," fait il, "une rien:
Je ne cuic pas, ains le sai bien
Que vos i ferrés volentiers.
Et cil se guart endementiers,   3450
Se il violt, qui a garder s'a,
U s'il nel fait que fols fera.
Segnor, jo que vos celeroie?
Mes enemis enconterroie
Se jo aloie o vos en France,   3455
Cho sachiés vos tolt a fiänce;
U s'o vos aloie en Espagne,
En Alvergne, u en Alemagne.
Si me vient chi miols remanoir,
Qu'aler allors por pis avoir.   3460
Jo remanrai, cho est la some,
Et vos end irés com prodome
Et bone gent, bien le savés.
Si com vos viers moi fait avés,
Vos rendie Dex le gueredon;   3465
Por tel deserte altretel don.
Moult m'avés fait, plus eüsciés
Se moi faire le peüssciés.
En vos servir ai jo perdu."
Li jogleör sont esperdu.   3470
Aportent le gaäig avant,
Se li ont dit par avenant:
"Sire, amis chiers, prendés vo part."
Et l'enfes .c. mars en depart. /
A çals en lasce plus de .c.,   3475
Et cil s'en vont hastivement.

Silence remaint a sejor
Avoec le duc a grant honor.
Puis li prent pités de son pere,
De ses parens et de sa mere.   3480
De ses .c. mars bien se conroie.
Al duc prent congié de sa voie,
Et passe la mer d'Engletierre.
Plus tost que pot vint en sa tierre.
Vient la u on plus le desire,   3485
Mais li alquant en avront ire
Anchois qu'il sachent qui il soit.
Al plus bel ostel que il voit

If they strike, we strike, too."
"I have something to say to you," said Silence.
"I think, or rather, I know very well,
that you will be only too happy to strike.
In the meantime, the one who has to protect himself   3450
had better be on his guard, if he wants to defend himself;
and if he doesn't do this, he is a fool.
Gentlemen, why should I not speak openly?
You know very well indeed
that I would encounter my enemies   3455
whether I went with you to France
or whether I went with you to Spain
or Auvergne or Germany.
Therefore, it would be much better for me to stay here
than to go somewhere else and be worse off.   3460
In short, I'm staying here.
And you will go off, like upright
and honest men, make no mistake about that.
As you have done to me,
may God do to you in return;   3465
may you receive your just desserts.
You have done much for me,
and would have done more if you could have.
I haven't been able to do quite enough for you."
The minstrels were undone.   3470
They took out the earnings
and graciously said to him,
"Dear friend, good sir, take your share."
Then the youth took a hundred marks as his portion,
and left them more than a hundred,   3475
and they took off in a hurry.

Silence stayed on a while
as a highly valued member of the ducal household.
Then he was seized with pity for his father
and mother and his relatives.   3480
With his hundred marks, he easily made arrangements.
He took leave of the duke, was on his way,
and crossed the English Channel.
He reached his own lands as quickly as possible.
He's arrived at the place where he's most wanted,   3485
but some people are going to be very upset
before they find out who he is.
The youth went immediately

S'est trais li enfes maintenant.
Et li ostes li vient devant   3490
Et molt dolcement le reçuit;
Mais tost a veü son deduit,
Cho sont li estrument celui.
"Sainte Marie! quel anui,
Amis," fait il, "et qué damage   3495
Ai requelloit de tel ostage!"
Silences enquiert et entierve
S'il a bon sens u se il derve.
"Amis," fait il, "cis diols est vostres—
Il est ambeure et miens et vostres.   3500

Or entendés a ma raison,
Si poés oïr l'oquoison.
Chi vindrent l'altre an jogleör.
Li cuens lor fist moult grant honor.
N'ot c'un enfant: celui enblerent.   3505
Nos ne savons u l'enmenerent.
Moult loig de nos l'ont espani.
Par ceste oquoison sont bani
Li jogleör de ceste terre,
Que rien n'i vienent mais aquierre.   3510
Ki un en prent, u il le renge,
Quel qu'il miols violt, u il se penge.
Menres mals est de vos a rendre
Que l'en me deüst por vos pendre.
Mais or ne l'aiés en despit.   3515
Trosqu'a demain avrés en respit.
"Non ai," fait il, "se Dex me salt,
Car respis sor nuit .c. mars valt.
Or menons nostre vie a joie:
Ki plus l'a longe si l'a poie."   3520
Dont prent sa harpe et sa viiele,
Si note avoec a sa vois biele. /
N'i a celui d'illuec entor
Ne face a l'ostel donc son tor.
Moult i a borjois assanblés,   3525
Car puis que l'enfes fu enblés
N'i ot oï harpe ne rote,
Viiele nule, cant ne note.*
Et dient tuit, cho est la some:
"Ainc mais ne fu tels forme d'ome!   3530
Com il a, las, povre sejor,

164

to the best inn he could find.
The innkeeper came out   3490
and greeted him most cordially,
but then saw at once what he had with him—
his instruments.
"Holy Mary!" he said,
"what trouble and sorrow   3495
I get from a guest like you, my friend."
Silence asked him
whether he was sane or crazy.
"Friend," said the man, "the sorrow is yours as well—
it is both of ours, mine and yours.   3500
Now listen to what I have to say,
and you will understand the reason why.
A few years ago, some minstrels came here.
The count bestowed great honors upon them.
He had only one son: they kidnapped him.   3505

We don't know where they took him;
they took him far away from us.
For this reason, all minstrels
have been banished from this land;
they can no longer seek their fortune here.   3510
Whoever catches one of them must hand him over
as best he can, or be hanged himself.
It's a lot easier on me to turn you in
than to be hanged in your place.
Butr don't get upset about that now—   3515
you have a reprieve until tomorrow."
"Well then, I won't," he said, "God help me,
a night's delay is well worth a hundred marks.
Now let's enjoy our life;
no matter how long, it's always too short."   3520
Then he took his harp and viele
and sang beautifully as he played.
Everyone from all around
came running to the inn.
There was a large crowd of townspeople,   3525
for they hadn't heard a harp or lute
or viele* or song or even a note
since the child had been kidnapped.
And they all exclaimed,
"There never was such a man!   3530
What a pity he'll be here for such a short time—

165

Car il pendra demain sor jor."
N'i a celui ne s'esmervelle.
Silences lor fait sorde orelle:
Maine sa joie et son deduit.   3535
Et l'ostes trait moult male nuit,
C'ainc ne le fina de gaitier,
Car al conte le violt ballier.

Qu'alongeroie plus mon conte?
L'endemain l'enmena al conte   3540
Tolt vielant amont le rue.
L'enfes le voit, si le salue.
Li cuens ne li volt mot respondre
Car il le pense bien confondre.
Silensce dist: "Sire, merchi,   3545
Car se jo ma vie perc chi
Nule rien n'i conquesterés
Ne ja plus riches n'en serés!"
Li cuens l'entent, parfont sospire.
Or [ot] tel dol ne pot mot dire.   3550
Grant dol demainent li baron
Et a privé et a laron,
Et forment plore la contesse.
Li cuens lor fait une promesse
Que il nen iert huimais pendus,   3555
Et il l'en ont grans grés rendus.
Mellent o joie lor anui,
Tolt por le biel deduit celui.

Uns viellars l'a bien ravisé
Et voit bien qu'il a desvisé.   3560
Al conte dist sa consience:
"Veés la vostre fil Silence,
Si a apris des estrumens."
Li cuens li dist: "Traistor, tu mens:
Cho m'est avis que tu rasotes,   3565
Bien est mais tans que tu radotes."
Et cil li a dit un respit:
"Cho est grans diols que povres vit.
Miols me venist estre teüs.
Plus est oïs uns desseüs/   3570
En toltes cors, s'il a avoir,
C'uns povres hom de grant savoir."
Li cuens li a dit que il derve.

166

for he'll hang tomorrow morning."
They were all amazed, every one of them.
But Silence turned a deaf ear
and continued to perform joyously.   3535
The innkeeper had a very bad night:
he didn't take his eyes off the youth,
for he wanted to hand him over to the count.

Why should I prolong the suspense?
The next day the youth was taken to the count,   3540
playing the viele as he went up the street.
When he saw the count, he greeted him.
The count didn't want to say a word in reply,
because he planned to have him killed.
Silence said, "Mercy, Sire!   3545
If I lose my life here,
you won't have gained any great advantage
or be at all the richer for it!"
The count heard him and sighed deeply.
He felt such pangs of grief that he couldn't utter a word.   3550
His noble companions grieved deeply,
although they betrayed no signs of it,
and the countess wept aloud.
The count promised them
that he wouldn't be hanged right away,   3555
and they expressed their profound gratitude.
Their joy was mingled with sorrow
at the thought of the youth's exquisite performance.

A certain old man* examined the youth closely,
and saw what he was up to.   3560
He spoke his mind to the count:
"That is your son Silence;
he has learned the minstrel's art."
The count replied, "Traitor, you're lying!
I think you're completely mad.   3565
You've picked a bad time to start babbling."
And the old man rebuked him, saying,
"It's a dreadful thing to be poor.
I would have done better to keep silent.
In every court, a wealthy ignoramus*   3570
is listened to more
than a poor but learned man."
The count told the old man that he was crazy.

167

Vait a l'enfant, son non enterve.
"Sire," fait il, "nel quier celer.   3575
Je me fac Malduit apieler."
Et li viellars dont li respont:
"Bien sai que vostres nons despont,
Car malduis cho est mal apris,
Si estes vos, qu'il n'i a pris   3580
Ne los a vos n'a vo parage
D'avoir mené si fait usage.
Cui calt? Or serés plus senés
Com plus avrés esté penés,
Qu'en une cort ne puet avoir   3585
Quanque wés home a [a] savoir.
Par une cort, cho est la some,
Ne verrés ja bien apris home.
Que que aiés fait, amis Scilence,
Amendés estes en science: 3590
Et se vos vesquisiés .m. ans
S'en seriés vos moult plus vallans."

[Q]ue que li viellars die u face,
Silence fait que mot ne sace
De quanque il onques li devise;   3595
Mais cil s'en a bien garde prise
Que cho est il, et vait al conte
Qui orains l'en dist lait et honte.
Et por le honte qu'il li fist
Or escoltés que il li dist.   3600
"Sire, or sai bien que jo mespris
De vostre fil, que jo vos dis.
Cho n'est il pas, mais j'ai oï,
Se Dex me doinst estre esjoï,
Que cis vos dira tels novieles,   3605
S'il violt, et vos, ki seront bieles.
De vostre enfant set la verror
Et si vos metra fors d'error."
"Fera, por Deu?" li cuens* respont.
"Oïl, par Deu, ki fist cest mont."   3610

Li cuens violt bien cel plait celer.
Le jogleör fait apieler
Et moult priveëment l'enmainne
Od lui en sa cambre demainne./
L'uis de la canbre apriés lui serre.   3615

But the old man went up to Silence and asked him his name.
"Sir," said the boy, "I won't try to hide it.   3575
I call myself Malduit."
And the old man replied,
"I know very well what your name means:
Malduit means 'badly brought up,'
and that suits you well, for neither you   3580
nor your family wins any praise or prizes
for such a counterfeit upbringing.
But what does it matter? You will be all the wiser now
for having endured greater hardships,
for one cannot learn everything   3585
one needs to know by staying at court;
in short, you will never see a wise man
who learned all he knows at court.
Whatever you have done, friend Silence,
you have made amends for it through wisdom,   3590
and if you lived a thousand years,
you would be all the more admirable."

Whatever the old man said or did,
Silence acted as if he hadn't understood a word
of what he was telling him.   3595
But the old man could see very well
that it was he, and he went to the count
who had just insulted him so shamefully.
And in return for the way the count has shamed him,
listen to what he told him: 3600
"Sire, I know now that I was mistaken
in what I told you regarding your son.
That's not he, but I have heard,
may God grant me the joy of it,
that this boy can tell you some wonderful news—   3605
if you and he are willing.
He knows the truth about your son
and will clear the matter up for you."
"Will he, by God?" the count replied.
"Yes, by God who created this world."   3610

The count wanted to keep this interview private.
He had the minstrel summoned
and brought him in strictest secrecy
to his private chamber
and locked the door behind him.   3615

Halt s'est assis et cil a terre.
Son fil a saisi par la destre,
Si enquiert u ses fils converse.
Son fil demande et il le tient;
Il le convoite et nel voit nient!   3620
Li cuens est en dure sentence,
Qu'il ainme plus son fil Silence
Qu'altre richoise n'altre avoir,
Et por quant ne le violt avoir!
Il va ja ravisant sa chiere: 3625
Com plus l'esgarde, plus l'a chiere.
Une hore pense: "Et Dex, est cil!"
Et en apriés: "Par foi, nenil!"
Ses cuers tamaint pense et* requelt,
Que iols ne voit, et cuers ne velt.   3630
De cho qu'il n'a son fil si pleure.
Ses filx le voit, plus n'i demeure,
Ciet li as piés, et plore, et crie.
"Sire," fait il, "vos fils vos prie
Que vos merchi aiés de lui.   3635
Bien reconois que grant anui
Avés eü por moi, bials pere,
Vos et mi parent et ma mere.
Merchi de vostre engendreüre!
Vos savés bien de ma nature: 3640
"Jo sui," fait il, "nel mescreés,
Com li malvais dras encreés
Ki samble bons, et ne l'est pas.
Si est de moi! N'ai que les dras,
Et le contenance et le halle   3645
Ki onques apartiegne a malle."
Sor diestre espaule li ensegne
Une crois qu'il ot a ensegne.
Ormais le puet li cuens bien croire:
Donc a baisié son fil en oire.   3650
De joie qui en lui fuisone
Li cuens dont tant basier li done
Que jo en ai perdu le nonbre,
Por le grant fuison qui m'enconbre.

Grant joie en mainne donc li pere,   3655
Tolt cil de la terre et la mere.
Ki donc veïst gens esjoïr
L'enfant vont veoir et oïr.

170

He sat on a chair, the boy, on the floor.
He took his son by the right hand
and asked where his son was living.
He asks for his son while holding him;
he wants to have him and can't see that he's there! 3620
The count is serving a harsh sentence,
for he loves his son Silence
more than any wealth or possessions,
and yet he doesn't want to have him!
Now he examines the boy's face carefully: 3625
the more he looks at it, the dearer it is to him.
One time he thinks, "My God, it's he!"
But an instant later: "I'd swear it's not!"
His heart is receptive to many things
that his eyes don't see and his mind can't accept. 3630
He weeps because he doesn't have his son.
When his son saw this, he didn't wait any longer.
He lay at his father's feet and cried and wept.
"Sire," he said. "your son begs you
to have pity on him. 3635
I see very well that you have endured dreadful suffering
on my account, dear father,
you and my family and my mother.
Have pity on your offspring!
You know my nature very well. 3640
I am," he said, "believe me,
like an inferior piece of cloth
powdered with chalk, that looks good, but isn't.
That's what I am! I have only the clothing
and bearing and complexion 3645
that belong to a man."
He showed him a birthmark shaped like a cross
that he had on his right shoulder.
Now the count had to believe him;
he immediately embraced his son. 3650
Bursting with joy,
he kissed him so many times
I lost track of the number,
overwhelmed by such profusion.

The father expressed his great joy, 3655
as did his mother and all the inhabitants of the land.
Then you could see joyful celebrations,
as the people came to see and hear the youth.

171

Silences siet as piés son pere.
Dist: "Sire, jo sui vos harpere,   3660
Si vos volrai servir anuit.
Por amor Deu, ne vos anuit/
Que j'en voel estre soldoiés.
Por mon service m'otroiés
Li jogleör tres ore mais   3665
Aient en vostre tiere pais,
Car on les a a tort banis
C'ainc ne fui par als espanis.
Li cuens respont: "Cho me delite
Qu'il soient por vostre amor cuite."   3670
Al viellart qui dist les novieles
Done li cuens soldeës bieles.
Por cho qu'il li dist verité
En a .x. mars en ireté.
Tols li païs est esclairiés   3675
Que Silences est repairié.
Trosques al roi va li noviele
Qu'il est venus, moult li fu biele.
Li cuens est mandés maintenant
Qu'il viegne al roi atolt l'enfant: 3680
Et il i vient plus tost qu'il puet.
Tolte la cors contre als s'esmuet.

Or est Silences bien venus.
Del roi Ebain est retenus:
De sa maisnie avoir le velt.   3685
Li cuens ses pere moult s'en duelt;
Et quant il altre ne puet estre,
Son fil a saisi par la destre
Et baze sa bouce et sa face,
Et prie moult que bien li face,   3690
Que bien se cuevre. Et donc s'en torne:
Et l'enfes o le roi sejorne,
Et siert le bien en mainte guise.
La roïne en est moult esprise
Por sa façon, por sa bialté.   3695
Or oiés quel desloialté
Avint et ques mesaventure,
Con faite rage et quele ardure
Cis Sathanas en soi aquelt:
Car onques Tristrans por Izelt,   3700
Ne dame Izeuls por dant Tristran

172

Silence sat at his father's feet.
He said, "Sir, I am your harper,   3660
and as such I'd like to serve you tonight.
For the love of God, don't be angry
if I want to be paid for it.
For my services, grant me
that from this very moment on   3665
all minstrels may enter your land in peace,
because they are wrongly banished:
I was never kidnapped by them."
The count replied, "I should be delighted
to acquit them for love of you."   3670
The count gave a generous reward
to the old man who had told him the news.
He received a bequest of ten marks
for having told the truth.
The whole country was glad   3675
that Silence had come home.
When the news of his return reached the king,
he was delighted.
The count was immediately ordered
to bring the youth to court.   3680
He went there as soon as possible.
The whole court came forth to greet them.

Now Silence received a cordial welcome:
King Evan chose him as retainer;
he wanted him to be part of his household.   3685
His father the count was very upset at this,
but since it couldn't be helped,
he took his son by the hand
and kissed his mouth and face
and prayed fervently that he would make a good job of it
and conceal his identity well. Then he departed,   3690
and the youth stayed on as the king's attendant
and served him well in various capacities.
The queen was much taken with the youth
because of his beauty and demeanor.   3695
Now you shall hear what treachery
and evil deeds transpired,
what deceitful madness and burning lust
lurked in this female Satan!
Tristan never suffered   3700
such anguished yearning for Isolde

173

N'ot tele angoisse ne ahan
Com eult Eufeme la roïne
Por le vallet ki ert meschine;
N'onques Jozeph, ki fu prisons   3705
Rois Pharaöns, si le lisons,
N'ot tele angoisse ne tel mal
Par la mollier al senescal,
Comme ut icis par la roïne.
Si l'orés, ains que l'uevre fine. /   3710

Un jor ala li rois en bois
Et mena od lui des Englois.
Eufeme se fait malhaitie
Ki de cel ouevre ert afaitie,
Et fait Silence remanoir   3715
Por cui le cuer el ventre a noir.
De la harpe le doit deduire,
Mais cho li porra anchois nuire
Que sa nature li canjast.
Anchois espoir que mals n'alast*   3720
Seroit la roïne sanee
Kist par sanblant moult enganee.
En la cambre fait apieler
Silence, et, por l'uevre celer,
Li fait sa harpe o soi porter,   3725
Quanses por li reconforter.
En la cambre painte et celee
Li violt s'amor dire a celee;
Et donc la fait a tols voidier
Qu'il ne la puissce sorcuidier.   3730
Si a le jor fait un dangier
Faintic que ne poroit mangier,
Et qu'el ne puet sofrir le noise
Ne ne violt pas c'on i estoise,
Ne mais que cil qui harpera.   3735
Cho dist qu'il l'asoägera.
Ele n'oirre pas sagement
Car ja voir assoägement
N'avra par lui fors de baisier.
Cel pora plus mesaäsier   3740
Quant al sorplus volra entendre
Qu'ele falra del tolt al prendre.

nor Lady Isolde for Lord Tristan
as did Queen Eufeme
for this young man who was a girl;
nor did Joseph, who was imprisoned   3705
by King Pharaoh, as the story goes,
suffer such trials and tribulations
at the hands of the captain's wife
as did Silence because of the queen.
You shall hear all about it before the end of this work.   3710

One day, the king went to the forest,
accompanied by some of his men.
Eufeme, who was highly skilled in such matters,
pretended to be indisposed,
and had Silence stay behind.   3715
Her heart and body were consumed with lust for him.
He's supposed to soothe her by playing the harp,
but he might get into trouble instead
for having changed his nature.
Perhaps [if Silence had looked like a girl]   3720
the queen, who was so sadly misled by external appearances,
might have been cured before anything bad happened.
She summoned Silence to her bedchamber,
and in order to conceal her intent,
she had him bring his harp along,   3725
as if in order to comfort her.
In her carved and gilded chamber,
she wanted to confess her secret love to him.
and so she made everyone else leave the room,
so that he could not snub her in public.   3730
All day she complained,
pretended that she couldn't eat,
that she couldn't stand the least bit of noise
or bear to have anyone come near her —
except the harper.   3735
She said he would relieve her distress.
She's on the wrong track,
because she'll never have any relief from him
beyond a kiss, believe me!
And this will upset her all the more   3740
when she goes after the rest
and doesn't get it.

175

Sa harpe a cil bien atenpree
Si a grant dolor destenpree
A oués la dame de roïne   3745
Ki sor lui s'apoie et acline:
Et plus et plus de cel s'esprent
Que cil harpe si dolcement. /
Et pense donc: "Jo li dirai
L'amor et tolt li gehirai."   3750
Et redist donc: "Viols li tu dire?
Vios te tu donques si despire?
O je, nel larai por despit,
Por reprover, ne por respit,
Ne li face orendroit savoir   3755
Que il porra m'amor avoir."
Et a itant l'acole et baise
Et dist li: "Or estes vos aise! /
Baisiés me, ne soiés hontels!
Por .i. baisier vos donrai .ii.   3760
Et ne vos sanble bien estrange
Que vos avrés si riche cange?"
"Oïl!" dist li vallés mescine.
"Donc, me baisiés," dist la roïne.
Joste la face, sos sa guinple   3765
Li dona cil .i. baisier sinple,
Car il n'entent pas, al voir dire,
Con fait baisier ele desire.
Et la dame, qui nen a cure
D'estre baisie en tel mesure,   3770
Li done .v. baisiers traitis,
Bien amorols et bien faitis,
Et ot les .ii. baisiers promis
Li a des altres tant tramis
Que il en est tols anuiés.   3775
Dist la dame: "Por Deu, fuiés?
Comment?" fait ele, "est cho dangiers?
Ene vos plaist si fais cangiers?"
"Oïl, roïne, il me delite,
Mais bien vus en lairoie cuite."   3780
"Cuite! Por quoi?" fait ele donques.
"Eut hom de vostre parage onques,
Tant fust de pris, ensi grant don?
Mon cors vos doinsc tolt a bandon!"
Et li vallés qui est mescine   3785
Est moult en dure descipline,

176

The youth's harp was in perfect tune.
This only caused our lady queen—
who was sitting next to him and leaning against him—
    unbearable pain.   3745
Her desire for the harper, who played so sweetly,
grew stronger every minute,
and she thought, "I'm going to tell him that I love him
and confess all to him."   3750
But then she said to herself, "Do you really want to tell him?
Do you want to lower yourself like that?
Yes, I do! I won't hold back for fear of rejection
or reproval or delay;
I'm going to tell him right here and now   3755
that he can have my love."
And then, right away, she embraced him and kissed him
and told him, "Now just relax!
Kiss me, don't be shy!
I'll give you two kisses for one.   3760
Don't you think that's an amazing
rate of exchange?"
"Yes," said the youth who was a girl.
"So kiss me!" said the queen.
Right on her forehead, just below her wimple,   3765
Silence gave her one chaste kiss—
for you can be very sure he had no intention
of kissing her the way she wanted.
But the lady, who did not care
to be kissed in this manner,   3770
gave him five long kisses,
exceedingly passionate and very skillful.
Besides the two kisses she had promised,
she gave him so many others
that he was extremely upset.   3775
The lady said, "My God! are you running away?
What's the matter?" she said, "is something wrong?
Don't you like the rate of exchange?"
"Oh yes, my queen, I am delighted with it,
but let's call it quits."   3780
"Quits? Whatever for?" she said then.
"Was any man of your lineage,
however exalted, ever offered such a glorious gift?
I'm offering you my body in complete surrender."
Now the youth who is a girl   3785
is in a really terrible situation—

Qu'il volroit miols estre .c. liues
U li eüst et pais et triues
Que en la cambre en tele anguisse,
Que il ne set que faire puisse. 3790

La dame son col desafice
D'un harponciel d'or qu'ele ot rice.
Blance est sa cars com nois negie:
N'est pas de fronces asegie,
Car ses aés n'a encor cure 3795
Que ele ait nule froncissure,
Ains ert roönde et tendre et mole.
Al vallet dist la dame fole:
"Veés quels bras et quels costés!"
"Dame," fait il, "por Deu, ostés! 3800
Jo vos requier por Deu merci.
Se jo ma loialté perc chi
Donques sui jo enfin honis
Et as piors del mont onis.
Meffait nen a el mont gregnor 3805
Car jo sui hom vostre segnor, /
Et ses parens ne sai con priés,
Ki me feroit jamais confiés?"
"Confés! Por Deu, et c'or me dites?
Serés vos monies, u hermites? 3810
Mandés le conte vostre pere
Et la contesse vostre mere
Que vos hermites devenrés
Et que religiön tenrés!
En vos avra moult bon abé!" 3815
"Roïne, or m'avés vus jabé."
"Non ai, se vos estes estables,
Mais jovenes sains est viés diäbles.
Lassciés, bons hom, tolt cho ester.
Ichi fait mellor arester 3820
Q'en bos por son cors afoler."
Dont le conmence a acoler,
Mais cil nen a de tolt cho cure
Car nel consent pas sa nature.
Ains li dist: "Dame, en pais soiés!" 3825
"Estes vus donc pris ne loiés?"
Dist la roïne. "Qui vos cache?
Ki vus laidist? ki vus man[a]ce?

178

he'd rather be a hundred miles away,
somewhere nice and peaceful and quiet,
than in that bedroom in such a tight spot
that he doesn't know how to get put of it.   3790

The lady was wearing a magnificent gold brooch
at her neck. She unfastened it.
Her skin was as white as fresh-fallen snow:
she had no problem with wrinkles;
she was not old enough yet   3795
to have to worry about creases,
not at all; she was round and smooth and soft.
This lascivious lady said to the youth,
"Take a look at these arms! Look at these curves!"
"Lady," he said, "for the love of God, stop!   3800
for God's sake, have mercy on me!
If I commit an act of treachery here,
I will be so dishonored by it
that I will be one of the worst men in the world.
There is no greater crime in the world,   3805
for I am your lord's vassal,
and his blood relation, I don't know to what degree.
Who could ever absolve me of such a sin?"
"Absolve you? My God, what are you telling me now?
That you want to be a monk or a hermit?   3810
Go tell your father the count
and your mother the countess
that you're going to take vows
and become a hermit.
You'd make a terrific abbot!"   3815
"My queen, now you're making fun of me."
"No I'm not, if you're normal.*
Don't you know a saintly youth makes for an old devil?*
Forget all that—be a man!
It's much better to romp in here   3820
than to let your body go to waste in some forest!"
Then she began to embrace him,
but he wasn't at all interested,
because his nature kept him from responding.
He said to her, "Lady, calm down!"   3825
"Are you a captive? Does somebody own you?"
said the queen. "Who is chasing you?
Who is mistreating or threatening you?

179

Ja n'a chaëns lyöns ne leus!
Avés paör d'estre o moi seus? 3830

Jo ne sui mie mordans beste!
Vos estes vilains, par ma teste.
Quant jo vos aig et car m'amés!
N'aiés paör, ne vus cremés;
Tolte la cors sera mais vostre. 3835
Vos serés miens, jo serai vostre.
Bials dols amis," cho dist la dame,
"Sor moi tornés trestolt le blasme.
Mais qui nos blasmeroit, caieles,
U qui en savroit ja novieles? 3840
Nus hom, voir, se vus voliiés.
Joés mains que vos ne solliés,
Amis, a moi, par coverture;
Mais si* vus fagniés par mesure
Que l'on n'ataigne en vo* faintise, 3845
Bials dols amis, vostre cointise.
Se del tolt vos abstenissciés
Que vos a moi ne venissciés
Et parler et joër et rire,
Dont poroit on cuidier et dire: 3850
Iceste gens de gré s'astienent
Qu'il ensanble ne vont ne vienent.
Se nos reveniens trop ensamble,
Folie seroit, cho me samble:/
Qu'en tolte rien valt moult mesure. 3855
Moienetés soit coverture,
Bials dols amis, de no faisance.
Bien le ferons, n'aiés dotance."

La dame por noient se painne
Et li vallés fort se demainne. 3860
Pense s'or li issoit des mains
N'i enterroit des mois al mains.
Mais li ostoirs qui joint a l'anne
Ne se paine plus ne ahane
De restraindre, quant il a fain, 3865
Qu'el l'enfant;* poisons a l'ain
Ne painne plus estre escapés
Que li vallés quist atrapés.
Il n'a poöir de li rien faire.

180

There's no lion or wolf around here!
Are you afraid of being here alone with me?   3830

I'm not a wild beast! I won't bite you!
God, what churlish behavior,
when I have made you my equal, and since you love me!
Have no fear, don't be afraid!
The whole court will be yours from now on.   3835
You shall be mine, I will be yours.
Sweet, handsome love," said the lady,
"put all the blame on me.
But who would be able to blame us, for heaven's sake,
and who could find out about it?   3840
No one, honestly, if you want to do it.
Play for me less often than you usually do,
my love, to conceal our relationhip,
but be sure to temper your deception with moderation,
so that no one sees that your prudent behavior   3845
is just a cover-up, sweet, handsome love.
If you stayed away altogether,
and never came to see me,
or play or speak or laugh with me,
people might notice that and say,   3850
'Those two are avoiding each other on purpose,
that's why they are never seen together.'
On the other hand, it would be unwise
to meet too often, it seems to me;
moderation is best in all things.   3855
Let moderation be the mask
that conceals our deeds, dear,sweet love.
We'll manage things well, never fear."

The lady was expending all this effort for nothing,
and the youth was in a state of extreme agitation.   3860
He was thinking that if he could escape her clutches now,
he wouldn't set foot in that place for at least a month.
But a hungry goshawk that has seized a wild duck
doesn't struggle harder
to hold onto its prey   3865
than did the queen with this youth, nor does a fish
caught on a hook try harder to escape
than did this youth who is trapped here.
He couldn't do anything for her;

181

N'ele ne puet s'amor retraire,   3870
Ne li vallés ki est mescine
Ne violt pas dire son covine,
De sa nature verité,
Qu'il perdroit donques s'ireté.
La nonpossance de celui   3875
Fait a la dame grant anui.
Li fols voloirs de la roïne
Fait al vallet moult grant cuerine.
Il li anuie trop et grieve.
De li s'estorst et si s'en lieve,   3880
Et la roïne le rahert.
Por poi qu'ele son sens ne pert.
Sospire a lonc gemisscement.
Dist li: "Est cho chierisscement?
Quant vus si chier vus savés rendre,   3885
Bien devriés achater et vendre!
Ciertes, bien savés contrefaire
Felon vilain de put afaire.
Nel fis fors vos a assaier.
Moult [me]* convenroit esmaier,   3890
S'il me tenoit ensi a certes.
Vostre cors doinst Dex males pertes,
Car fait eüsciés altretel
Se bien le volsisse et nïent el."

Atant le lassce et cil s'en vait.   3895
Desor volra bastir mal plait,
Male aventure o sa jovente,
La dame cui Dex mal consente.
Ains l'ama plus que creäture,
Et or le het a desmesure: 3900
Car feme n'est mie laniere
D'amor cangier en tel maniere. /
Celui que plus amera fort,
U soit a droit u soit a tort,
Repuet de moult legier haïr.   3905
Feme oze tres bien envaïr
L'amor d'un home fierement.
Ja nel laira por cri de gent.
Mais s'amor nen est mie ferme,
Ains est moult fole et moult enferme.   3910
De moult legier et ainme et het.
Celui el mont qui miols li set,

182

she couldn't stop loving him.   3870
Nor did the youth who is a girl
wish to reveal her secret,
the truth about her nature,
because he would lose his inheritance.
The youth's inertia   3875
was causing the lady considerable distress.
The licentious desires of the queen
were upsetting the youth a great deal.
It was really getting to be too much for him.
He twisted free of her grasp and staggered to his feet,
but the queen hung on to him.   3880
On the verge of fainting,
she let out a long, low moan.
She said to him, "Are you trying to jack up the price?
If you are such an expert at selling yourself dear,   3885
you should go into the business.
You certainly do a very good imitation
of a cheap, vulgar tradesman.
I only did it to test you.
I certainly would have reason to be annoyed   3890
if I had been serious about it;
may God curse you,
because you wouldn't have hesitated to do it,
if I had really wanted you to."

And then she let go of the youth and he left.   3895
From now on, the lady would scheme
and plot against the youth,
may God confound her!
Before, she loved him more than anything;
now she hated him beyond measure.   3900
A woman never wearies
of changing her feelings like this.
It is easy for her to hate
the man she loves most,
whether or not she has reason to.   3905
Woman does not hesitate to claim
a man's love openly and fiercely;
she'll never leave him for fear of public opinion.
But her love is not steadfast;
it's irrational and unstable.   3910
She loves and hates with equal ease.
If she begins to find fault

183

S'ele commence a enlaidir,
Sel prent si fort a enhaïr
Com s'il eüst tols mors lé siens.   3915
Ja ne li sovenra des biens
Que fait li ait, s'un poi li lance.
En feme a grant desmesurance
Quant ire le sorporte et vaint.
Mais n'i a nule qui trop aint: 3920
De trop amer se gardent bien.
Mais jo vos dirai une rien:
Tres puis qu'ele a home en cuerine,
Ne ciet de legier sa haïne.

Ceste dame estoit moult engrant   3925
Com honir peüst cel enfant.
Ses cuers i point: ne li dolroit
S'il fust pendus, ainz le volroit.
Et pense donc: "Se cis pensast
Viers feme, rien ne s'en tensast   3930
Qu'orains n'eüst a moi joé.
U gel verrai tolt desjoé,
En fin honi, se gel puis faire,
U ja n'iere mais sans contraire.
Certes, gel croi bien a erite   3935
Quant a feme ne se delite.
Quant jo li mostrai mes costés,
Que il me dist: 'Por Deu, ostés!',
Ene fu cho moult bone ensaigne
Qu'il despist femes et desdaigne?   3940
Il dist qu'il apartient le roi
Mais nel fait guaires plus qu'a moi.
Ainc nel lassça por parenté,
Mais el a en sa volenté.
As vallés fait moult bele chiere   3945
Et a lor compagnie chiere.
Herites est, gel sai de fi,
Et jo de m'amor le deffi.
Honte li volrai porcacier."
Atant repaire de chacier/   3950
Li rois, si corne la menee.
Grant joie i ot le soir menee
Fors de la dame la roïne
Et del vallet ki est mescine.

184

with the one she is closest to,
she starts to hate him as passionately
as if he had killed her entire family. 3915
The least criticism makes her forget
all the good things he may have done for her.
When a woman is dominated by anger,
she is completely out of control.
There's not one of them who loves too much — 3920
they're careful not to love to excess —
but I'll tell you one thing:
as soon as she has a grudge against a man,
she doesn't give up hating easily.

This lady was thinking very hard 3925
about ways to harm this youth.
Her heart spurred her on: she wouldn't care
if he were hanged — in fact, she'd like that.
Then she thought, "If he were interested
in women, nothing could have prevented him 3930
from taking his pleasure with me just now.
Either I will see him totally dishonored,
completely destroyed, if I can manage it,
or I will never know a moment's peace.
In fact, I'm sure he's a queer, 3935
since a woman doesn't arouse him at all.
When I showed him my gorgeous body,
he said, 'O God, stop that!'
Isn;t that proof enough
that he has nothing but contempt for women? 3940
He claims to be the king's man,
but he belongs just as much to me!
He didn't reject me because he's related to the king;
he did it because he has something else on his mind.
He likes young men a lot 3945
and really enjoys their company.
He's a fag, I'd swear to it,
and my love threatens him.
I will see that he is totally disgraced."
Then, to the sound of long notes on the horn, 3950
the king returned from the hunt.
That evening, the whole court made merry,
except for the queen
and the youth who was a girl.

La roïne est en grant angoissce   3955
Par quel engien honir le poissce.
Silences ra moult grant contrarie,
Car il ne set par quel affaire
Il puist sa bone amor avoir.
Mais ele puet tres bien savoir   3960
Quant il li est ore escapés
Qu'il n'iert mais en canbre atrapés,
A la pensee qu'il a ore.
Mais il i entrera encore
A se moult grant male aventure.   3965
Por quant s'afice bien et jure
Que por plain bacin de deniers
N'i enterroit le mois entiers.
Si passe avant c'onques n'i entre.
Il va bien od li u soëntre   3970
Trosques a l'uis et dont retorne.
Dont est la dame e sinple et morne
Et pense u ele en iert vengie
U ja nen iert longhes engie
De quanque ele est roïne et dame.   3975
Li cuers li art, ele entre en flame.

La dame est plainne de grant rage.
Or oiés qu'ele a en corage.
Le vallet violt bel sanblant faire,
Sel poroit en sa cambre atraire,   3980
Et s'une fois dedens l'atrape,
Anchois que il mais li escape
U il fera quanqu'el volra
U a tols jors mais s'en dolra.
Silences s'est .v. mois tenus   3985
Qu'il en la cambre n'est venus.
Ele nel torne mie a geu.
Un jor quant ele voit son leu
Si l'ararole faintement.
Or escoltés confaitement: 3990
"Silence, jo vos ai trové
Por moult loial et esprové.
Jo le vos di endroit de moi
Et d'endroit mon segnor le roi.
Ne vos sovient c'o vos giuai   3995
Ens en ma cambre, et vos priai
Que vos m'amissciés par amors,

The queen was desperately searching   3955
for a means to destroy Silence.
The young man, for his part, was under considerable stress,
because he couldn't think of a way
to get back into her good graces.
The queen knew very well that   3960
since his narrow escape, it wouldn't
be easy to trap him in the bedroom again,
given the knowledge he now had.
(But he will enter it again,
at terrible cost to himself,   3965
even though he swore that
he wouldn't go there again for a whole month,
not even for a basketful of money.)
He often passed by, but he never went in.
He would accompany the queen, or follow a little   3970
behind her, as far as the door, and then turn back.
This made the lady wretched and miserable.
She thought that either she would soon have her revenge
or she would not enjoy the advantages
of her position as lady and queen for long.   3975
Her heart was on fire; she was aflame.

The lady was consumed with dreadful rage.
Now wait till you hear what she had in mind!
She would pretend to be nice to the youth
in order to lure him into her room.   3980
Once he was trapped inside,
before he could make his escape again,
either he would do what she wanted him to,
or he would regret it permanently.
Silence held out for five months   3985
without entering the bedchamber.
She didn't take this lightly at all.
One day, she saw her opportunity
and spoke to him, intending to deceive.
Listen to how well she did it: 3990
"Silence, I have found you to be
very loyal and trustworthy.
I say this to you on my own behalf
and on behalf of my lord the king.
Don't you remember how I joked with you   3995
in my bedroom, and begged you
to make love to me,

Et vos fesistes vos clamors?/
Donc seuc jo bien sans devinalle
Que vos loials estes sans falle.   4000
Mais savés por quoi jo le fis?
Li rois mes sire m'a requis
Et cho a bien un an duré
Qu'il m'a tant sovent conjuré
Que le plus loial eslesisse   4005
Des vallés, et se li desisse.
Se Dex me porgart m'ireté,
Ne li seuc dire verité,
Et il me tint tols jors engrant.
Jo si vos vi moult simple enfant   4010
Et par vostre sinple viaire
Me fu, bials amis, a viaire
Qu'en vos ot gregnor loialté
Qu'en vallet de se roialté.
Jel cuidai, s'en fui en error,   4015
Mais or sai jo bien la verror.
Et si ne sai pas, al voir dire,
Por quoi l'a fait li rois mes sire,
Mais que jo cuit que cil avra,
Cui li rois plus loial savra,   4020
Alcune grant bone aventure.
Cho serés vos, car c'est droiture."
"Dame," fait il, "ne fu cho el?"
"Nenil, se Dex me gart de mel!"
Respont encontre la roïne.   4025
Cil l'en merchie, si encline.

[O]r a la roïne oquoison
De celui honir sans raison,
Car li vallés le servira,
Venra entor li et ira   4030
Ens en la cambre com ains siolt.
Un jor est si que li rois violt
Aler en bois, com fait sovent.
Oiés con dolerols covent
Ués le vallet apparellier,   4035
Cui Damerdex puist consellier.

Li rois en est el bois alés.
Silences a adevalés
Les degrés avoec la roïne

188

and you made such a fuss about it?
From then on, I knew for a fact
that you are completely trustworthy.   4000
But do you know why I did it?
The king, my lord, had been after me
for a whole year to do it.
He repeatedly asked me
to test the most loyal youth   4005
and report back to him.
So help me God,
I didn't know what to say to him,
and he kept on insisting.
You looked like an innocent lad to me,   4010
and, judging from your harmless appearance,
it seemed obvious to me, my friend,
that you were more trustworthy
than any other youth in this kingdom.
I wondered whether I was wrong about you,   4015
but now I know for certain I was right.
And although I honestly don't know
why my lord king has made this request,
I do think that whoever
the king knows to be most loyal   4020
has some great adventure in store for him.
That one will be you — it's only right."
"Lady," he said, "it was a test and nothing more?"
"That's all there was to it, so help me God!"
the queen replied.   4025
The youth thanked her and bowed deeply.

Now the queen would have ample opportunity
to harm the guiltless youth,
for he would serve her,
attend her, and enter the   4030
bedroom the way he used to.
One day, it so happened that the king wanted
to go off hunting, as he frequently did.
Listen to what a terrible trap
is being set for the youth,   4035
may God help him!

The king had gone off hunting.
Silence had gone down
the steps with the queen

En la maistre cambre parrine.   4040
Ele a l'uis moult tost verellié:
Et cil s'en a moult mervellié, /
Et enviers l'uis se trait et sache.*
Ele le saisist par l'atache.
Dist li: "U viols tu aler ore?"   4045
"Dame, la fors." "Cho n'est encore!"
Respont encontre la roïne.
"Por quoi nos fais tu tel covine?
Jo t'ai moult longement amé.
Tu m'as mon cors moult adamé: 4050
Jo t'ai forment acoragié,
Et tu mon cors as damagié.
L'altrier te mostrai mes amors
Et t'en fesis par tolt clamors.
Ne me degnas pas escolter,   4055
Ains me presis a deboter.
Ne degnas puis chaëns venir.
Jo ne t'i seu comment tenir,
Mais tant ai fait par mon engien,
Enon Deu, que jo vos i tiengn;   4060
Et par meïsme le catel,
Prent chi mon cors, il n'i a tel.
Faisons com amis et amie."
"Roïne, cho n'i avra mie!
Par cele foi que jo doi vos   4065
Par moi n'iert honis vostre espols,
Non! non! par Deu l'esperitable!"
"Comment?" fait ele. "Est cho estable?
"Oïl, par Deu, qui me cria!
Jo vos ai dit quanqu'il i a."   4070
Or voit la dame qu'il refuse.
S'amor crient qu'al roi ne l'encuse
U qu'il l'ait lasscié par despit,
Si l'a torné en mal respit.
Commence ses cevials detraire   4075
Si com diäbles le fait faire.
Fiert soi el nés de puign a ente:
Del sanc se solle et ensanglente.
Plore sans noise et sans criër
Qu'el velt le fait tant detriër   4080
Que li rois Ebayns vient de cache.
N'i violt qu'altres que il le sache.
Defole sos ses piés se guinple

190

into the master bedroom, which was made of solid stone.   4040
Right away, she locked the door securely.
The youth, very surprised at this,
ran to the door and shook it.
But she grabbed him by the belt
and said, "Now where do you think you're going?"   4045
"Out, Lady!" "Not just yet,"
replied the queen.
"Why are you spoiling things for us?
I have loved you for a long time,
and you insulted me terribly.   4050
I gave you every encouragement,
and you spurned me.
Not long ago, I demonstrated my love for you,
and you yelled and screamed
and wouldn't listen to me;   4055
in fact, you even argued with me.
You wouldn't deign to come here any more.
I couldn't figure out how to get hold of you.,
but, by God, I've tricked you,
and I've got you here now.   4060
And by very right of possession,
I command you to take my matchless body now.
Let's make love!"
"My queen, I will do no such thing!
By the fidelity I owe you,   4065
your spouse will not be dishonored by me.
No! No! By God in heaven!"
"What?" she said. "Is that your final word?"
"Yes, by the God who created me!
I've said all there is to say."   4070
Now the lady saw that he really was refusing her,
and she was worried he might denounce her to the king,
or that he had rejected her offer because he despised her.
She decided to turn the situation to her own evil advantage.
Prompted by the Devil,   4075
she began to tear her hair.
She gave herself a punch in the nose,
so that she was covered with blood.
She shed tears, but without making noise or crying,
because she wanted to keep this up   4080
until the king returned from the hunt,
and she didn't want anyone else to know.
She trampled her wimple underfoot,

Et tient bien ferm le vallet sinple.
"Fils a gloton!" fait ele, "fols!   4085
Dehet ait hui li vostre cors!
Fils a encrieme paltonier!
Li rois n'a soig de parçoignier
A sa mollier en tel maniere.
Malvaise sui et moult laniere/   4090
Se ne te fac vif escorcier
Ki si me volsis efforcier.
As me tu por cho losengie?
J'en serai, se Deu plaist, vengie.
Mais que li rois meïsmes viegne   4095
Et que il droit de toi me tiegne."

Or a grant dol icil al mains:
Sue d'angoisse et tort ses mains,
Gemist, fremist forment et pleure.
Li rois Ebains plus n'i demeure.   4100
Dessendus est desos un arbre
Sor un perron qui est de marbre;
Vient trosques a l'uis de la canbre
Ki estoit pavee de lanbre.
"Ovrés!" fait [il]. "A i nullui?"   4105
"Oïl, tel ki moult a d'anui!"
Dist la roïne. "Bials dols sire,
Tel a chaëns qui vos desire
Et ki de vos a grant mestier,
Itel que por plain un sestier   4110
De fins besans n'i volroit estre."
La roïne est huissiere miestre:
Ouevre l'uis et li rois i entre.
Reclot la cambre et vient soëntre.
Sa feme voit li rois sanglente   4115
Et ensegnie moult a ente,
Ronpus ses crins, mollié son vis.
Or n'i a il ne giu ne ris.
"Biele," fait il, "qui vos fist cho?"
"Bials sire, jal vos dirai jo.   4120
Veés chi devant vos celui
Ki m'a faite cestui anui.
Cuida sa fole avoir trovee.
Il m'a soventes fois provee:
Cuidai quel fesist par son giu,   4125
Mais orains quant il vit son liu

192

while keeping a firm hand on the wretched youth.
"You swine!" she said, "you crazy bastard!   4085
Damn your filthy hide,
you dirty scum!
THe king doesn't like to share his wife
with the likes of you!
I would be culpable and cowardly   4090
if I didn't have you skinned alive
for trying to rape me like this!
Do you think I'm bluffing?
I will be avenged, God willing,
as soon as the king himself arrives   4095
and gives me the right to deal with you."

Then she went into fits of agony;
she perspired with anguish and wrung her hands,
she moaned, shuddered dreadfully, and wept.
At this point, King Evan returned.   4100
He dismounted at the tree-shaded
marble steps
and came to the door
of the paneled room.
"Open up!" he said. "Is anyone there?"   4105
"Yes, one who has a terrible grievance,"
said the queen. "Dear, sweet lord,
there is someone inside who wants you
and needs you terribly;
one who would give a full measure   4110
of fine gold coins to be elsewhere."
The queen was an expert locksmith:
she unlocked the door and the king entered;
then she locked the door again and followed him in.
The king saw his wife bleeding   4115
and dreadfully bloodied all over;
her hair disheveled and her face wet with tears.
This was no laughing matter to him.
"My dear," he said, "who did this to you?"
"My lord, I will tell you everything.   4120
The one who did this to me
is right here in front of you.
He thought he had found a loose woman to suit him.
He has tried things several times.
I thought he was only joking,   4125
but just now, he saw his chance,

193

Et vos fustes el bos alés,
Les degrés ot tost sormontés,
Entre en la canbre et ferme l'uis.
Sire, veés qu'il m'a fait puis! 4130
Silences l'a fait, sire, sire,
Par sa folor, par sa grant ire.
Ne lairai ore sa folie
Que trestolte ne le vos die.
Quant il m'ot, sire, si blecie 4135
Ma guinple rote et depecie,
Et il vit bien que g'ere caste,
De si faite folie gaste/
Pria que jo li pardonasse
Et que itant le me lassasce; 4140
Mais jo ne vol mie lasscier
Por vostre honor si abasscier.
Moult volentiers s'en volt estordre.
Bials sire, por le desamordre
Tolte gens mais de tel oltrage, 4145
De tel folie, de tel rage,
Prendés de cestui vengement
C'onques n'atendés jugement!"

Li rois en a si gros le cuer:
Ne desist .i. mot a nul fuer, 4150
Mais que les ioils celui roöille.
Et li roïne s'agenolle
As piés le roi et plore et crie
Car la venjance li detrie
Par plorer le violt engignier 4155
Qu'ele ne violt pas forlignier:
Car feme plore par voidie
Quant aënplir violt sa boisdie.
Et li vallés est en angoisse,
Ne set sos ciel que faire puisse. 4160
Por poi de duel que il ne muert;
Et la roïne se detuert.
Moult li est grief que la roïne
Li a esmute tel haïne.
Entre ses dens dist bielement: 4165
"Ele meffait moult malement,
Mais, que que face, ele est ma dame:
Ne li doi pas alever blasme.
Encor desisse al roi le voire

194

when you had gone off hunting.
He climbed the stairs right away,
entered the bedchamber, and locked the door.
And look what he did to me then, Sire!   4130
Silence did this, Sire, he did it;
he was mad with lust!
I will tell you
how vile he was:
after he had beaten me, Sire,   4135
and torn my wimple to shreds,
and saw that I still wouldn't yield,
he begged me to forgive him
for such vicious and depraved behavior,
and just let him go.   4140
But I don't ever want to let your honor
be so abased as to let him off.
He would be very glad to worm his way out of this.
Dear lord, in order to deter others
from such acts of fury,   4145
violence and outrage,
take your vengeance on this man immediately!
Don't wait for a trial!"

The king's heart was so heavy
he couldn't say a word   4150
without rolling his eyeballs.
And the queen was kneeling
at the king's feet and weeping and crying
because he was delaying her vengeance.
She wanted to trick him with her tears   4155
into thinking she was innocent,
for a woman always cries as a strategy
when she wants to accomplish something deceitful.
The youth was in such distress
he didn't know what on earth to do;   4160
he was almost dead of grief.
And there was the queen, writhing in agony.
He profoundly regretted
that the queen felt such intense loathing for him.
He muttered softly, between his teeth,   4165
"She is gravely in the wrong,
but whatever she does, she is my lady:
I must not sully her reputation.
Even were I to tell the king the truth,

Il ne m'en poroit mie croire,   4170
Se il ne seüst ma nature:
Adonc perdroie ma droiture,
L'onor mon pere et m'ireté.
Et si sai bien, par verité,
La roïne estroit malballie   4175
Et de s'onor seroit fallie.
Certes," fait il, "que que [je] face,
Conques li rois Ebayns me hace,
Ja n'en sera par moi adrece
Se jo nel fac par grant destrece.   4180
Dex ki tolt set me puet garir:
Cui violt aidier ne puet marir."
La roïne fort se demente.
Sachiés que moult li est a ente
Qu'ele ne voit ardoir en cendre   4185
Le vallet, u a forces pendre. /
Mais el roi a bon home et sage
Et atenpret de son corage;
Et set bien de .ii. mals eslire
Quels est li mioldres et quel pire.   4190
Voit se venjance nen est prise,
Foible est, malvaise sa justice.
Pis est de honir cel enfant,
Car il seroit honis par tant,
Se honte esparse et esmeüe   4195
Ki pas nen est encor seüe.
Por cho se violt il miols retraire
De la justice que trop faire.
Et cascuns hom se doit pener
Por cho qu'il i puist assener   4200
De s'onor salver, se il puet:
Et se il voit que lui estuet
De .ii. mals tols jors l'un passer,
Son sens doit en soi amasser
Veïr liquels li puist mains nuire.   4205
Ne se doit pas li hom destruire
Por une soie mesestance.
Quels hom li fera honerance
Tres puis qu'il meïsmes s'aville?
Par sa folie tels s'escille*   4210
Et lance tel parole avant
Dont on le tient plus por enfant.
Nus ne puet en cest siecle vivre

there's no way he would believe me 4170
unless he knew my real nature.
And then I would lose my standing,
my father's honor and my inheritance.
And I know for certain
that the queen would be punished 4175
and deprived of her honor.
Clearly," he said, "whatever I do,
however much King Evan may hate me,
I will never be able to set things right
without great cost to myself. 4180
Only God the all-knowing can save me:
anyone he helps cannot come to a bad end."
The queen was throwing a dreadful fit.
You must realize that it was very upsetting for her
not to see the youth burned to a crisp 4185
or swinging from a gallows.
But the king was a wise
and moderate fellow at heart,
one who knew very well
how to choose the lesser of two evils. 4190
He saw that if he didn't take vengeance,
his reputation for justice would be undermined.
But it seemed worse to dishonor this youth,
because he himself would also be dishonored,
if he should spread the news about the shameful deed 4195
that nobody knew about yet.
Because of this, he would rather do too little
justice than overdo it.
For each man must do his utmost
to figure out a way 4200
to save his honor, if he can.
And if he sees that he has to
choose definitively between two evils,
he must be able to make an intelligent choice
as to which will harm him less. 4205
A man should. not destroy himself
merely to avenge an injury done him.
Who would respect him
if he brought about his own disgrace?
A man may be driven by folly to disgrace himself 4210
and say things
that make him look childish.
No one can live in this world

Ki longhes puist estre a delivre
Qu'il n'ait encombrier de son cors.   4215
Doit il por cho crier alhors
Cascune fois que lui mesciet
U que se cose li messiet?
Si enemi ki l'orront dire
N'en feront fors joër et rire.   4220
De cho se pense bien li rois;
N'est pas ireuls a fuer d'Irois
Por faire d'un damage .ii.
Le vallet fait traire ensus d'els
Et a dit a la dame en oire: 4225
"Biele, se vos me volés croire,
Bon consel porons de cho prendre."
"Comment?" fail ele. "El que del pendre?"
"Oïl! n'avra pas tel martyre."
"Que li volés donc faire, sire?   4230
Ardoir, u a chevals detraire?"
"Ne mie, bele; on doit moult faire
Solvent contre sa volenté.
Cis est moult de halt parenté, /
Et si est fils a moult prodome.   4235
Or en gardons tolte la some.
Cho qu'il a fait est par enfance:
Et vos savés bien a fiance
Se gel faisoie ardoir u pendre
Par cel feroie as gens entendre   4240
Que jo l'aroie o vos trové
Ens en la canbre et pris prové.
Et, en non Deu, cho est tels plais
Que plus l'esmuet on plus est lais.
Mais or tornons cho a mençoige,   4245
Ma biele amie dolce, a songe:
Niens fu, niens est, a rien ne tagne."
Or a li dame grant engagne
Mais ne l'ose pas contredire.
Or oiés que li dist ses sire.   4250
"Grant dol avés, et jo gregnor.
Mais oiés: j'ai un mien segnor,
Le roi de France, par mon cief,
U jo l'envoierai par brief.
Jo sui ses hom, il est mes sire,   4255

for very long without
having something go wrong.   4215
Is that any reason to carry on and let everyone know
every time something happens to you
or things don't turn out right?
That way, you will only give your enemies
something to celebrate when they hear about it.   4220
The king considered all this very carefully;
he was not inclined to anger, like the Irish,
who make everything twice as bad as it is.
He had the youth removed from the room
and then said at once to the lady,   4225
"Trust me, darling,
we'll work something out."
"What?" she said, "and what about hanging him?"
"Yes, well. . .that won't be his punishment."
"Then what do you intend to do with him, Sire?   4230
Burn him? Have him torn apart by wild horses?"
"No, no, dearest. One has to do a lot of things
one doesn't want to.
Now, this youth comes from a very good family
and is the son of an important man.   4235
That's the situation in a nutshell.
He just acted out of youthful high spirits;
and you know very well
that if I have him burned or hanged,
people are bound to believe   4240
that I not only found him with you in the bedroom,
but caught him in the act as well.
Damn it all, with this kind of mess,
the more you stir it up, the more it stinks.
So let's pretend it didn't happen.   4245
Just think of it all as a dream, sweetheart.
Nothing happened, nothing's wrong, nothing should come of
    it."
The lady was furious at this,
but she didn't dare to contradict him.
Now listen to what her lord told her: 4250
"You have received an injury, and I an even greater one.
But listen: the king of France
is my liege lord. My idea is
to send Silence to him with a letter.
Since I am his loyal subject and he is pledged to me,   4255

199

Et, quant il ora mon brief lire,
Ne falroit mie por Monmartre
Ne face quanque dist la cartre.
Biele, bien en serés vengie."
Li rois l'a forment losengie   4260
Qu'oster le violt fors de ses mains;
Qu'il n'estoit pas fols ne vilains
Quil destruisist par sa fole ire,
Por quanqu'ele li sace dire.
Mais ne volt son dit blastengier,   4265
Car feme quant se violt vengier
En tel maniere est moult trençans,
Cho set li rois, et trop tençans,
Est el. Quant on le roeve taire
Dont s'esforce de noise faire.   4270
Sil violt li rois miols aquoisier
Ensi qu'il le fesist noisier.
Mais ne li valt pas une tille,
Car la roïne est bien gopille
En son corage et moult destroite.   4275
Pense que se li briés esploite
Que li rois violt en cire metre
Qu'ele mesme fera tel letre
Dont cil avra grant destorbance,
S'el puet quil portera en France.   4280

Cho dist li rois: "Ma dolce suer,
Or faites huimais lié vo cuer."
"Bials sire, jo moult volentiers."
"Loira il," fait il, "dementiers.
Biele, por faire bel sanblant   4285
Par coverture a cel enfant,
Jel voel trametre dela mer
Al roi qui moult me siolt amer,
De France, biele, cui moult aim,
De cui, sos Deu, jo me reclaim,   4290
Car mes sire est, si teng en fief
Engletiere. Vois m'en: .i. brief
Ferai escrire en parcemin,
Et le vallet metre al cemin."
Dont vait a lui, si l'aseüre,   4295
Se li a mostré a droiture
U il ira et qu'il fera

once he has my letter read,
I assure you that even were Montmartre at stake,
he won't fail to do exactly as it says.
Dearest, you shall have your revenge."
The king told her a tremendous lie,   4260
in order to get Silence out of her clutches.
He wasn't crazy or foolish enough
to destroy the lad because of her terrible rage,
no matter what kind of story she told.
But he also didn't want to contradict her,   4265
because he knew that a woman, when she is out to avenge
    herself,
has a very sharp tongue
and will never stop arguing.
When she is told to keep quiet,
she tries all the harder to make noise.   4270
So the king thought to appease her [by lying],
just as he let her continue to rage.
But it didn't do him a bit of good:
the queen was cunning as a vixen
by nature, and extremely shrewd.   4275
She thought that if the message the king planned
to seal with wax would really be so efficacious,
she herself would send a letter
that would cause the youth a great deal of trouble,
if she could see to it that hers was the one he carried to France.   4280

The king said, "My sweet sister,
take heart and cheer up."
"Dear lord and master, I'll be happy to."
"You'll have reason to from now on," he said.
"Sweetheart, in order to keep up appearances   4285
and conceal this youth's deed,
I want to send him overseas
to the king of France, who has been a true friend to me,
and whom I trust, dearest.
By God, I can rely on him,   4290
because he is my liege lord, from whom I hold
England in fief. Look: I will have a letter
written on parchment,
and send the youth on his way."
Then he went to the youth and reassured him,   4295
and told him the truth about
where he would be going and what he would do

201

Et con le brief enportera.
Al cancelier vait donc li sire
Et maintenant li prent a dire: 4300
"Amis, escris me tost un brief,
.d. salus el premier cief,
A mon segnor le roi de France
En cui jo ai moult grant fiänce.
Met i que jo li pri et mant,   4305
Com hom sor cui il a commant,
Silences li soit bien venus,
De sa maisnie retenus.
Armes li doinst quant il volra
Quant ore et tans l'en requerra.   4310
Et trosqu'atant od lui le tiengne
Que jo le manc et dont se viegne."
Cho dist li rois et dont s'en torne,
Et cil d'escrire tost s'atorne.

La roïne en la canbre enclose   4315
A sor le brief escrit tel cose
Ki oués Silence est moult gagnarde,
Se Dameldex ne l'en porgarde.
Crualté n'oïstes gregnor.
De par roi Ebayn, son segnor,   4320
Escrist al roi de France un brief
Qu'il tolle al message le cief
Qui les letres a lui enporte;
Que il por rien ne l'en deporte,
Car il a fait al roi tel honte   4325
Qu'il ne le violt pas metre en conte.
Il est forment de halt parage,
Por cho l'a tramis al message.
Li rois ne l'ose pas desfaire
Por cho qu'il est de halt affaire. /   4330
Cest brief a la roïne escrit.
Mar l'a cil eü en despit.
Cho dist la dame: "Par mon cief!"
Ploié enporte puis le brief
Desos son doit la u cil est   4335
Ki le brief roi Ebayn a prest.
"Amis," fait ele, "que est cho?"
"Ma dame, jal vos dirai jo.
Silences iert tramis en France
De par le roi por remanance   4340

and how he would bring the letter with him.
And then the king went to the chancellor,
and this is what he said to him: 4300
"My friend, write a letter for me at once.
First convey five hundred greetings
to my lord the king of France,
in whom I have the utmost confidence.
Tell him that I request and entreat of him, 4305
as his vassal,
that Silence be welcomed at his court
and made a member of his household.
He should knight him at his discretion,
at the appropriate time and place, 4310
and keep the youth with him
until I ask for him, and then he should return."
That's what the king said. Then he left,
and the chancellor got busy writing immediately.

In the privacy of her bedchamber, 4315
the queen had written the kind of letter
that would do Silence a lot of harm,
if God didn't save him.
You never heard of anything more cruel.
In the name of her lord, King Evan, 4320
she wrote the king of France a letter
saying that he should behead
the bearer of this message,
and not spare him for any reason,
for the disgrace he had brought on the king 4325
was too shameful to commit to writing.
He was of very high lineage,
and that was why he had been sent with a message:
the king didn't dare to have him executed
because he was from a prominent family. 4330
This was the letter the queen wrote.
"He'll be sorry for spurning me,"
said the lady. "I swear it!"
Then she folded the letter and carried it,
concealed in her hand, to the chancellor, 4335
who had King Evan's letter ready.
"My friend," she said, "what's that?"
"Madam, I will tell you.
The king is sending Silence to France
to be part of the royal household 4340

Por sens aprendre et cortesie."
La dame respont par boidie:
"Cho poise moi se il i vait."
"Si fait il moi, dame, entresait."
"Jo cuit," fait ele, "cho est gas." 4345
"Roïne, par Deu, non est pas;
Et ces letres enportera."
"Amis, jo cuit que no fera.
Jo ne cuit pas qu'ensi s'en alle."
Li canceliers le brief li balle. 4350
"Veés," fait il, "que dist l'escris,
Puis que vos mescreés mes dis."
Et la roïne el ne demande.
Le brief a ore en se commande.
Moult [tost] esgarde sor la letre. 4355
El n'i violt mie longes metre,
Ains a le brief moult tost ploié,
Voiant celui, et ferm loié.
Retient celui, le fals li piure,
Et cil le saiele a droiture; 4360
Si l'a la dame decheü
Qu'il ne s'en a apercheü
Que li briés qu'il en cire mist
Ne soit cil meïsmes qu'il fist.
Li canceliers puis ne s'atarge. 4365
Il vient al roi, le brief li carge,
Et il le balle al vallet donques, —
Se Dex nel fait, quil mar vit onques! —
Et dont l'a fait bien atorner.
Cil n'i ose plus sejorner. 4370
Se harpe et sa viiele enporte,
Si s'en ist plorant de la porte.
Bien doit plorer et avoir ire
Car sa mort porte escrite en cire,
Se Dex n'en pense, quil cria 4375
Et fist el monde quanque il a.
O li plusor mainnent grant duel
Por le vallet de Tintaguel/
Ki s'a fait moult a tols amer.
Plus tost qu'il pot passe la mer 4380
Et si s'en vient tolt droit en France.
Le roi i trueve sans fallance.
Devant lui vient moult bielement.
Salué l'a si faitement:

and be schooled in courtly behavior."
Deceitfully, the lady replied,
"I shall be sorry to see him go."
"Indeed, so shall I, Lady."
"I think it's all a joke," she said.   4345
"No, my queen, it's not.
He is going to take this message."
"Friend, I bet he's not.
I don't believe he's leaving like that."
The chancellor handed her the letter.   4350
"See for yourself what it says," he said,
"since you won't take my word for it."
The queen didn't ask for more.
Now she had the letter in her possession.
She read it carefully;   4355
it didn't take her long.
She unfolded it very quickly,
in full view of the chancellor, and closed it again.
She kept this letter, and gave him the false one,
and the man sealed it in good faith.   4360
The lady deceived him so thoroughly
that he didn't notice
the letter he sealed with wax
wasn't the one he had written.
Without further delay, the chancellor   4365
went to the king and gave him the letter,
and he handed it over to the youth,
who is doomed if God doesn't help him!
With that, he had given the youth everything he needed.
Silence didn't dare postpone his departure.   4370
He took his harp and viele
and went forth weeping.
He had every reason to weep and be upset,
for he carried his death sealed with wax,
unless God, who created him   4375
and made the world and all things in it, is mindful of him.
Most people were very sorry
to lose the youth from Tintagel,
who had made himself very popular with everyone.
He crossed the sea as soon as he could   4380
and thus went directly to France.
He arrived at court straightaway,
made a most charming appearance before the king,
and greeted him like this:

205

"Sire, cil Dex de majesté   4385
Ki tols jors iert et a esté
Et tolt le mont a en sa main
Vos salt de par le roi Ebain."
"Amis, et Dex li doinst grant joie."
Silences son saiel desploie;   4390
Livre le al roi qui fraint le cire
Et rueve lués les letres lire.
Li canceliers ki tient le brief
L'a tost veü de cief en cief:
Et quant il voit qu'il senefie   4395
Que le vallet de mort desfie,
Tel dol en a por poi ne muert.
En soi meïsme se detuert
Et pense: "Dex! quel creäture!
Com chi a biele engendreüre!   4400
Com fait damage a ses amis
Qu'il en tel message est tramis!
Jo ne volroie por Monmartre
Qu'il m'esteüst lire la cartre:
Ja se jel di cho iert pechiés,   4405
Qu'il iert deffais et depechiés.
Pitiés me rueve al roi mentir;
Paörs nel violt pas consentir.
Pitié ai grant se il i muert;
Paör s'il par moi en estuert.   4410
De .ii. mals estuet ore eslire
Le mains malvais, cho est le dire:
Se ne disoie qu'a el brief
Li rois me tolroit tost le cief.
Mains me nuist donc la vertés dire   4415
Que por lui sofrir tel martyre."

A le bialté de cel enfant
Sont li Franchois moult entendant.
Li rois li a dit: "Amis, frere,
Car me di ore quist tes pere."   4420
"Sire," fait il, "se Dex me valle,
Li cuens Cador de Cornuälle."
Li rois l'acole dont et baize
Si fort que il oblie enaize
Le brief, tant por lui conjoïr,   4425
Tant por novieles a oïr/
Del roi Ebain, dont il demande.

"Sire, may God enthroned in majesty,   4385
who always has been and always will be
and holds the whole world in his hands,
save you: this is the fervent wish of King Evan."
"And may God grant him happiness, my friend."
Silence took out his sealed letter   4390
and presented it to the king, who broke the wax
and asked to have the letter read immediately.
The chancellor, who was holding the letter,
quickly skimmed it from top to bottom,
and when he saw what it contained—   4395
that it condemned the youth to death—
he was so stricken with grief he nearly died.
Wracked with sorrow, he thought
to himself, "My God, what a gorgeous creature!
He must come from a very good family.   4400
What a pity for his friends
that he has been sent with such a message!
By Montmartre, I don't want
to have this letter read aloud;
if I tell what it says, it will be a pity,   4405
for the youth will be executed.
Pity tells me to lie to the king,
but fear won't let me.
I will feel great pity if he dies,
but fear if he is spared because of me.   4410
Of two evils, I must now choose
the lesser, that is, to tell.
For if I didn't say what was in the letter,
the king would soon have me beheaded.
It will harm me less to tell the truth   4415
than to suffer such a fate for this youth."

The French were extremely responsive
to this young lad's beauty and bearing.
The king said to him, "Friend, brother,
why don't you tell me who your father is."   4420
"Sire," he said, "as God is my witness,
Count Cador of Cornwall."
Then the king embraced him and kissed him
so heartily that he nearly forgot the letter,
he so enjoyed talking with the youth   4425
and hearing news of
King Evan, whom he asked about.

207

Puis piece al cancelier conmande
A dire que li briés despont.
"Volentiers, sire, cil respont.   4430
Vos me rovés lé letres lire.
Jes lis envis, mais, bials dols sire,
Mais que ne vos doi rien taisir,
Sire, encontre vostre plaisir,
Vos hom, vos parens, vos amis,   4435
Rois Ebayns le vos a tramis
Por le vallet faire afoler,
Que je vos vi ore acoler.
Por lui honir et damagier
En a fait, sire, messagier.   4440
Dex, com mar fu tels creäture!
Cho me dist ceste letreüre
Que il a fait al roi tel honte
Que il ne violt pas metre en conte.
Ensi com vos amés s'onor   4445
Qu'il ne le perde u ait menor
Si com il a en vos fiänce
De son honte prendés venjance.
Por cho l'a tramis a message,
Qu'il est forment de halt parage   4450
Et si nel violt mie deffaire
Por cho qu'il est de halt affaire.
Del dire ai fait grant cruelté
Mais jo vos doi tel feëlté
Que ne vos doi mençoigne traire."   4455
Li rois a bassé son viaire.
Tel dol a qu'il ne puet mot dire:
Puis que fu nés n'ot mais tel ire.

Cho dist li rois: "J'ai grant anguissce.
Ne sai sos ciel que faire puissce,   4460
Car li hom el mont ki plus m'ainme
De cest message a moi se claime.
Forfais li est, jo ne sai dont,
Por cho me prie et me semont
Sor quanque il m'a fait d'onerance   4465
Que jo en prenge la venjance.
Engig[n]ié m'ai et decheü,
Que jo si biel l'ai recheü.
Sa grans bialtés m'a afolé
Que baizié l'ai et acolé./   4470

208

After a while, he ordered the chancellor
to tell him what the letter said.
"As you wish, Sire," was the reply.   4430
"You ask me to read the letter:
I do so with the utmost reluctance, dear, kind lord,
but for the fact that I must not conceal anything from you.
Sire, contrary to your pleasure, King Evan,
your vassal, relative and ally,   4435
has sent you this letter
in order to cause the death of this youth,
whom I saw you embrace a short while ago.
He has made him a messenger
in order to destroy him, Sire.   4440
God, what an unfortunate creature!
The letter says
that what he did to the king
was too shameful to be told.
And as you hold his honor dear,   4445
and would not wish to see it lost or diminished,
he has every confidence
that you will avenge his shame.
He sent the youth as a messenger
because he is of high lineage,   4450
and he doesn't want to execute him
because his family is very prominent.
I have committed an act of terrible cruelty
by telling you this, but it is my duty
to tell you the truth."   4455
The king bowed his head.
He felt such grief he could not utter a word;
he had never felt such pain in his life.

The king said, "I am in a dreadful dilemma.
I don't know what in the world I can do,   4460
for the man requesting my help in this message
is my most faithful ally.
It is contemptible of him; I don't understand
why he is asking me secretly,
in the name of all the honors he has paid me,   4465
to avenge him.
As for me, I was a fool
to greet the youth so heartily.
His beauty and noble bearing moved me
to kiss and embrace him.   4470

209

Ki s'apensast de tel affaire
Qu'il fust envoiés por deffaire?
Nel puis par raison malballir
Ne par raison le roi fallir
Qu'il a eü por moi maint soig: 4475
Et s'or li fal a cest besoig
Dont porra il tols jors bien dire
Que jo del mont sui tols li pire
Quant por bienfait ne por franchize
Ne puet trover en moi servisce. 4480
Et se jo cestui li desfac
Grant mal et pechié m'i porcac.
Et tols li mons me doit haïr
Se jo commenc or a traïr.
Gel baizai certes, c'est la voire. 4485
Ki me porra jamais puis croire?
Nus hom voir ne me kerra mais.
Li baiziers senefie pais.
Nel puis deffaire ne lasscier,
Certes, sans moi trop abasscier. 4490
Ne sai so ciel que faire puissce
En cest estrif, en ceste anguissce."
Li rois .iii. contes en apiele:
Dire lor violt ceste noviele.
Des trois contes m'a un conté: 4495
L'uns tenoit de Blois la conté,
L'autres cuens ert de Navers sire,
Li tiers de Clermont, ch'oï dire.

Li rois ne lor dist plus ne mains
Ne mais: "Segnor, li rois Ebayns, 4500
Mes hom, mes parens, mes amis,
A cest message a moi tramis.
Et savés vus por quel affaire?
Il le m'a tramis por desfaire;
Car cis vallés, ne sai li sien, 4505
Ont fait roi Ebayn el que bien,
Cho dist li briés, voire, tel honte
Qu'il ne le violt pas metre en conte.
Et il m'a chier a desmesure
Et jo lui plus que criäture. 4510
Ja savés vos, n'i a celui,
L'amor quist entre moi et lui.
Il m'a ja fait tamaint servisce.

Whoever would have thought
he was sent here to be killed?
I cannot, in justice, do him wrong,
nor can I rightly fail the king,
who has done a good deal for me.   4475
And if I fail to grant him this request,
he will always be able to say
that I am the most dishonorable man in the world
because I would not help him
either as a favor or from a sense of obligation.   4480
And if I kill the youth for him,
I will be guilty of a terrible crime.
Everyone will have reason to hate me
if I betray him now.
I greeted him formally, with a kiss. I can't go back on that.   4485
Who would ever trust me again?
No one would ever return my greeting again.
That is the kiss of peace.
I cannot undo it or disregard it
without bringing terrible dishonor upon myself.   4490
I simply don't know what to do
in the face of this conflict, this dilemma."
The king then summoned three counts,
to tell them the news.
According to my information,   4495
one was the count of Blois,
the second the count of Nevers,
and the third, the count of Clermont, or so I've heard.

The king said this to them, no more, no less:
"Lords, King Evan,   4500
my vassal, my relative, my ally,
has sent me this messenger.
And do you know why?
He sent him here to be killed.
This youth, or maybe one of his relatives,   4505
has done something terrible to King Evan,
that's what the letter says, something so shameful
he doesn't want to talk about it.
And he is utterly devoted to me,
and I value him more than anyone else in the world.   4510
You all know, each and every one of you,
how devoted we are to each another.
He has done many things for me;

211

Or si violt prover ma francisce.
Cho qu'il m'a fait violt que li solle   4515
Que a cestui le cief en tolle;
Et vos si ravés bien veü
Coment j'ai cestui recheü./
Ne doit trahir li hom qui baize.
Segnor, jo sui a grant mesaize.   4520
Ne me donai garde de cho!
Segnor, por Deu que ferai jo?
Selonc l'amor qu'ai viers le roi
Et qu'ai bazié cestui en foi,
Esgardés que m'est miols a faire   4525
U mains puet torner a contraire.
Et cil respondent: "Volentiers.
Et vos alés endementiers
O vos barons ester, bials sire,
Qu'enon Deu chi a moult a dire."   4530

Li rois s'en vait et cil remainnent
Ki del esgart forment se painnent,
Cascuns selonc cho qu'il set miols.
Li cuens de Blois ert li plus viols:
Por cho si a bele oquoison   4535
De parler avant par raison.
"Segnor," fait il, "volés le vos
Que jo parole?" "Sire, o nos."
"Jo volentiers! Si entendés:
Si jo mesdi, si m'amendés.   4540
Jo ne fac chi nul jugement:
Ains parol par amendement
De cest esgart u nos a mis
Li rois; nos sire est. Ses amis,
Segnor, rois Ebayns d'Engletiere   4545
Est venus nostre roi requiere
Par son seël et par son brief
Qu'il tolle a cest vallet le cief.
Et vos savés e non Deu bien
Onques mais nel requist de rien.   4550
Jo croi moult bien qu'encor n'eüst
Se il enmioldrer le peüst,
Et il n'eüst or moult grant soig.
Son ami voit on al besoig.
Il s'est por mon segnor penés   4555
Plus que hom qui soit de mere nés.

212

now he wishes to put my good will to the test:
in return for his services,   4515
he is asking me to behead this youth.
But all of you saw quite clearly
how I greeted the lad.
One cannot kiss a man and betray him.
My lords, I am in a quandary.   4520
I wasn't expecting this!
Lords, what shall I do?
On the basis of the obligation I feel towards the king,
and the kiss I gave the youth in good faith,
I want you to decide which course of action is better,
or has less chance of going wrong."   4525
They replied, "As you wish, Sire,
and in the meantime, you should
return to your barons, Sire,
in the name of God, who is the best counsellor."   4530

The king left, and those who had to
struggle with such a difficult decision remained.
Each one did the best he could.
The count of Blois was the oldest,
therefore it was only fitting   4535
that he should give his opinion first.
"My lords," he said, "may I speak?"
"By all means, good sir."
"I should be glad to, then. But first let it be understood
that you should correct me if I'm wrong,   4540
for I am not trying to pass judgment here,
I am trying to find a solution
to the matter put before us
by our lord the king. Lords,
his friend, King Evan of England,   4545
has requested our king
by means of seal and letter
to cut off this youth's head.
And, by God, you know very well
that he has never asked anything of our king before,   4550
and I firmly believe that he wouldn't be now,
if he had any choice in the matter,
and if he weren't in dire straits.
A friend in need is a friend indeed.
He has done more for my lord   4555
than any other man alive.

213

Et por cho fait on c'on reface
Bien sovent plus que por man[a]ce.
Et uns bezoins altre requiert.
Vos savés bien qu'il i affiert: 4560
Ki mon ami honore, et moi,
Ki li fait honte, il le fait moi.
Ne proise gaires ma possance
Ki mon ami fait mesestance.
Li brief tesmoigne de cestui   4565
Qu'il a fait al roi tel anui/
Qu'il ne le violt pas metre en conte.
Dont a il fait mon segnor honte.
De honte se doit on vengier,
L'onor son ami calengier.   4570
Cis vallés est pris a la trape:
Ne voi raison com il escape.
Mais ne doit avoir mal ne painne
En la premiere quarentainne.
.xl. jors doit avoir pais   4575
Por amor del baisier, ne mais;
Tant doit bien nostre rois atendre.
Se il le fait adonques pendre
U il le fait ardoir en flame
Ne li doit on torner a blasme.   4580
Cho est al miols que jo sai dire."
Li cuens de Clermont s'en aïre.
En sa main tint un baston brief:
Si vait rumant de cief en cief.
A paines qu'il puet dire mot   4585
De maltalent de cho qu'il ot;
Mais qu'il refrainst son maltalent
Com sages hom, si parla gent.
Ne le violt mie desmentir
Al premier mot, ne consentir: 4590
Car cil met le fu en l'estoppe
Ki al premier le bouce estoppe
De celui que voel contredire.
Hom qui cho fait, son plait empire,
Ainz doit premiers tolt otroier,   4595
Por miols son per amoloier.
Si fist li cuens de Clermont donques.
Hom plus atemprés ne fu onques.
Otroie al conte tols ses buens
Qu'il li otroie tols les suens.   4600

214

You can catch more flies with honey
than with vinegar.
One good turn deserves another.
You know what it comes down to: 4560
honor me, honor my friend;
shame him, and you shame me, too.
Lay a hand on my friend,
and you'll have me to deal with.
This letter states that the lad   4565
injured the king so seriously
that he doesn't want to talk about it.
In that case, he has harmed my lord as well.
Every wrong must be avenged.
The honor of one's friend must be upheld.   4570
This youth is trapped.
I don't see how he can escape.
But he should not be harmed
for the next forty days.
He should be granted forty days' reprieve   4575
on account of the kiss, no more than that.
Our king should wait that long.
If he should then have him hanged
or burned at the stake,
he should not be blamed.   4580
That is the best advice I can give."
The count of Clermont grew very angry at that.
He clenched a short staff in his hand
and paced back and forth, muttering.
He was so angered by what he had heard   4585
that he could scarcely utter a word.
But he repressed his anger
and spoke softly, like a wise man.
He didn't want to start off by contradicting
the count of Blois, nor did he want to agree with him.
He who begins   4590
by squelching his opponent
only adds fuel to the fire.
A man who does that harms his own cause.
Instead, he should agree to everything at first,   4595
in order to soften up his adversary.
That is what the count of Clermont did.
There never was a man with more self-control.
He agreed with all the count's suggestions,
so that he would agree with his.   4600

215

Et si set tres bien nequedent
Qu'il a parlé malvaisement.
"Jo sai bien," fait il, "une rien:
Li cuens de Blois a dit moult bien.
Ichi ne peüst home avoir   4605
Ki parlast par si grant savoir.
Car moult doit on celui haïr
Quant il son segnor violt traïr.
Mais que li rois ne sot qu'il fist
Quant il cha oltre le tramist: 4610
Il l'a delivré par itant
Que il envoié l'a avant.
Or l'a baisié li rois, messire.
Ne li puet faire dont soit pire,/
Par nule raison que j'en voie,   4615
Tant com il est en ceste voie.
Et nos somes si loial conte,
Ne li devons loër son honte.
Encor fust rois Ebains nos pere
Et cis eüst ocis no frere,   4620
Ne deveriemes consellier
No roi cestui a essillier.
N'a loialté el mont gregnor
Que salver l'onor son segnor.
Bien gart li sires que tels soit   4625
Viers ses homes com estre doit.
Il soit por lui et nos por nos,
Segnor," fait il, "qu'en dites vos?"

Quant l'entent li cuens de Naviers
Si l'a esgardé d'entraviers.   4630
"Cuens de Clermont, qu'est que vos dites?
Doit en dont cis aler si quites?
Car prendés garde a vostre dit!
Dont n'a il ens el brief escrit
Qu'i a fait al roi tel anui   4635
Que ne le violt dire nului?
Dont a il fait mon segnor honte
Se cho est voirs que li briés conte.
Jo ne puis veïr de cestui
Coment puist aler sans anui: 4640
Mais ne doit avoir mal ne painne
En le premiere quarentainne.
Mais puis le puet, cho m'est viaire,

216

And yet, he knew very well
that what the count of Blois had said was wrong.
"I know one thing for certain," he said,
"the count of Blois has given us excellent advice.
There's no one else here   4605
who could have spoken so knowledgeably.
Indeed, it is a man's duty to be the enemy
of anyone who wants to betray his lord.
However, the king didn't know what he was doing
when he sent the youth elsewhere.   4610
He freed him by the very act
of sending him away.
Our king has given the youth the kiss of peace, my lords.
I do not see how there can be any justification
for his doing him any harm,   4615
since he started out this way.
And we, as the king's loyal subjects,
must not give advice that would cause him dishonor.
Even if King Evan were our father,
and even if the youth had killed our brother,   4620
we should not advise
our king to have him killed.
The first duty of any subject
is to safeguard his lord's honor,
just as it is the lord's duty   4625
to see that he fulfills his obligation to his men.
He should do his part and we should do ours.
My lords," he said, "What do you say to that?"

When the count of Nevers heard this,
he looked at him askance.   4630
"Count Clermont, what are you saying?
Are we to let him off scot-free?
You'd better watch what you are saying!
Didn't it say in the letter
that he did such a terrible thing to the king   4635
that he didn't even want to tell anyone about it?
Therefore, he brought dishonor on my lord as well,
if what the letter says is true.
I cannot see
how we can let this youth go free.   4640
He must not be harmed
for forty days.
But after that, as I see it,

217

Li rois envoier por deffaire
A un de ses lontains amis.   4645
Li rois Ebayns qui l'a tramis
Por cho qu'il est de halt parage
Nel violt deffaire par hontage."

Li cuens de Clermont respont donques:
"Cuens de Navers, cho n'avint onques!   4650
Volés vos le roi consellier
Por altrui soi mesme avellier?
Quant il le lassça por son honte,
Al roi de France puis que il monte,
Ki mie avellier ne se violt?   4655
Mais se li rois Ebayns se diolt
Qu'il a por no roi despendu,
Or pensons qu'il li ait rendu!
C'est al miols que jo puis savoir
Qu'avoir li rende por avoir,   4660
Anchois tols jors por .i. marc deus
Qu'il devigne por lui honteuls,/
C'est miols que il s'abandonast,
Et por avoir s'anor donast.
Tels piert le sien qui puis recuevre,   4665
Mais ne puis veïr par quele ouevre
On puist s'onor puis recovrer
Quant on le pert par mal ovrer.
Tant com li argens valt mains d'or,
Si valt honors miols de tresor.   4670
Ja ne l'eüst baisié messire
Nel poroit livrer a martyre
Lués se presenta por message.
Ne tieng pas roi Ebayn a sage
Por cho qu'il ait forfait le cief   4675
Quant il l'envoia par son brief
Al roi de France por desfaire.
E n'avés vos oï retraire
C'on ne puet faire jugement
S'on ne set bien premierement   4680
Le fait? Car l'ouevre juge l'ome:
Cho est sivable, c'est la some,
Qu'a salver l'a li rois messire.
Cho est al miols que jo sai dire
Que de lui metre a salveté,   4685
Car baisié l'a en feëlté.

the king can send him to be killed
by some ally of his who lives far away. 4645
King Evan only sent him here
because he is from a prominent family and he wanted
to avoid the disgrace of a public execution."

To this, the count of Clermont replied,
"Count of Nevers, that would never do! 4650
Would you advise the king
to sully his reputation to preserve someone else's?
Since the king of England declined to do it for fear of shame,
why should it be the king of France's business,
when he doesn't want to degrade himself either? 4655
But if King Evan complains
that he has spent large sums on our king's behalf,
let us see him reimbursed.
That's the best solution I can suggest:
that our king give back the money, 4660
and at the rate of two marks for every one.
Rather than be dishonored for King Evan's sake,
it's better for our lord to spend freely
and pay the money to retain his honor.
A man may lose his property and recover it later, 4665
but I can see no way
to retrieve honor lost
through a dishonorable act.
Just as silver is worth less than gold,
honor is worth more than wealth. 4670
Even if my lord had not kissed him,
he couldn't order him executed,
because he came here as a messenger.
In my opinion, King Evan acted unwisely:
he forfeited the right to the lad's head 4675
when he sent him as messenger
to the king of France to be killed.
And haven't you heard it said
that one cannot pass judgment
without knowing the facts first? 4680
A man is judged by his actions.
In short, it follows, then,
that my lord the king must spare him.
That is the best solution I can offer:
save the youth's life, 4685
because he kissed him in good faith.

219

Garnir le doit de son contraire.
Jo vos ai dit trestolt l'afaire:
N'en dirai el, foi que doi vos.
Volés le ensi?" "Bials sire, o nos,   4690
Mais que li rois ne vos desdie."
"Biel segnor, cho ne di jo mie
Que li rois ne puist faire bien
Trestolt son plaisir malgré mien.
Mais puis que dit li averai   4695
Al miols que dire li sarai,
Puet il faire tolt son plaisir.
Doi li jo donc por cho taisir
Consel de droit, s'il le demande?
Nenil, par foi! s'il le conmande,   4700
Consel li doi doner et dire,
Et puis si face comme sire!
Ja diäbles tant ne m'esmarge
Que jo del tolt ne me descarge
Viers mon segnor, cui amer doi,   4705
Quant conjuré m'avra en foi!
Se jo li di le miols tols dis,
Quel blasme i ai s'il fait le pis?
Encor li soit il contrecuer,
Nen istrai del droit a nul fuer/   4710
Por cho que g'i puissce assener.
Car alons le roi amener
A une part, se li disomes
L'esgart que nos ci fait avomes."
Donques l'ont d'une part mené   4715
Et cil ki miols a assené,
C'est cil de Clermont, cil a dit:
"Bials sire, entendés un petit.

Vostre commandement avons
Fait tolt al miols que nos poöns.   4720
Nos connissons tolt troi tres bien
Que se vos aviés une rien
Que rois Ebayns volsist avoir,
Si le vos eüst fait savoir,
Tel ki valsist .m. mars et plus,   4725
Doner le devriés sans refus.
Mais honir ne vos devés mie
Por nul home ki soit en vie.
Por quanque li rois vos a fait

Our king should warn him that King Evan is seeking vengeance.
I've told you what I think;
that's the way I see it, so help me God.
Are you with me?" "My lord, we are,   4690
but we hope the king doesn't go against you."
"My lords, I have never said
that the king cannot act as he sees fit,
despite my considered opinion.
Even after I have given him   4695
the best advice I could,
he can still do just as he wants.
Is this any reason to keep silent
and deny him proper counsel, if he requests it?
By God, no! If he asks for it,   4700
I am duty bound to give him sound advice,
and then let him act as befits a king!
Were I tormented by the very Devil,
I would still discharge my duty
to my lord, whom I am bound to serve,   4705
since he asked me in good faith!
If I always tell him the best course of action to take,
it is not my fault if he takes the worst.
Even if I incur the king's displeasure,
I will not stray from the right path at any price,   4710
as far as I can determine it.
Why don't we go and take the king
aside, and tell him
the results of our deliberations."
So they took him aside,   4715
and the one who had given the soundest advice,
that is, the count of Clermont, said,
"Sire, be so kind as to hear us out.

We have followed your instructions
to the best of our ability.   4720
All three of us know very well
that if you had something
King Evan wanted,
and he let you know about it,
even if it cost a thousand marks or more,   4725
you ought to give it to him without hesitation.
But you must not bring dishonor upon yourself
for any man alive.
No matter what the king has done for you, Sire,

221

Ne por quanque il servi vos ait 4730
Ne poriés vos pas voloir, sire,
C'on peüst de vos honte dire.
S'uns hom trestolt le mont eüst,
Par nul engien que il seüst
N'en poroit plus c'uns hom user. 4735
Por cho ne doit nus refuser
Honor por tantelet d'avoir.
Cil n'oirre mie par savoir
Ki por richoise honor refuse,
Por tantelet que il en use. 4740
Nient plus que cierges sans luör
Ne luist riçoise sans honor.
Por rien que nus de nos en voie
Ne poés vos en ceste voie,
Bials sire dols, cest messagier 4745
En cest message damagier.
Et si a plus: bien le savés,
Por cho que vos baisié l'avés,
Encor l'eüst il envoié
Comme larron pris et loié, 4750
Nel poriés vos deffaire pas.
Saciés que cho n'est mie a gas,
Ne on ne doit pas deffaire home
Se on ne set de fait la some:
Car del fait prent on l'oquoison 4755
Del jugement, qui fait raison.
Entendés, sire, un poi a mi.
Amer devés bien vostre ami/
Mais haïr devés sa folie:
Car certes jo ne vos lo mie 4760
De faire ja ceste mervelle
Se vostre cuers le vos conselle.
Icho ne manda hom mais onques."
Cho dist li rois: "Que ferai donques
Bien? Car vos estes mi feël 4765
Et donet m'avés bon consel.
N'ai soing de faire felenie.
Mais or crieng jo a vilonie
Le m'atort li rois d'Engletiere:
Si vos en voel jo consel quierre." 4770

Li cuens de Clermont dist: "Bials sire,
Se bon vos est, lasciés me dire.

and however he may have assisted you, 4730
you could not possibly, Sire, want
anyone to be able to say you are without honor.
If a man possessed the entire world,
no matter how ingenious he was,
he couldn't use up more than one man can. 4735
Therefore, no man should give up honor
for some piddling amount of money.
He never acts wisely
who gives up honor for wealth,
for he will have little use for it. 4740
Wealth without honor has no more luster
than a candle without a flame.
However we may analyze the situation,
you cannot, considering the circumstances,
Sire, harm this messenger 4745
while he is fulfilling his mission.
And that's not all: as you know very well,
given the fact that you kissed the youth,
even if he had been sent
as a thief, caught and properly sentenced, 4750
you could not have killed him.
You should know this is a serious matter.
One doesn't kill a man
before all the facts are in:
one bases a just verdict 4755
on the facts of the case.
Be so kind as to listen to me, Sire.
You should love your friend,
but hate his folly.
I certainly don't deny 4760
your right to fulfill this strange request,
if you can do so in good conscience.
But I've never heard of anyone sending such a letter."
The king said, "What shall I do, then?
You are very loyal 4765
and have given me excellent advice.
I do not care to perpetrate an unjust act,
but I am afraid that the king of England
will accuse me of misconduct:
I'd like to hear your advice about that." 4770

The count of Clermont replied, "Sire,
if you please, allow me to tell you.

Vos cremés vilonie a faire
D'endroit le roi de cest affaire.
Ki bien volroit la garde prendre   4775
El roi Ebayn poroit entendre
Moult plus qu'en vos de vilonie
Quant vos manda tel felonie.
De felonie octroier, sire,
Est hontes, honors d'escondire.   4780

[S]e jo ai un mien buen ami,
Honor li doi, et il a mi.
Il n'est mes hom ne jo li siens
Ne mais c'onors, service et biens
Fait l'un de nos viers l'altre sopple,   4785
Et en amistié nos acople.
Mais puis qu'il cose me querra
Que il meïsmes bien verra
Qu'il me sera torné a honte,
De nostre amor deffait le conte.   4790
N'ai cure puis de son dangier
Por son avoir m'onor cangier.
Ne pris s'amor puis .ii. fordines
Car c'est li dols miols sor espines.
Puis qu'il me violt a honte atraire   4795
Ses biensfais me valt un contraire.
Mais por les biens qu'il me fist ja,
Et por l'amor qu'eüe i a,
Le doi haïr mains c'un altre home.
Or vos ai jo dite la some.   4800
Nel doi amer ne bien haïr
S'il ne me prent a envaïr, /
Mais s'il me laidist et sorquiert,
Ferir le doi, se il me fiert.
Hom cui ne devrai point d'omage,   4805
Et il me quera par halsage
Que jo face honte por lui,
Il me fait, certes, grant anui.
Mais se il est mes liges sire,
Ne li puis pas si escondire   4810
Une grant cose par amor,
Encor me quiere deshonor.
Et s'il me mande en liu ho[n]tels,
Jo n'i ai pas le honte sels,
Ne vient ains l'a mes sire tolt   4815

You fear you will wrong
the king in this matter.
But a careful assessment of the situation   4775
would attribute far more blame
to King Evan than to you
for asking you to do such a shameful deed.
To consent to a vile deed, Sire,
is shameful; to reject it is honorable.   4780

If I have a good friend,
I owe him honor, and he owes me the same.
He is not my friend, nor am I his,
unless honors, favors and material rewards
bind us in mutual exchange   4785
and ties of friendship.
But if he should ask something of me,
and he himself could see very well
that it would damage my reputation,
that would be the end of our friendship.   4790
I would not care on his account
to exchange my honor for his wealth.
I wouldn't assess his loyalty at two cents;
it would be like honey hiding sharp thorns.
Since he wants to bring shame upon me,   4795
his kindnesses are the same as hostile acts to me.
But for the sake of past favors
and previous bonds of friendship,
I should be less hostile to him than to another man.
Now I have told you what I think.   4800
I wouldn't be his friend, or foe, either,
unless he should undertake to attack me.
But if he should do me wrong and ask more than his due,
I must strike him, if he strikes me.
A man to whom I owe no homage,   4805
and who asks me out of arrogance
to do a shameful deed for him
is surely doing me an injury.
But if he is my liege lord,
I cannot refuse him such an   4810
important request, because I owe him loyalty,
even if it means dishonor.
And if he orders me to do something shameful,
the shame is not mine alone: on the contrary,
as my superior, hasn't he taken it upon himself,   4815

A cui jo doi servir de bolt.
Alsi com il a del bien los
Sor tols ses homes, dire l'os
Que s'il me mainne en liu honi
Le blasme en doit avoir alsi   4820
Mes sires ki me puet pener
Et comme sen home mener;
Mais s'il me quiert trop grant hontage
Guerpir li puis bien son omage.
Guerpir li puis, guerpir li doi,   4825
Se jo aim tant honor et foi,
Se j'ai plus cier Deu que mon fief,
Guerpir li doi tolt, par mon cief,
Ançois que jo tel cose face
Dont Dex et li pules me hace.   4830
Certes, moult fait a home lait
Ki le requiert de hontels plait.
Et rois Ebayns est vostre hom, sire,
Si me consalt Dex nostre sire
Que jo l'aim or mains que ne suel   4835
Por cest oltrage et cest orguel.
Ne mais jo cuit le roi si sage
Que ne croi mie en mon corage
Si grant sorcuiderie el roi.
Ainc ne pensa tel estreloi!   4840
Jo ne cuic mie, par mon cief,
Qu'il onques envoiast tel brief."
"Qui l'envoiast donc, sire cuens?"
"Puet s'estre, sire, alcuns hom suens
Canja son saiel par envie   4845
Por tolir a l'enfant la vie,
Ki het u lui u son parage.
Mais or envoiés un message
O vostre brief, sel commandés
Al roi Ebayn, se li mandés/   4850
Que il ne seut preu que il fist
Quant il cestui si vos tramist.
Et vostre cors ne loe mie
Qu'il i perde menbre ne vie.
Le brief que cis aporta, sire,   4855
Faites enseëler en cire.
Se li mandés par vostre brief
Que il escrist el sien mescief

226

since I am bound to obey him without hesitation?
And just as he earns praise for the courageous deeds
of all his men, I dare say
that if he leads me into dishonor,
he should receive the blame for it as well,   4820
since he is my lord and I am his man
to command and to punish.
But if he asks too shameful a deed of me,
I can leave his service.
I can and I must leave him,   4825
if I hold faith and honor as dear,
if God is dearer to me than my holdings,
I must renounce him completely, so help me,
rather than do a deed
for which God and man would despise me.   4830
Certainly, any man who calls upon another
to do something dishonorable, does him great harm.
And since King Evan is your man, Sire,
our lord God advises me
that I should esteem him far less than before   4835
for this outrageous and arrogant behavior.
However, in my heart of hearts,
I believe the king is too wise
to be capable of such presumption.
He has never thought of anything so outrageous before!
In fact, Sire, I would swear to it   4840
that he never sent such a letter."
"Then who sent it, my lord Count?"
"Perhaps, Sire, one of his men
changed the seal, wanting   4845
to kill the boy
because of some grudge against him or his family.
But now send a messenger
with a letter directly to
King Evan, letting him know   4850
that he scarcely knew what he was doing
when he sent you this youth,
and that you yourself do not recommend
that he lose life or limb.
Also, you should enclose with it the letter   4855
the youth brought you, Sire,
and let him know in your letter
that he has damaged your reputation

A home qui tant doit valoir.
N'avés pas mis en noncaloir   4860
Ne vostre pris ne vostre los
Por metre honor ariere dos.
Trop vos a costé ja ariere
Honors por perdre en tel maniere.
Ki honor porcace et desert   4865
Mal fait s'il por petit le pert.
Mandé vos a trop grant oltrage.
Que tenés, sire, cest message?
Se li faites honor et bien;
Mais qu'il sos ciel n'en sace rien   4870
Coment il est de cest affaire.
Trosque li messages repaire,
Tant li sera cis plais celés."
Li canceliers est apielés.
El parcemin le lettre a mise   4875
Tolt si com li cuens li devise.
Tost a ensaëlé cel brief
Et le fals alsi de recief.

A un vallet de sa maison
Ki miols sace entendre raison   4880
Carge li rois ces letres donques.
Et li vallés ne fina onques
Trosques il vint en Engletiere.
Ne li covint pas le roi quierre
Plus loig que sor mer a Hantone.   4885
Cil vint a lui, le brief li done.
Priveëment l'a salué.
Li brief ne sunt pas eskivé.
Li rois meïsmes prent le cire
Et voit bien tost que voloit dire.   4890
Il a ansdeus les letres lites,
Primes les grans, puis les petites.
Ens el brief grant si trueve escrit
Coment se complaint del petit
Li rois de France, ses amis,   4895
De cho que il li fu tramis.
En l'altre cartre plus petite
La est la mors Silence escrite/
Que il devoit avoir tramise.

by writing such a thing to a man whom he should hold in the
   highest esteem.
You have never slighted   4860
your worth or reputation
by turning your back on honor.
You have invested too much in the past
to lose your honor in such a way.
A man who has spent his life in the pursuit and service of
   honor   4865
is wrong to throw it away for a trifle.
His request was terribly insulting.
Why don't you keep the messenger here, Sire,
and treat him well and honorably,
and not let him know a single thing   4870
about this matter;
until the messenger returns,
this whole business must be kept secret from him."
The chancellor was summoned.
He committed the letter to parchment   4875
just as the count dictated it.
Then he quickly sealed this letter
and resealed the false one as well.

The king entrusted these letters
to the most dependable young man   4880
in his household,
and the youth didn't stop
until he arrived in England.
He didn't have to look for the king
any farther than the port of Southampton.   4885
He came to him in private,
greeted him, and gave him the letters,
which did not go astray.
The king himself broke the wax
and soon saw what it was all about.   4890
He read both letters,
first the long one, then the short one.
The long letter contained
the complaint of his ally,
the king of France, about the fact that   4895
the short one had been sent to him.
In the other, shorter letter
was Silence's death sentence,
which he himself was supposed to have written and sent.

Por Londres, de deso*r* Tamise, 4900
S'ele fust tolte confundue
U trosqu'en abisme fondue
Ne fust il pas si dolans donques:
Il nen ot mais si grant dol onques.
Dolans est que li rois de France 4905
Cuide ore en lui si grant enfance
D'avoir nes pensé tel mervelle.
La face l'en devint vermelle
De maltalent, d'angoisce et d'ire.
Ne set sos ciel qu'il en puist dire. 4910
Celer le velt et si ne puet.
Le cancelier savoir l'estuet,
Celui l'estuet ore savoir
Ki grant honor en puet avoir!
Si vait, tant mains hom est bleciés 4915
D'altrui mesfais, d'altrui pechiés,
Et cil remaint tols sains et sals
Par cui est esmeüs li mals.

Li rois le cancelier apiele.
Dire li violt tele noviele. 4920
Rolle les iolx, crosle le cief.
"Conniscés vos," fait il, "cest brief?"
Et puis li a dit en secroi:
"Vos le veïstes ja, cho croi!"
Cil voit l'escrit, li cuers li tramble. 4925
Cho dist li rois: "Que vos en samble?"
Li canceliers ne sot que dire
Car il ne puet nul bien eslire
Ne el dire ne el taisir
Por quoi il puist al roi plaisir. 4930
Et s'on le deüst desmenbrer
Ne li poroit il ramenbrer
Dont cil escris peüst venir
Qu'il voit illuec al roi tenir.
Tols esmaris al roi a dit: 4935
"Bials sire ciers, se Dex m'aït,
Jo nel li ainc mais que jo sace
Cest brief, se ja Dex bien me face."
"Comment?" fait il, "fals clers prové!
Donc ne t'euc jo l'altrier rové 4940
A faire un brief, et tu fesis,

If all of Londontown-on-Thames   4900
had been destroyed
or had fallen into an abyss,
the king wouldn't have been as upset.
He had never felt such pain before.
He was pained to think that the king of France   4905
could think him enough of an imbecile
as to even imagine anything that crazy.
His face turned crimson
with frustration, anguish, and fury.
He didn't know what on earth to say.   4910
He wanted to keep the matter a secret, but couldn't.
The chancellor would have to hear about this,
oh, yes! he would have to hear about it;
it would certainly redound to his honor!
That's the way it goes: how often men suffer   4915
for the misdeeds and sins of others,
while those responsible for the mischief
remain safe and sound.

The king summoned the chancellor.
He wanted to tell him this piece of news.   4920
He was rolling his eyes, his head shook with rage.
"Do you recognize this letter?" he said.
Then he said so that only he could hear,
"I think you've seen it before."
The chancellor saw the letter; his heart quivered
     inside him.   4925
The king said, "What about it?"
The chancellor didn't know what to say,
for he could not see how it would do him any good
to speak or to remain silent;
neither would please the king.   4930
Even if he had been torn limb from limb,
he couldn't have remembered
where the letter that he saw
in the king's hand came from.
Nearly mad with fear, he said to the king,   4935
"Beloved Sire, as God is my witness,
to the best of my knowledge, I have never set eyes
on this letter before, so help me God."
"What?" he said. "You're caught in the act, false scribe!
Do you deny that the other day I asked you   4940
to write a letter, which you did,

231

Et en le main le me mesis,
Et jel ballai Silence en oire?"
"Bials sire," fait il, "c'est la voire."
"Ba! se tu escresis celui   4945
Que tu me ballas et jo lui,/
Donques escresis tu cest brief!
Car nus nel canja, par mon cief,
Puis que al vallet l'euc cargié!
Mar acointas, voir, cest marcié!"   4950
Et cil n'en set sos ciel que dire.
Li rois ki puet avoir grant ire
Le fait en sa cartre jeter.
De traïson le violt reter,
Qu'en lui, cho dist, ne remaint mie   4955
Silences n'ait perdu la vie.
N'i a celui en la maison
Le roi ki sace l'oquoison
Por qu'il fu jetés en la cartre.
Mar fu escrite cele cartre   4960
Par cui est mis en tel martyre.
Cho puet Silences et il dire:
Mais cil a le pis parti ore
Si avra pis puet s'estre encore.
Silences ne les crient ormais   4965
Qu'il est en France a tote pais,
A moult grant joie et a deduit.
Moult l'aiment et honorent tuit.
Dient buer passast il la mer.
Droit ont, qu'il fait moult a amer: 4970
De se harpe, de se viiele,
Comme vallés, bone puciele,
Siert bien le roi et le roïne,
Mais ne set mie le covine
Del fals brief qu'i porta en oire.   4975
Ançois li fait li rois acroire
Qu'il fu tramis al roi en France
Par les letres por remanance.
Ne li desist el por Monmartre.
Li canceliers est en la cartre   4980
A Wincestre a moult grant torment
Et pense nuit et jor forment
Dont li briés puist estre venus
Par cui est en tele tenus.
Il pensa moult, se li covint,   4985

and you delivered it into my own hands
and I gave it at once to Silence?"
"Sire," he said, "that is true."
"Well, if you wrote that letter   4945
which you gave to me and I to him,
then you wrote this letter!
Nobody had a chance to tamper with it, clearly,
after I gave it to the youth.
You're going to be sorry you ever started this!"   4950
And the chancellor didn't know what on earth to say.
The king, who was in a very bad temper,
had the chancellor thrown into prison.
He wanted to have him accused of treason,
because, he said, if Silence was still alive,   4955
it was no thanks to him.
No one in the royal household knew
the reason why
the chancellor had been thrown into jail.
What a misfortune for him that letter was ever written—   4960
he was suffering terribly for it.
That can be said for both Silence and the chancellor,
but right now, the latter is having the worse time of it,
and worse may happen to him yet.
Silence has nothing to fear from it, now   4965
that he is enjoying a peaceful
and pleasurable existence in France,
where everyone loves and honors him greatly.
They blessed the hour he crossed the sea.
They were right—he did many other endearing things;   4970
with his harp, with his viele,
as youth who is a lovely maiden,
he served the king and queen well.
But he never knew the secret
of the false letter he had brought there in such haste.
Instead, the king led him to believe   4975
that he had been sent to France
with a recommendation, to be raised at court.
He wouldn't have told him otherwise for Montmartre.
But the chancellor was in prison   4980
at Winchester, suffering terrible torments,
asking himself night and day
where the letter might have come from
that had caused his incarceration.
He thought a great deal about it (and rightly so),   4985

233

Tant qu'al tierc jor se li sovint
Que li roïne tint son brief.
"Si nel list pas de cief en cief
Non la moitié," fait il, "par foi,
Quant ele clost et mist en ploi   4990
Tolt alsi qu'ele n'eüst cure
Que jo veïssce l'escriture!
Mais se jo seüsce a nul fuer
Qu'ele l'enfant eüst sor cuer/
Bien le poroie cuidier donques,   4995
Qu'altres qu'ele ne le tint onques.
E las! quels pechiés m'a traï!
Ainc, que jo sace, nel haï,
Ains li mostra moult biele ciere
Qu'a tols les altres, m'ert a viere.   5000
Mais nus hom ne puet feme ataindre
Quant el se violt covrir et faindre.
Feme vait par son bel samblant
Le sens del siecle tolt enblant.
Sens d'ome sage poi ataint   5005
Por feme ataindre qui se faint.
Jo ne cuit nul bien entresait
El biel samblant qu'ele li fait;
Si ne sai de Silence mie
Se la roïne quist folie   5010
Dont ele eüst le cuer irié
De lui avoir si empirié.
Car feme nen est pas laniere
D'engiens trover en tel maniere.
Engignose est por home nuire   5015
Plus que por un grant bien estruire.
Las! com jo sui en grant anguissce!
Ne sai cui jo mescroire en puissce.
Mais jo ne puis nul bien noter
Que ma dame se vint froter   5020
Si priés de moi et tint mon brief.
Li en mescroi jo, par mon cief!
Onques mais ne li vi venir
Mes letres lire, ne tenir.
Mal de l'eure qu'ele i vint ore!   5025
Se Deu plaist, on sara encore
La fin dont li brief est venus,
Car Dex nen est ne sors ne mus.

234

and he thought so hard that on the third day he remembered
that the queen had held his letter.
"She didn't read it from beginning to end;
she hadn't read half of it," he said, "upon my word,
when she closed it and folded it up— 4900
just as if she had been afraid
I might see the handwriting.
If I were to find out by some means or other
that she had a grudge against the boy,
then I could be reasonably certain 4905
that no one else had got hold of the letter.
Alas! What have I done to deserve this?
As far as I know, she has nothing against him.
On the contrary, she used to favor him
far above all the others, it seems to me. 5000
But no man is a match for a woman
when she is bent on concealment and deception.
A woman goes about putting up such a false front
that she fools everyone.
A wise man's reason can achieve little 5005
against a woman who wants to deceive.
I suspect that she was up to no good
when she was being so charming to him.
I wonder whether the queen
tried to seduce Silence, 5010
and whether something happened that made her angry
    enough
to seek revenge on him like that.
A woman is always quick
to think of something clever in such circumstances.
She is much quicker at finding ways to harm a man 5015
than at thinking up something beneficial.
Alas! I am in terrible straits!
I don't know whom to suspect.
But I can see no good in the fact
that my lady came nosing around 5020
so close to me and had her hands on my letter.
She is the one I suspect, so help me!
I have never known her to come around
and read or touch my letters before.
What bad luck for me that she came this time! 5025
But if it pleases God, the reason why
the letter was brought will yet be revealed,
for God is neither deaf nor dumb.

Si voirement, Dex, com Tu vois,
Tols tans seras et aidier dois   5030
Çals qui T'apielent de bon cuer,
Ne suefres Tu ja a nul fuer
Mon cors a tort estre blecié
Si vilment por altrui pechié.
Mais li viés pechiet ki m'enconbrent—   5035
Si m'aït Dex, jo cuit m'enconbrent.
Li viés pechié, on le tiesmoigne,
Renovielent sovent vergoigne.
La moie vergoigne est parans,
Mais Dameldex me soit garans   5040
Viers cui riens ne se puet mucier."
Le cartrier prent dont a hucier:/
"Amis," fait il, "por Deu merchi,
Car di al roi que jo perc chi
Ma vie, a tort me fait destruire.   5045
Fai m'i parler ains que jo muire.
Por Deu, ne m'ait si en despit
Que jo n'aie de moi respit."
Et cil l'a fait al roi savoir
Ki li a fait respit avoir.   5050
Et quant il vient devant le roi
Ne l'aparole par derroi.
Chiet li as piés et s'umelie:
Com cil ki a mestier si prie.
"Merchi!" fait il, "bials sire ciers!   5055
Jo ne fui onques costumiers
D'enseëler faus brief, bials sire."
"Comment? viens tu chi por cho dire?"
Respont li rois. "Ne fu cho el?"
"Sire, se Dex me gart de mel,   5060
Et por icho dire et por plus
Desirai jo venir cha sus.
Ensi puissce jo Deu avoir
Com jo sos ciel ne puis savoir
Dont cis fals briés [vos] peut venir;   5065
Mais il me prist a sovenir
D'une rien, mais jo vos criem si."
Li rois respont: "Di tost! di! di!"

"[S]ire, ma dame vint a moi.
Ne sai sos ciel por quoi, n'a quoi,   5070
Mais forment m'ala costiant,

236

If it is true, God, that you see all,
and are eternal, and help   5030
those who call upon you in good faith,
you will certainly not allow
me to suffer unjustly
and so wretchedly for the sins of another.
True, I am burdened with the weight of former sins —   5035
yes, I know they weigh me down, so help me God!
Old sins, as we all know,
are a constantly renewed source of shame.
My shame is all too apparent.
But may the lord God from whom no creature can hide   5040
preserve me from harm."
Then he began to shout for the jailer.
"Friend," he cried, "for the love of God,
tell the king I am perishing here,
that he is doing me in unjustly.   5045
Let me speak to him once before I die.
For God's sake, don't let him be so angry with me
that I am not allowed a reprieve."
And the jailer notified the king,
who granted him a reprieve.   5050
And when he came before the king,
he was so distraught he couldn't speak.
He fell at his feet and prostrated himself,
like a churchgoer saying his prayers.
"Mercy, dear, sweet Sire!" he cried,   5055
"I have never made a habit
of sealing false letters, Sire!"
"What? Did you come here to tell me that?
replied the king. "Nothing else?"
"Sire, may God preserve me from evil,   5060
I wanted to come here
to tell you this and more.
I swear to God,
there is no way I can ever know for certain
where this false letter could have come from;   5065
however, I did start to remember something,
but I'm so afraid of you."
The king replied, "Speak up! Out with it!"

"Sire, my lady came to see me.
I don't have the faintest idea why or for what purpose,   5070
but she came and stood very close to me

237

Mes lettres, sire, manoiant;
Et quant ele ot mon brief ploié
Sil me rendi bien ferm loié
Et jo l'enseëlai en oire.   5075
Ne puis bien croire, ne mescroire,
Car ne me denai de l[i] garde.
Mals fus et male flame m'arde,
Ne sai s'ele l'enfant haï,
Mais moult malement m'a trahi.   5080
Ensi me consalt Dex, bials sire,
Jo n'en sai altre verté dire,
Et s'escondire me leüst
Feroie quanque vos pleüst,
Et quanque diroit vostre cors."   5085
Li rois n'est pas ne fols ne lors. /
Il nen a soig de faire rien
C'on li atort a el qu'a bien,
Ne de faire tel commençalle
Ki ait malvaise definalle.   5090
Ne proise gaires sa venjance
Qui li acroisce sa viltance.
Il rueve al cancelier qu'il cuevre,
Si com a chiers ses menbres, [l]'ouevre.
Car il set bien que la roïne   5095
Escrist le faus brief par haïne;
Et se blastange en a la dame
Bien set que il i avra blasme.
Al cancelier coile son honte;
Dist que li brief vint par un conte   5100
Ki het l'enfant et son parage.
Un brief fait cargier al message
Ki mioldres fu del premerain.
Cil prent congié al roi Ebayn.
Plus tost qu'il puet en France vient,   5105
Droit a Paris son cemin tient.
Le roi i trueve en un praël
Se li presente son seël.
Salue le de par le roi
Et se li a dit en secroi   5110
Com li escrivans fu ballis
Et c'uns cuens paltoniers fallis
Canja les letres par envie
Por tolir a l'enfant la vie.

238

and picked up my letter, Sire.
And when she had folded my letter,
she returned it to me all tightly fastened,
and I sealed it right away.   5075
I can't prove a thing one way or another,
since I wasn't paying close attention to what she was doing.
[If I'm lying] may an evil fire consume me,
I don't know whether she had it in for the boy,
but she played a terrible trick on me.   5080
That's the God's truth, Sire,
I don't know any other.
And if it is possible to pardon me,
I will do whatever you wish,
whatever you say."   5085
The king was neither a fool nor a madman.
He did not wish to take any action
that could possibly be used against him,
or begin anything
that might not end well.   5090
He had no use for the sort of vengeance
that might reflect badly on him.
He told the chancellor to cover up the matter,
as he valued life and limb.
For he knew very well that the queen   5095
had written the false letter out of hatred,
and if suspicion should fall upon the lady,
he knew he would bear the blame.
He concealed his shame from the chancellor,
and said the letter came from a count   5100
who had a grudge against the boy and his family.
He gave the messenger a letter
that was a big improvement over the first one.
He took leave of King Evan,
came to France as quickly as he could,   5105
and made his way straight to Paris.
He found the king in a meadow
and presented him with the sealed letter.
He gave him King Evan's greetings
and told him privately   5110
how the scribe had been imprisoned
and that a deceitful, wicked count
had switched the letters because he hated
the boy and wanted to kill him.

Quant li rois entent la noviele 5115
Moult par li est amee et biele.
Et quant il ot le cartre lire
Dont par est il liés al voir dire.
Or est Silences bien de cort:
Le roi est por qu'il i demort, 5120
Qu'il est moult frans et honorables,
Cortois et pros et amiables.
Et si vos puet on dire bien
Si per ne valent a lui rien.
Ses los torne le lor a blasme, 5125
Que tant en est bone la fame
C'on ne parole tant ne quant
Des altres fors de cel enfant.
Par les novieles qui en sunt,
Dont si ami joiols s'en funt, 5130
Sont moult dolant si enemi.
A .xvii. ans et a demi
Tolt droit a une Pentecoste,
Cui qu'il soit biel, ne cui il coste, /
L'adoba li rois a Paris, 5135
Et por s'amor bien jusque a dis.
Es prés dejoste Saint Germain
Vit on liquel erent certain
D'armes porter et de bien poindre
Et de lor josteörs bien joindre, 5140
Car moult i ot bons behordis.
Liquels qui i fust estordis
Silence en ot le jor le pris
Por cui li behordis fu pris.

Moult le fist bien ens en l'arainne 5145
Entre .ii. rens a la quintainne.
Ainc feme ne fu mains laniere
De contoier en tel maniere.
Kil veïst joster sans mantel
Et l'escu porter en cantiel 5150
Et faire donques l'ademise,
La lance sor le faltre mise,
Dire peüst que Noreture
Puet moult ovrer contre Nature,
Quant ele aprent si et escole 5155
A tel us feme et tendre et mole.
Tels chevaliers par li i vierse

The king was very happy   5115
to hear this welcome news.
and when he had the letter read,
he was absolutely delighted, to tell the truth.
Now Silence was really part of the court;
the king wanted him in his household   5120
because he was so noble, honorable,
courteous, valiant, and kind.
Anyone will tell you
that his peers were nothing compared to him;
the praise he won put theirs to shame.   5125
He was so famous
that no one talked of anyone else
except this boy.
The news of his successes
gladdened his friends   5130
and saddened his enemies.
When Silence was seventeen and a half,
exactly at Pentecost,
whether it was a good thing or not,
the king dubbed him knight in Paris,   5135
and, in his honor, ten others with him.
In the meadows beside Saint-Germain
you could see which knights
excelled in bearing arms and leading the charge
and joining with their opponents courageously.   5140
The jousting was superb.
Many were knocked senseless that day,
but Silence, for whom the tournament had been held,
won the prize.

In the tilting-field, between the two rows,   5145
Silence excelled at hitting the target.
There never was a woman less reluctant
to engage in armed combat.
Whoever saw him jousting, stripped of his mantle,
carrying his shield on his left arm,   5150
charging in the tournament
with well-positioned lance,
might well say that Nurture
can do a great deal to overcome Nature,
if she can teach such behavior   5155
to a soft and tender woman.
Many a knight unhorsed by Silence,

241

Que se il le tenist envierse
Et il peüst la fin savoir
Que grant honte en peüst avoir   5160
Que feme tendre, fainte et malle,
Ki rien n'a d'ome fors le halle,
Et fors les dras et contenance,
L'eüst abatu de sa lance.
Et savés que dist mes corages?   5165
Que bien ait tols jors bons usages.
Bons us tolt moult vilonie
Et fait mener cortoise vie.
Car bons us a qui bone vie uze
Et vilonie le refuse.   5170
Mains hom fait tols jors desonor
Que s'il eüst flairié honor
Et maintenue dé l'enfance
Ki n'avroit cure de viltance.
S'il fait le honte n'en puet nient   5175
Qu'a cho qu'il a apris se tient.
Silences ne se repent rien
De son usage, ains l'ainme bien.
Chevaliers est vallans et buens,
Mellor n'engendra rois ne cuens.   5180
Ne vos puis dire la moitié
De si com il a esploitié./
Ains que li ans trasist a fin
A bon chevalier et a fin
Le tienent tolt cil de la terre.   5185
La avint si qu'en Engleterre
Mut une guerre fors et fiere,
Qu'avierse gent et poltoniere
Se revelerent viers le roi
Par grant orguel et par derroi.   5190

De Silence vait la noviele
En maintes terres bone et biele.
Ja set on bien par fais, par dis,
Qu'il est pros, sages et hardis.
Quant li rois Ebayns l'a seü   5195
Ne l'a mie longes teü.
A la roïne anchois a dit:
"Suer dolce, or m'oiés un petit.
Un don vos quier, sel me donés."

242

if he had known the truth
at the time she knocked him down,
would have been terribly ashamed   5160
that a tender, soft, faint-hearted woman,
who had only the complexion,
clothing and bearing of a man,
could have struck him down with her lance.
And do you know what I really think?   5165
One should behave properly every day.
Good manners refine one's behavior
and help one lead a courtly life.
Proper behavior is the sign of a good life
and of moral refinement.   5170
Many act dishonorably every day,
but if they had had a taste of honor
and had been raised with it from infancy,
they would reject base deeds.
If they behave improperly. they can't help it;   5175
they're only practicing what they've learned.
Silence had no regrets
about his upbringing, in fact, he loved it.
He was a valiant and noble knight;
no king or count was ever better.   5180
I can't tell you the half
of his exploits.
Before the year was over,
all the people in the land
considered him an outstanding and accomplished knight.
Then it so happened that   5185
a fierce war broke out in England:
hostile and dastardly men
rebelled against the king
out of great pride and folly.   5190

Silence's fame spread
throughout many lands.
Everyone knew that he was valiant,
wise, and brave in word and deed.
When King Evan heard the news,   5195
he didn't keep it to himself for long,
oh, no indeed! He said to the queen,
"Listen, my sweet,
I have a favor to ask of you, if you're willing."

243

"Et il vos soit abandonés," 5200
Dist la roïne. "Que est cho?"
"Gel vos dirai, avrai le jo?"
"Bials sire, o vos, jel vos creänt."
Cho dist li rois: "Plus ne demant.
Or ne vos soit contre cuer mie, 5205
Ma dolce suer, bele Eufemie.
Jo voel Silence o moi ravoir,
Car on m'a fait bien asavoir
Que il n'a chevalier en Franche
Tant valle d'escu ne de lance. 5210
Et vos veés le grant besoig."
La roïne ot le bon tesmoig
Et le vallance de celui,
Et qu'il n'a eü nul anui
Par le fals brief que li canja. 5215
Onques ne but, ne ne manja,
Ki tel dol eüst com ele eut
Quant ele sain et sauf le seut.
Mais d'altre part, por sa bonté,
Por les biens c'on en a conté 5220
Si l'aime un petit la roïne
Cui amors valt une haïne.
Ele ainme, oiés en quel maniere,
Qu'ele ne sera pas laniere
De porcacier son honte et querre 5225
Se il repaire en Engleterre,
Por cho qu'il ne le voelle amer.
Einsi amer est moult amer,
Ensi amer est amertume,
Maldehait ait hui sa costume./ 5230
Ensi amer est bien haïr
Et home mordrir, et traïr.
Faintice feme paltoniere,
Quant violt d'ome estre parçoniere,
Pasmer et plorer est sa guise. 5235
Mais ja n'iert d'ome si soprise,
Por cho qu'il n'ait de s'amor cure,
Ne voelle sa male aventure.
Feme faintice n'ainme mie,
Ains faint pur furnir sa folie. 5240
Moult a a dire en fainte feme.
"Sire," dist la roïne Eufeme,

"Whatever you want, it's yours,"   5200
said the queen. "What is it?"
"If I tell you, can I still have it?"
"Absolutely, dear sir, I promise."
Then the king said, "I can't ask for more.
Now please don't get upset,   5205
my lovely Eufeme, sweet sister mine—
I want to have Silence back with me,
because I have heard
that of all the knights in France
he is the most skillful with shield and lance.   5210
And you must be aware of the fact that we need him badly."
The queen then learned of the youth's
prowess and excellent reputation,
and found out that her switching the letters
hadn't hurt him a bit.   5215
She was sure she would never eat or drink again,
she was so distressed
to learn that he was safe and sound.
Yet, on the other hand, his prowess
and the flattering things people were saying about him   5220
made the queen fall a little bit in love with him again.
But for her, love was the same as hate.
She loved him, but wait till you hear how:
she won't hesitate
to seek his disgrace and pursue his destruction   5225
if he returns to England,
because he refuses to be her lover.
This kind of love is very bitter;
this love is bitterness itself.
A curse on the queen's behavior!   5230
This kind of love is really hatred,
betraying a man and killing him.
When a treacherous whore of a woman
wants to get her claws into a man,
she gets her way by weeping and swooning.   5235
Yet she's never so taken with a man
that she doesn't want to destroy him
if he rejects her advances.
A deceitful woman never loves,
she only deceives to feed her lust.   5240
There is much that could be said on the subject of woman's
    deceitfulness.
"Sire," said Queen Eufeme,

245

"Ne cuidiés vos ja a nul fuer
Silences me soit contre cuer,
Se il vos puet mestier avoir." 5245
"Suer dolce, or dites vos savoir."
"Bials sire, cuidiés que jo soie
Si fole que jo haïr doie
Home qui vos puist rien aidier?
Se jel peüssce soshaidier, 5250
Jo l'i* soshaideroie, sire."
Li rois fait metre un brief en cire:
.d. salus al roi de France
Et grans merchis de l'onerance
Que pur s'amor Silence a fait. 5255
Or le violt ravoir entresait.
Viegnent od lui si compagnon,
Car si voisin li sont gagnon
Entre icele gent haïe,
Car or ont grant mestier d'aïe 5260
Ke* moult l'ont assalli de guierre.
Li mes s'en part tost d'Engletierre.
Passe la mer tost d'Engletierre,
Par le plus droit cemin atierre.
A Mont Loön en France vient. 5265
Li rois i est, grant fieste i tient,
Et cil les lettres li presente
Cui li esploitiers atalente.
Cho qu'il dut dire, cho li dist.
Ki lire dut le brief si list, 5270
Et si a fait al roi savoir
Que li rois Ebayns violt ravoir
Silence ariere en Engletierre,
Et de ses pers, qu'il a grant guierre.

Li rois fait Silence atorner 5275
Ki plus ne violt la sejorner.
De ses pers mainne trosqu'a .xxx.
Tolte la cors en est dolente;/
Plorent Silence a desmesure:
"Ahi!" font il, "quel noreture 5280
Et quels atrais est d'estrange home!
Quant on l'a norri, c'est la some,
Et miols apris, sil pert on donques."
Mais Silences ne fina onques

246

"you mustn't think that I bear
any sort of grudge against Silence,
if you have need of him."   5245
"My sweet sister, tell me your thoughts."
"Dear sir, do you think I am
so foolish as to be the enemy
of a man who can be of service to you in any way?
If I could wish him here,   5250
I would, Sire."
The king had a message prepared and sealed:
he sent five hundred greetings to the king of France
and thanked him for having honored Silence
for the sake of their friendship.   5255
But now he wanted him back at once,
and his companions should come with him,
because his neighbors were turning against him,
together with these rebels,
and he and his men were in urgent need of reinforcements,   5260
for his assailants were numerous in this war.
This messenger left England at once,
quickly crossed the English Channel,
and landed at the nearest port.
In France, he went to Laon,   5265
where the king was holding a great feast.
Eager to accomplish his mission,
the messenger greeted the king properly
and presented him with the letter.
The appropriate official read the letter   5270
and informed the king
that King Evan wanted to have
Silence back in England,
and his peers with him, because he was faced with a serious
     uprising.

The king had Silence prepare for departure;   5275
he left at once,
taking thirty of his companions with him.
The whole court was plunged into sorrow;
they mourned Silence's absence.
"Alas!" they cried, "see what happens when you   5280
raise a stranger in your midst!*
It's always the same story! You nurture him,
you teach him all you know, and then he leaves you."
But Silence didn't stop

247

Ne por haïr ne por amer   5285
Entros qu'il a passé la mer.
Et quant il vint en Engletierre
A Cestre se traist a la guierre.
Al roi en vait grant aleüre
A sa moult grant male aventure,   5290
Et tols ses compagnons enmainne.
Tres or conmence sa grans painne.
Al roi est venus, lui trentisme.
Or est entrés en male lime.
Trestolt i sont moult bien venu,   5295
Si com drois est, et retenu.
Tolt mainnent de Silence joie
Gregnor que jo dire vos doie.

Droit al tierc jor que li François
Vinrent al roi, un poi ançois   5300
Que il presist a ajorner,
Li rois fait sa gent atorner,
Car aler violt desor un conte
Ki li a fait et tort et honte.
Trois contes ot ains amatis.   5305
Or s'est moult forment aätis
Que de cestui sera vengiés,
U ja nen iert longes engiés
De quanque il el siecle tient.
En la contree al conte en vient   5310
Ki li a cele honte faite.
Li rois del vengier s'en afaite.
Joste le mont, en un pendant,
Vait li rois sa gent atendant.
Descendent dont, si s'arment tuit,   5315
Cols i avra ferus ains nuit.
Li cuens avoit Cestre tenue
Sor cui l'os le roi est venue.
Li rois li toli par effors,
Mais moult i ot navrés et mors   5320
Ains que li cuens partist de Cestre.
Or puet li rois tres bien fis estre
Que li cuens a or tel ferté
Ki n'iert prise a oan, par verté,
Si n'est par oltrecuiderie   5325
Ki honist moult chevalerie. /

248

for love or hate   5285
until he had crossed the sea.
And when he arrived in England,
he made his way to the war at Chester.
He hastened to join the king,
to his very great misfortune,   5290
and took his companions with him
(his troubles will start very soon now).
He came to the king, his thirty men with him.
Now he has fallen into a nasty trap.
They were all warmly welcomed,   5295
as was fitting, and urged to remain.
Everyone was overjoyed at Silence's arrival,
more than I can tell you.

Right on the third day after the French
had joined the king, a little before   5300
it began to grow light,
the king ordered his men to arm themselves,
for he wanted to attack a count
who had wronged and betrayed him.
He had already defeated three counts;   5305
now he had sworn a solemn oath
to get revenge on this one,
or else forfeit
all his earthly possessions.
The king reached the estates   5310
of the count who had defied him so.
He prepared to take vengeance.
Next to a mountain, on a sloping plain,
the king went to await his men.
They all came down and armed themselves.   5315
There would be blows exchanged before nightfall.
The count whom the king's army
was attacking had held Chester.
The king had wrested it from him,
but there were many dead and wounded   5320
before the count left Chester.
Now the king could be very sure of the fact that
the count held a fortress
that certainly wouldn't be taken quickly,
unless reckless chances were taken,   5325
with heavy loss of life.

Segnor, dejoste la montagne
Dont jo vos di, ens en la plagne,
S'arme rois Ebayns et li sien;
Car il le set et dist tres bien   5330
Que li cuens lués l'enconterra
Quant en sa tiere les verra.
Se bon vos est, et atalente,
De Silence et des François .xxx.
Dirai, mais qu'escoltés en soie.   5335
Desor un ganbizon de soie
Giete l'obierc malié menu
Que li rois de France ot tenu
En tel cierté qu'il nel donast
Por rien c'on li abandonast.   5340
Legiers est, ne puet faire falle.
Calces de meïsmes la malle
Li lacent qui moult bones sunt.
Si esporon a proisier funt:
De fin or sunt bien avenant,   5345
Se li fremerent maintenant.
Doi sien vallet de gregnor los
Li gietent donc l'obierc el dos.
Sa bone espee a donques çainte
C'uns siens vallés li a atainnte.   5350
Et maintenant ainz qu'il s'en alle
Li ont fremee la ventalle.
Moult tost li ont puis lacié l'elme:
Nen a si bon en nul roialme.
Pieres i a et cercle d'or   5355
Ki valent bien tolt un tressor.
Li rois de France li dona.
Bien ait quant il l'abandona.
Il ot esté a un sien oncle:
El nasal a un escarboncle.   5360
Li auferrans est amenés.
Uns siens vallés li plus senés
L'estraint moult bien et donc li rent.
Puis monta sus, qu'arçon n'i prent.
Des esporons d'or qu'il avoit   5365
Com cil qui faire le savoit
Le tolce es costés et il salt
.xiiii. piés, que rien n'i falt.

Lords, from the mountainside
I just mentioned to the plain,
King Evan and his men were arming themselves,
for he knew very well, and let it be known,   5330
that the count would attack him
as soon as he saw them on his land.
If it amuses and pleases you,
I shall tell you of Silence and the thirty Frenchmen,
as long as you care to listen.   5335
Over a padded silken tunic,
Silence put on the finely-meshed hauberk
which the king of France had valued
so highly that he wouldn't have exchanged it
for anything anyone could have offered him.   5340
It was light and flawless.
Leggings of the same mesh
and of excellent quality were laced upon him.
His spurs were very valuable,
they were of fine gold and very beautiful;   5345
these were fastened upon him now.
Two of his most renowned young companions
now pulled the hauberk down over his back.
Then he girt on his good sword,
which one of the youths handed to him.   5350
And now, before he left,
they fastened his mesh hood
and quickly laced his helmet upon him.
There wasn't another like it anywhere.
It was covered with precious stones and a golden circlet
that were worth a fortune.   5355
It was a gift from the king of France—
may he prosper for having given it to him—
and had belonged to an uncle of his.
The nose-piece held a deep-red ruby.   5360
The war-horse was led forth;
one of the most seasoned squires
curbed it well and gave him the reins.
He mounted without holding onto the saddle-bow.
With his golden spurs   5365
he expertly
touched its flanks and it leapt
a full fourteen feet.

251

Armé sunt li .xxx. François
Alsi tost com il, u ançois,   5370
Et montent o lor avoé,
Dont ont soshaidié et voé
Que ja ne puist entrer en glize
Uns d'als, s'il i fait coärdize. /
Scilense parla com senés: 5375
"Segnor, jo vos ai amenés
Par vos mercis en ceste tiere.
Or si vos voel jo moult requierre
Que vos soiés ensi par vos
Que nus ne puist dire de nos   5380
Orguel, oltrage, ne folie,
Se il nel dist par droite envie.
Jo sui a vos et vos a mi."
Et cil respondent com ami:
"Sire," funt il, "tolt somes un,   5385
Et bien et mal avrons commun."

Li François sunt bien a conroi.
Bien pert qu'il vienent de bon roi.
Il ont tramis estor furnis,
Des obiers, des elmes burnis,   5390
Et des escus a l'or d'Espagne
Dont resplendist tolte la plagne.
Jo le vos di, bien le sachiés,
Que li cuens ot esté cachiés
De Cestre, car n'ert pas garnis,   5395
Et uns siens fils bien enbarnis
I fu ochis. Cho poise lui,
Et moult li torne a grant anui.
Mais or a grant gent aünee,
Viande atraite et amassee.   5400
Dist bien qu'il iert vengiés del roi
Car il li a fait grant desroi.
Li cuens a moult de gent haïe
Et les .iii. contes en s'aïe
Cui li rois ot jetet d'estor.   5405
Mais jo vos di li tors fu lor.
Car li .iii. et li cuens de Cestre
Volrent par force segnor estre
Desor le roi, qui nen ot cure
De perdre vilment sa droiture,   5410

252

The thirty French were armed
as soon as he was, or sooner.   5370
They mounted together with their chosen leader,
for whose sake they had sworn a vow
that not one of them might ever enter a church again
if he showed any signs of cowardice.
Silence spoke as an experienced leader: 5375
"Lords, you have consented
to follow me to this land.
Now I should like to urge you
to conduct yourselves in such a way
that none may accuse us   5380
of arrogance, excess, or folly
unless they do it out of sheer envy.
I am pledged to you and you to me."
And they replied as loyal companions:
"Sire," they said, "we are all one;   5385
we will face triumph or defeat together."

The French were a well-disciplined troop.
It was clear that a good king had sent them.
They were extremely well equipped:
hauberks, shining helmets,   5390
and shields embossed with Spanish gold;
the entire plain was ablaze with their splendor.
I've already told you, as you well know,
that the count had been driven from Chester,
because it wasn't fortified;   5395
also, one of his sons, a seasoned warrior,
was killed there. This was a heavy blow,
and he suffered terribly from it.
But now he had gathered large numbers of men,
and was very well provisioned.   5400
He declared he would take vengeance on the king
for causing him such serious losses.
The count had many rebels on his side
and three counts as his allies,
the ones the king had defeated in battle.   5405
But I want you to know they were in the wrong,
for the three counts and the count of Chester
wanted to usurp supreme power
from the king, who didn't care
to lose his rights illegitimately.   5410

Ains lor fera, cho dist, anui.
Il remanacent forment lui.

Encor ne furent pas veü
Icil de l'ost quant l'a seü
Li cuens, dont s'arme isnielement   5415
Et s'en ist moult hasteëment,
Il et li .iii. conte en s'aïe
Ki moult mainnent de gent haïe.
Durement vont aproçant l'ost
Et li roial le sevent tost.   5420
Trestolte l'os est la montee,
Cui la noviele estoit contee/
Que li cuens estoit issus fors.
Mervellols soneïs de cors
Et de buisines i a donques;   5425
Et li roial ne finent onques
Trosques il sunt en la montagne.
Lor enemis ens en la plagne
Voient porprendre les lairis.
Sempres i avra des mari[s].   5430
Li hardeme[n]s qui les atise
Et li haste qui les justisce
De conbatre et venir ensanble
Les desmesure, cho me sanble,
Si qu'il n'i a eschiele faite: 5435
L'une os viers l'autre s'est atraite.

Moult par est biele la contree.
Li une oz a l'altre encontree.
Cui qu'il fust biel, ne cui costast,
Nus ne devisa qui jostast.   5440
Tolt i ferirent premerain,
U tolt ferirent daërrain,
Car tolt ont feru a un frois,
Ainc nus hom n'oï mais tel crois.
Quant vint as lances abasscier   5445
.m. en covint a mort quasscier.
Dont veïssciés tronçons voler,
Tamainte jovente afoler,
Escus estroër et percier.
Nus hom ne poroit entiercier   5450
Ne savoir el premier enbronc
Al quel fu miols u pis adonc.

Rather than that, he said, he would oppose them.
But they presented a considerable threat to him.

The king's army was still out of sight
when the count learned of its approach.
He armed himself at once   5415
and left with the utmost haste,
he and the three counts who were his allies,
and with them many hostile forces.
They rode hard toward the enemy,
and the royal forces were soon aware of it.   5420
The entire army was mounted
as soon as they heard the news
that the count had sallied forth.
Then there were terrible blasts
of horns and trumpets,   5425
and the royal troops didn't stop
until they reached the mountain.
From the plain, their enemies
saw that the heights were occupied:
someone always has to lose.   5430
Fearlessly daring, eager to attack,
driven by the urge
to close and fight,
they are out of control, it seems to me.
They didn't even pause to regroup: 5435
each army rushed upon the other.

The countryside was very beautiful.
The armies closed upon each other.
Whoever would win or lose,
the sides were evenly matched.   5440
Everyone was first—
or last—to strike,
for everyone struck at the same time.
You never heard such a clash of weapons.
When it came to lowering of lances,   5445
a thousand were determined to strike a fatal blow.
You could see shattered fragments fly,
and many young men in battle-frenzy,
and shields pierced and perforated.
As soon as battle was joined,   5450
no one could tell
who was getting the better or worse of it.

255

Mais cui qu'il fust u pis u miols
Si s'entrefierent des espiols
Qu'escu n'i vallent plus que palle,   5455
N'obierc, tant aient bone malle,
O les trenchans de alemieles
N'estuece espandre lé boieles.
Et quant les lances sont perdues
Dont traient les espees nues.   5460
A l'acointier des brans tallans
Parut liquels fu plus vallans.
La commencierent tel estor
Dont li plus hardis ot paör.
Li brant de l'acier poitevin   5465
Sont a tels .m. si mal voisin,
Ja ne rediront en lor tierre
A cui estait pis de la guerre.
Mais bien vos puis par verté dire
C'ainc mais n'oï gregnor martyre. /   5470
Gregnor! Ba, Dex! comment gregnor?
.m. per de castials et d'onor
I sont ochis, fust drois u tors,
Dont i a moult des altres mors.

Li .iiii. conte desloial   5475
Ont ja tant fait que li roial
Vont durement afoibloiant.
Moult vilment les vont manoiant.
N'est hom qui tolt le vos pardie
Com le cuens ot la car hardie   5480
Ki Cestre tint, tant com lui lut.
Mais or a il tel plait esmut
Jamais n'i enterra al mains
Mais que li rois le tiegne as mains.

Li rois est forment de grant ire   5485
Et li cuens alsi, al voir dire.
Il voit le roi, li rois voit lui;
L'uns fera sempres l'altre anui.
L'uns ne violt l'altre deporter.
Tant com chevals les puet porter   5490
Et randoner les sals menus
Est l'uns d'als viers l'altre venus.
Si s'entrefierent de ces lances
U ot moult bones conisances,

256

But whoever was winning or losing,
they struck each other so hard with their lances
that shields were as much use as straw,   5455
as were hauberks, no matter how strong their mesh;
nor did the sharp edge of the lance's blade
spare the spilling of entrails.
And when the lances were gone,
they drew their naked swords.   5460
And when the sharp swords met,
it was clear who the most valiant were.
The hand-to-hand combat was so violent
that even the bravest were afraid.
The blade of a Poitevin sword   5465
was an unwelcome intruder to some thousand men
who would never tell stories at home
about who had won or lost the war.
I can tell you in all honesty, however,
that I have never heard of a greater slaughter.   5470
Greater? Bah, how can I say greater,
when a thousand men with castles and fiefdoms
were killed, whether they deserved it or not,
along with many others.

The four rebel counts   5475
had already done so much damage
that the royal troops were seriously weakened.
They were under savage attack.
No one could possibly tell you
how bravely the count of Chester   5480
defended himself, as long as he could.
And now he had unleashed such a serious conflict
that he would never be beaten
unless he fell into the king's hands.

The king was furiously eager for combat;   5485
so was the count.
He saw the king; the king saw him.
One was bound to harm the other;
neither wished to spare the other.
As quickly as the horses, galloping,   5490
with short strides, could carry them,
they rushed upon each other.
They struck each other with those lances
whose pennants bore such noble coats-of-arms,

257

Et li tronçon en volent sus.   5495
Li rois versa et chaï jus.
Li cuens sovine sor l'arçon,
N'ot pas senti colp de garçon.
Li rois est cheüs en la presse.
.c. en i muerent sans confesse.   5500
Un chevalier i pert li cuens,
Li rois i pert .iiii. des suens.
El conte ot chevalier moult fort
Mais que il ot viers le roi tort.
Li rois l'ot bien priés desjué   5505
Ki n'avoit mie a lui jué;
Mais [il] recovra tost sans falle.
Çals a mostré que ses brans talle
Ki vinrent la le roi secorre:
Com leus les moltons lor cort sore.   5510
Fiert sor ces helmes gentiors
Qu'il en abat pieres et flors.
Durement les vait costiänt.
As grans cols qu'il lor va donant
Il fait ces helmes enbarer   5515
Et maint chevalier esgarer:
Sanc et cerviele fait espandre.
Il contrefait roi Alixandre. /
Se li rois n'a proçaine aïe
La le prendront la gens haïe.   5520

Silence en l'ost est d'altre part.
O ses François fait grant essart.
Il ont piece a les lances fraites
Et si ont les espees traites
Et fierent tolt en un tenant: 5525
Moult les vont laidement menant.
Entre Silence et ses Franchois
Orent fait pais de .c. anchois
Qu'il onques oïsscent noviele
Del roi, ki lor fust laide u biele.   5530
Moult vont les rens aclaroiant.
Il nes vont mie tariänt
Li Franchois a fuer de garçons:
Des fols voidierent les arçons
Par tel covent que puis n'i montent.   5535
Doi chevalier Silence content
Coment li rois est contenus.

and sent the splinters flying.   5495
The king was unseated and fell to the ground.
The count reeled in his saddle;
he had been dealt a manly blow.
The king fell in the thick of the fray.
A hundred were dying there unshriven.   5500
The count lost a knight there;
the king lost four of his.
The count was a very valiant knight,
except for the fact that he was a traitor.
He dealt the king a blow that was no joke;   5505
the king came close to ending his game,
but the count rallied immediately.
He showed those who came to the king's aid
that his sword was sharp enough:
he fell upon them like a wolf among sheep.   5510
He rained such heavy blows upon their helmets
that he struck off jewels and ornaments.
He closed on them relentlessly.
The terrible blows he kept on giving them
smashed through the helmets   5515
and befuddled many knights:
their blood and brains were spattered all over.
He was a second Alexander.*
If the king didn't get help soon,
the enemy would capture him right then and there.   5520

Silence was on the other side of the fray,
mowing down the foe with his Frenchmen.
They had shattered their lances some time ago,
and drawn their swords
and rained blows ceaselessly: 5525
they inflicted terrible wounds upon them.
Between them, Silence and the French
had finished off more than a hundred,
before they ever heard any news
of the king, whether good or bad.   5530
They thinned out the enemy ranks considerably.
The French weren't fighting
at all like mercenaries:
they cleared the foolhardy from their saddles
in a way that ensured thay would never remount.   5535
Two knights informed Silence
that the king was surrounded.

259

Silences i est tost venus.
L'espee tint que fist uns Mors: 5540
Ne se trast pas a l'un des cors
De le grant presse, mais enmi.
Mar l'i virent si enemi.
Sor ces helmes fait retentir
Son brant, que il lor fait sentir. 5545
Riens ne lor puet avoir garant.
Al conte fait honte aparant,
C'un sien neveu a estoné,
Car un tel colp li a doné
Qu'il chiet devant le conte mors. 5550
Li Franchois voient son effors.
Acuellent gregnor hardement
Quant voient son contenement.
"Tels hom," font il, "fait a amer.
Bien ait quant il nos passa mer. 5555
Monjoie!" escrient. "Dex i valle!
C'est li vallés de Cornuälle!"

[U]ns des Franchois, Gui de Calmont,
Et uns Rogiers nés de Bialmont,
Et Hyebles de Castiel Landon 5560
Se lasscent chaïr a bandon
Desor le roi. Font li bonté,
Car par effors l'ont remonté. /
Silences lor voide la place.
Il tua un ki tant le hace 5565
Qu'il voelle son acointement.
Or vait al conte malement.
Enviers Silence a gros le cuer.
Il nel puet amer a nul fuer
Ne les Franchois, et si ne set 5570
Quels gens il sunt, mais moult les het.
Orains oï en la batalle:
"C'est li vallés de Cornuälle!"
Mais ne set pas la verté fine,
Tant c'uns des suens viers lui s'acline, 5575
Se li a dit: "Dont estes nés?
Et des Franchois qua[nz] amenés?"
Dont ont reconmencié l'estor
Ki sera tornés a tristor
A tels i a, ains qu'il anuite.

Silence rode there at once,
brandishing a Moorish sword.
He didn't skirt the edge of the battle,   5540
but went straight through the middle.
His presence there was not to the enemy's advantage.
He made them feel the weight of his sword
and made their helmets resound with the blows.
Nothing could save them.   5545
He did the count some obvious damage:
he dealt one of his nephews
such a stunning blow
that he fell dead at the count's feet.
The French saw this exploit   5550
and redoubled their own efforts
at the sight of his exemplary conduct.
"A man like this," they said, "inspires loyalty.
We did well to follow him across the sea.
Montjoie!" they cried. "May God prevail!   5555
Hurrah for the youth of Cornwall!"

One of the Frenchmen, Guy de Calmont,
and another, Roger de Belmont,
and Ibles de Castel Landon*
dismounted, exposing themselves to terrible danger,   5560
and by their efforts succeeded
in helping the king remount.
Silence cleared the way for them,
killing one who rushed upon him,
eager to attack.   5565
Now things were going badly for the count.
He was filled with hatred for Silence.
He simply couldn't manage to like him
or the French. He didn't know
who they were, but he certainly disliked them.   5570
Just a moment ago, he had heard a shout in the midst of
    battle:
"Hurrah for the youth of Cornwall!"
But he didn't know who he was
until one of his men leaned toward Silence
and asked him, "Where are you from?   5575
And how many French did you bring with you?"
Then they started up the fight again,
which would prove disastrous to
many of those present before nightfall.

Li cuens est forment en grant luite 5580
Qu'il soit acointiés as Franchois:
Si sera il, jo cuit, anchois
Que il gaäint ne tant ne quant.
Prent une lance d'un enfant.
Silences en a une prise 5585
Deseur le cheval qu'il justise.
Tant com chevals puet randoner
Se vont donques entredoner.
Çaingles n'estrier n'i ont valu
Ne çaient andoi el palu. 5590
Salent en piés isnielement,
Si se requierent vivement
Des brans forbis trenchans d'acier.
Se Dex Silence nen a chier
Que il le mece en noncaloir, 5595
Ne li pora gaires valoir
Elmes, ne brogne, ne escus.
Li cuens est forment irascus,
Et vos savés benignement
Que il rest plains de hard[em]ent. 5600
Grans cols i ot a l'envaïr.
Li uns fiert l'altre par aïr
Qu'il funt de lor escus astieles.
Silences dist: "Bials Dex, chaieles,
Ki m'a jeté de maint anui, 5605
Done moi vertu viers cestui!
Cho qu'afoiblie en moi Nature
Cho puist efforcier T'aventure.
Mais se Tu viols ne me puet nuire
Rois, n'amirals o son empire." / 5610
Li cuens atant son elme enpire
[Li cuens atant son elme enpire]
Qu'il en abat pieres et flors.
Ja l'eüst mort, cho fust dolors,
De l'espee que tint trenchant, 5615
Mais que li brans torna en chant:*
Par tant est guaris de la mort.
Silences dist: "Trop s'i amort
Li cuens Conans* a moi ferir.
Jo li volrai sempres merir 5620
Et le torture et le desroi
Que il a fait enviers le roi."
Moult vivement dont le requiert.

The count was making a desperate effort   5580
to get acquainted with the French.
And so he will, I think,
but it will hardly be to his advantage.
He seized a lance from one of his men.
Silence positioned his own weapon firmly,   5585
spurred his horse forward,
and they both galloped toward each other
as fast as their horses could carry tham.
Neither cinch nor stirrup prevented
either of them from falling into the mud.   5590
They jumped to their feet immediately
and went at each other fiercely
with sharp and furbished sword-blades.
If God is indifferent
to Silence's plight,   5595
neither helm nor cuirass nor shield
can help him!
The count was in a frenzy,
and you know very well
that Silence was resisting with all his strength.   5600
He was assailed by dreadful blows.
They struck each other so savagely
that their shields were shivered to pieces.
Silence said, "Dear God, for heaven's sake,
you who have rescued me from many a peril,   5605
let me prevail against this foe!
Only your intervention can strengthen
that in me which Nature has made weak.
If it is your will, none can harm me,
neither king nor emir with his whole army."   5610
Just then the count damaged Silence's helmet so badly
[line repeated]
that he knocked gems and ornaments off it.
He would have killed Silence with his sharp sword,
which would have been a pity,   5615
except that the blow was deflected;
only this saved Silence from death.
Silence said, "Count Conant is relentless
in his efforts to strike me down.
I must continue to seek vengeance   5620
for my own suffering and for his rebellion
against the king."
Then he went at the count with renewed vigor

Del branc d'acier le conte fiert
Si que del destre brac l'afole.   5625
Del puig perdu l'espee vole,
Et li cuens chiet, pert sa valor,
Pasmés chaï por la calor.
Silence l'a feru a ente.
Or est li cuens en grant tormente.   5630
Mais que valt longes aconter?
Silences le fist remonter.
Al roi le rent, revient en l'ost,
Ne mais icil de la, si tost
Com il sorent lor segnor pris   5635
Dont Silences a tolt le pris,
S'en vont fuiant a moult grant honte.
O als s'enfuient li .iii. conte.

Silences n'a soig de juër:
Ne violt pas le guerre atriuër,   5640
Cui colpe jambe, u piet, u puig.
Li Franchois vienent al besoig;
A "Monjoie!" que il escrie
N'i a un seul qui se detrie,
Cil del fuïr, cil del cacier.   5645
Savoir poés que Dex l'a cier,
Silence, ki le guerre fine.
Et quant l'ot dire la roïne
Qu'ele a le verté entervee
Dont par est ele si dervee   5650
Enaise li sens ne marist.
Donc dist, se Dex celui guarist,
Qu'il le garra de sa dolor.
Mue le jor .m. fois color.
"U il," fait ele, "me garra,   5655
U ses orghols voir li parra."

La roïne est de maint porpens:
Ne cuide ja veïr le tens, /
S'il violt u por son cors deduire
U s'il ne violt por li destruire.   5660
En le viés derverie rentre.
Maldis soit li cuers de son ventre!
Mar le vit ainc Silences nee!
Il a le guerre al roi finee,
Les .iiii. contes pris, et mors   5665

and struck him with his steel blade,
severing his right arm.   5625
The sword flew from the severed fist;
the count fell, lost his strength,
and fainted from the searing pain.
Silence had dealt him a dreadful blow.
Now the count was in terrible anguish.   5630
But why prolong the story?
Silence had him remount,
handed him over to the king, and returned to the fight.
But as soon as the enemy knew
that their leader had been taken prisoner—   5635
for which the full credit belonged to Silence—
they turned tail and fled ignominiously,
and the three counts with them.

Silence didn't feel like fooling around,
he didn't want to stop fighting;   5640
he kept on slicing off enemy legs and feet and fists.
The French came and helped him.
There was not one who failed to respond
to his cry of "Montjoie!":
the enemy fled; the French pursued.   5645
God was on Silence's side, as you can plainly see,
for he won the war.
And when the queen heard the news,
and knew it was true beyond a doubt,
she flew into such a rage   5650
that she nearly lost her senses.
Then she said to herself, if God had saved Silence,
then Silence could cure her of her pain.
She changed color a thousand times in one day.
"Either he will cure what ails me," she said,   5655
"or he will be punished for his insolence."

The queen was obsessed with thoughts of Silence:
she could not wait to find out
whether he would agree to be her lover
or choose his own destruction.   5660
Her old mad passion was renewed.
Damn her, body and soul!
It was a sad day for Silence when she set eyes on him!
Through his efforts, he had put an end to the rebellion,
captured the four counts, and killed   5665

265

Moult de lor gent par son effors.
De le cort al roi est moult bien.
Li rois nen aime avant lui rien.
A Cestre sunt puis revenu.
Issent li viel et li kenu.   5670
Por veïr Silence et coisir.
Li Franchois puis par bon loisir
Prendent congié. Bien les soldoie
Li rois, adonc s'en vont a joie.
Moult [est] Silences dolans ore,   5675
Mais il iert plus dolans encore.
Il mar vit onques sa bonté:
Et les biens c'on en a conté
Et les bons cols del brant d'acier
Eufeme li vendera chier,   5680
Car moult [est] plainne de grant rage.
Or est il priés de son damage.
Car quant li hom plus s'aseüre
Dont sorvient sa male aventure
Bien sovent por ses grans pechiés;   5685
Et mains hom est sovent blechiés
Par les pechiés qu'il ainc ne fist.
Mais nostre sire Jhesu Crist
Le set tres bien qu'il les feroit
Quant il et liu et tans verroit,   5690
Por cho que faire li leüst
Et que il lassor en eüst;
Mais ains qu'il ait le plait basti
Le retrait Dex par son casti.
Mais Silences ainc ne forfist   5695
Ne ne fesist, se il vesquist
.m. ans, les mals que li violt faire
La dame, cui Dex doinst contraire.
Piuls Dex, et plains de pasience,
Or Te soviegne de Silence!   5700
Car il ne se set preu gaitier.
Eufeme le cuide afaitier
D'aspre dit, ains que il anuite,
Se ses espoirs ne li afruite.
Ele a ja tant a lui jenglé   5705
Qu'a une part l'a enanglé. /
"Sovient vos or," fait ele, "amis,
De la viés amor de jadis?"
"Dame," fait il a la roïne,

266

many of the enemy.
He was the darling of the court
and the favorite of the king.
When the army returned from Chester to Winchester,
the elders of the city came forth   5670
to admire Silence and honor him.
The French were given leave to depart
at their leisure. The king rewarded them generously,
and they left in high spirits.
Silence was very sorry to see them go,   5675
but he would be even sorrier before long.
His admirable behavior had done him little good:
Eufeme would make him pay dearly
for the good deeds to his credit
and the fine blows of his steel blade,   5680
for she was filled with dreadful rage.
Now Silence was threatened with destruction.
When a man is feeling most secure,
that is when misfortune strikes.
Frequently, it is a punishment for sin,   5685
but often a man is punished
for sins he never committed.
This is because our lord Jesus Christ
knows very well that a man might commit
such crimes if he saw the proper time and place   5690
and occasion to do so,
and felt the urge;
so before he even decides to sin,
God deters him by chastizing him.
But Silence had never committed,   5695
nor would he, even if he lived
to be a thousand, commit the sins that the lady,
confound her, wanted him to.
Merciful, patient God,
may you now be mindful of Silence,   5700
because he's defenseless in this situation.
Eufeme plans to dispose of him
in a most unpleasant way
if her hopes don't come to fruition before nightfall.
She has already sweet-talked him so much   5705
that she has pretty well cornered him.
"Do you remember, friend," she said,
"the love we used to share?"
"Lady," he said to the queen,

"L'amors valut une haïne. 5710
Et quant si fait sont vostre amer
Et por noient, dame, clamer,
Bien doit on vostre amor haïr,
Car vostre amer valt bien traïr,
Et tuer home, et desmenbrer." 5715
"Amis, trop vos puet ramenbrer
De males ouevres d'en arriere.
Nos somes or d'altre maniere.
Plus sage et plus atenpré somes,
Bials dols amis, qu'adonc ne fomes. 5720
Dur vos trovai et vos moi dure,
L'un contre l'altre. N'aiés cure."
"Si ai, ja nel vos celerai.
A nul jor ne vos amerai,
Cho ne cuidiés vos jamais mie, 5725
Car allors ai faite une amie.
Nient plus que vos cangiés vo cuer
Ne puis jo le mien a nul fuer.
Vos ne poés vo cuer retraire
De moi amer, ne jo tant faire 5730
Que m'amors vos soit ja donee,
Car altrui l'ai abandonee.
Ja ne l'arés, n'ensi, n'ensi,
Ensi me consalt Dex, espi!"
Dist la dame: "Creés vos cho? 5735
Creés vos cho, dites, que jo
Vos aparlasse ensi a certes?
Anchois vos doinst Dex males pertes
Que jo deüsce a vos entendre;
Ains me lairoie ardoir en cendre. 5740
Ahi!" fait ele, "quel delit
Avroit en vos!" Dont vait el lit.
Tranble d'angoissce et de pute ire.
"Ahi!" fait ele, "u est mes sire?"
"Dame," cho dist sa camberiere, 5745
"Li rois est alés en riviere."

Contre le soir li rois repaire:
Vient a la dame de pute aire
Et si a trové le malfet,
Son cors espris, et escalfet. 5750
"Biele," fait il, "com vos esta?"
"Bials sire, vos le sarés ja.

268

"that love was the same as being hated.　　　　5710
When your love is so false
that you scream for no reason,
one should obviously shun it,
for what you call love is betrayal;
it kills and dismembers a man."　　　　5715
"Friend, you seem to dwell too much
on past grievances.
We have both changed now:
we are older and wiser,
dear sweet friend, than we were before.　　　　5720
I found you harsh, as you did me.
We were adversaries then. Don't worry about that now."
"But I am worried, and I want you to know it.
I won't ever be your lover;
get that out of your head once and for all.　　　　5725
I am in love with someone else.
I can't change my feelings,
any more than you can change yours.
You can't stop loving me,
and I can never　　　　5730
give my love to you,
for I have given my heart to someone else.
You will never have it, no way, never!
so help me God! Understand?"
The lady said, "Is that what you think?　　　　5735
Do you really believe that I
would talk to you this way seriously?
I'd rather have God strike me dead
than listen to another word from you.
I'd rather be burned to a crisp!　　　　5740
But ah!" she said, "what pleasure
you could give me!" Then she retired.
She was trembling with anguish and impure rage.
"Alas!" she said, "Where is my lord?"
"Lady," her lady-in-waiting said to her,　　　　5745
"the king has gone to hunt waterfowl."

Toward evening, the king returned.
He came to this whorish lady
and found the wicked slut
aroused, inflamed with lust.　　　　5750
"Sweetheart," he said, "how are you?"
"Good Sir, you'll soon find out,

269

Mais ne vos calt preu que jo face,
Ki maint sos ciel, ne qui me hace. /
Tres donc que vos veïstes, sire,　　　　　5755
Que Silences me volt ochire
Por cho que jo nel vol amer,
Quant l'envoiastes de la mer
Ne vos calut gaires de moi.
Vos me proisiés, certes, moult poi　　　　5760
Quant vos le sofrés en vo terre.
S'il a fenie vostre guerre
Trop violt chier vendre son servisce,
Car il se painne en tolte guise
De vostre honor, sire, abasscier,　　　　5765
Qu'il ne me violt en pais lasscier."

Li rois l'entent, sin a tel ire
C'on nel vos puet conter ne dire.
Soffle de maltalent, s'a dit
A la roïne: "Prent respit!　　　　　　　5770
Mains hom porcace et quiert son honte
Por fol atrait et se desmonte
Si com j'ai fait par mon fol sens.
Or sai jo bien et voi et pens
Que j'ai tort et vos avés droit.　　　　　5775
Savés vos or en nul endroit
Coment jo vengier m'en peüïssce
Sans moi honir, gré vos seüïssce."

La dame est plaine de grant rage.
L'engien a prest en son corage,　　　　　5780
Et dist al roi: "Bien le ferés
Que vos ja blasmés n'en serés."
"Puis donc ensi c'on ne men fierne?"
"Oïl!" "Comment?" "Rois Fortigierne
Fist une tor jadis ovrer　　　　　　　5785
Mais ne pot machon recovrer
Ki peüst faire ester la tor.
Ja tant n'i atrasist d'ator,
L'uevre del jor fondi la nuit.
Sire, oiés, si ne vos anuit.　　　　　　5790
La tor ne pot nus faire estable
Fors sol Merlin, fil al diäble,
Car altre pere n'oit il onques.
Merlins ert petis enfes donques.

although you obviously don't care what happens to me
or what's going on or who my enemies are.
From the time, Sire, that you saw   5755
that Silence wanted to kill me
because I wouldn't sleep with him,
and you just sent him abroad,
you haven't cared a thing about me.
You certainly think very little of me   5760
by tolerating his presence in this land.
He may have won the war for you,
but he's asking too much for his services:
he never stops trying to reduce
the value of your honor at any cost, Sire;   5765
he doesn't give me a minute's peace."

When the king heard this, he was so furious
that there are no words to describe it.
He was panting with rage, and said
to the queen, "Enough!   5770
Many a man is crazy enough to seek
his own disgrace and undoing,
as I have been fool enough to do.
Now I can see very well, I think, I know
that I was wrong and you were right.   5775
Now, if you know of any way
I could get revenge
without getting caught, I would appreciate hearing it."

The lady was filled with violent rage.
She had a clever plan all prepared,   5780
and said to the king, "There is a way to do it
so that you will never be blamed for it."
"Can I really do it without losing face?"
"Yes!" "How?" "King Vortigern
once wanted a tower built,*   5785
but couldn't find a mason
who could make the tower stand.
Whatever was built by day
collapsed during the night.
Listen to me, Sire, if you please.   5790
No one could make the tower stand
but Merlin—son of the devil,
for he had no other father—
who was only a child at the time.

271

Il fist la tor al roi ester,   5795
Et donc n'i volt plus arester;
Mais il dist donc, ains qu'en alast
Et que la tor adevalast,
Qu'il seroit encor si salvages
Et si fuitils par ces boscages,   5800
Ja n'estroit pris, n'ensi, n'ensi,
C'est verité que jo vos di,/
Se ne fust par engien de feme.
Bials chiers sire," cho dist Eufeme,
"Il a bien averé encore.   5805
Et savés que vos ferés ore?
Dites Silence que il pregne
Merlin et prison le vos renge
Por une visiön despondre.
S'orés qu'il vos volra respondre;   5810
Et, se il Merlin ne puet prendre
Faites li, sire, bien entendre
Mar renterra en ceste tierre.
Mais il le pora .m. ans quierre
Anchois que il le prenge mie.   5815
U cho n'est mie prophezie
Icho que Merlins dist adonques,
U cis ne revenra mais onques.
Et se chose est que Merlins mente,
Qu'il pris soit, drois est qu'il s'en sente."   5820
"Biele, vos avés dit moult bien.
Se Dameldex me face rien,
Tost si ferai." Fiert sor sa main.
Et quant cho vint a l'endemain
Si a fait Silence apieler.   5825
"Amis," fait il, "nel quier celer,
Vos m'avés fait moult grant servize.
Or si vos pri par vo franchize
Et conmanc un gregnor affaire
Por moi geter d'un grant contraire."   5830
"Sire, cho sachiés vos tres bien,
Jo volentiers. N'a sos ciel rien
C'om de mon poöir faire puet."
Cho dist li rois: "Cho vos estuet.

Or escoltés que vos dirai.   5835
Tolt mon consel vos gehirai.
Jo et ma feme giziöns

272

He made the king's tower stand,   5795
and then was ready to leave.
But before he left,
before he came down from the tower,
he said that he would take to the woods
and be so wild and hard to catch   5800
that he could never be taken,
I'm telling you the truth,
except by a woman's trick.
Dear, sweet lord," said Eufeme,
"the prophecy still holds true.   5805
And you know what to do now:
tell Silence to capture Merlin
and bring him back to you as prisoner
in order to interpret a vision.
See what he has to say to that!   5810
And make it very clear to him, Sire,
that if he can't capture Merlin,
he will return to this land at his peril.
But he could search a thousand years
without ever being able to capture him.   5815
Either Merlin is no prophet,
or Silence will never come back.
And if Merlin happens to be lying,
it is only right that he be caught
and have to face the consequences."   5820
"Well said, dearest.
So help me God,
I'll do it right away." He gave her his hand on it.
And the very next day
he had Silence summoned.   5825
"Friend," he said, "I do not deny
that you have been of great service to me.
Now I am appealing to your generous nature
and asking an even greater favor of you,
to help me out of serious trouble."   5830
"Sire, you know very well
that I will do it willingly. There is nothing on earth
I wouldn't do for you."
"So be it," said the king.

"Now listen to what I tell you.   5835
I will confide in you completely.
When my wife and I were asleep

273

L'altrier *et* une viziöns
Me vint devant qui m'espoënte.
Or si vos convient metre entente   5840
Que Merlins soit pris, qui me die
La visiöns que senefie
Car il set bien qu'ele despont,"
"Coment, sire?" cil le respont.
"Coment prendroie jo celui   5845
C'ainc ne se lassça a nului
Baisier, ne prendre, ne tenir,
N'a cui nus hom puist avenir?"
Li rois respont: "Bien vos coviegne.
Mais il n'est hom qui vos retiegne/   5850
Tant com sos ciel ma tiere dure.
Se il vos falt, par aventure,
Que vos Merlin nen amenés,
Vos n'estes mie bien senés
Qui mon conmant avés desdit."   5855
Silences n'a poi[n]t de respit.
Vait a son ostel, si s'atorne,
Monte el cheval et seuls s'en torne,
Pensius et tristres, tolt plorant
Et Dameldeu sovent orant   5860
Que il son traval li aliege,
Qu'il puist prendre Merlin a/ piege
Et qu'il soit vengiés de la dame
Ki por noient l'alieve blame.
Li grant traval et li dur lit   5865
Li atenuisscent son delit.
Atenuisscent? Nenil pas!
Car il n'a nul delit, li las!
Et quant en lui n'a point de joie,
N'a delit nul, plus que je voie,   5870
Car de joie naist li delis:
Il est moult las et moult delis.
Tant ne porquant d'anchois assés
Que li demis ans fust passés
Li vient uns hom tols blans al dos,   5875
Tolt droit a l'oriere d'un bos.
Salue le moult gentement,
Or escoltés confaitement:

"[C]il qui fait son solel luisir,
Doinst que riens ne vos puist nuisir.   5880

274

the other day, I had a dream
that frightened me.
If you could manage   5840
to capture Merlin, he will tell
me what the dream meant,
for he is skilled in interpretation."
"What, Sire?" Silence replied to him.
"How could I capture the one   5845
who has never let anyone
kiss, catch, hold
or come anywhere near him?"
The king replied, "You'd better find a way.
Otherwise, no one will accept you as retainer   5850
as long as my kingdom endures on this earth.
If you should by any chance fail
to bring back Merlin,
you will find it wasn't such a good idea
to have disobeyed my command."   5855
Silence hadn't a moment's reprieve.
He went to his room, got his things together,
mounted his horse and went off alone,
pensive and sad, weeping bitterly,
and praying frequently to God   5860
to ease his burden
and help him trap Merlin
and let him be avenged on the lady
who persecuted him for no reason.
The difficult task and physical discomfort   5865
attenuated his happiness.
No, wait, that's hardly the way to put it,
for he hasn't any happiness at all, poor wretch!
Because he had no joy,
as I see it, he had no happiness,   5870
for happiness is born of joy.
He was very miserable and discouraged.
And yet, not quite
half a year later,
a man with long white hair flowing down his back   5875
came right up to him at the edge of a grove
and greeted him very courteously.
This is what he said:

"May he who makes the sun shine
protect you from all harm,   5880

275

Et vos otroit si bien ovrer
Que vos puissciés Deu recovrer."
Silences li respont: "Bials sire,
Vos dites bien, Dex le vos mire."
"Amis," fait il, "se Dex vos salt,   5885
Quels bezoins vos chace en cest galt?
Chi n'a cemins, ci n'a sentiers,
Si passe bien li ans entiers
C'om ne repaire en ceste agaise.
Jo cuit vos avés grant mesaise."   5890
"Ciertes, bials sire, cho ai mon,
Car trés le tans al viel Aimon
Ne cuit c'uns hom fust vis ne nés
Ki por nïent fust si penés."
"S'il fait a dire, dites moi   5895
Que vos querés et se jo voi
Qu'aidier vos puissce si n'ensi,
Gel ferai, por voir le vos di."
Silences respont: "Par ma vie,
Jo ne sai preu que jo vos die   5900
Ne que jo vois querant, amis.
Mais [par] haïne m'a tramis
Li rois Merlin cerkier et querre
Por moi banir fors de la terre:
'N'i rentre mais,' cho m'a rové,   5905
'Trosque Merlin aie trové.'
Et par les .ii. iols de ma tieste,
Ne sai s'il est u hom u bieste;
Ne nus ne sot ainc qu'il devint
Tres puis que Fortg[i]e[r]ne le tint   5910
Por la soie tor conpasser.
Mais on me fait nïent lasser."

Cil voit celui, si l'enorta
D'esleechier, sel conforta.
"Amis, lasscier le dementer.   5915
Jo ai veü jadis enter
Sovent sor sur estoc dolce ente,
Par tel engien et tele entente
Que li estos et li surece
Escrut trestolt puis en haltece.   5920
Alsi pora en ceste voie
Sor vostre dol naistre tels joie
Ki tolte amenrira encore

276

and may you succeed in your undertaking,
with the help of God."
Silence replied, "Good sir,
these are courteous words. May God reward you for them."
"Friend," he said, "God save you,   5885
what harsh necessity drives you forth into this wasteland?
No roads or pathways lead to it;
whole years can go by
without anyone coming to this place of desolation.
I think you are in desperate trouble."   5890
"Yes, good sir, I am indeed,
Since the time of old Aymon,
I don't think a man was ever born
who was so tormented for no reason."
"If you deem it appropriate, tell me   5895
what it is you are seeking, and if I see
that I can help you in any way,
I will certainly do so."
Silence replied, "Upon my soul,
I scarcely know what to tell you   5900
or what I'm looking for, friend,
except that the king has sent me
to seek out Merlin, because he hates me
and wants to banish me from the land.
'Do not return,' he said to me,   5905
'until you have found Merlin.'
And I swear by the two eyes I have in my head,
I don't know if he's man or beast,
and no one has any idea what has become of him
since he was commissioned by Vortigern   5910
to build his tower.
I am being made to suffer for no reason."

The old man looked closely at the youth
and told him to rejoice and be comforted.
"Friend, cease your lamentation.   5915
I have often seen
a young bud grafted onto a sterile stock
with such skill and purposefulness
that both stock and graft
soon grew and flourished.   5920
Similarly,
such joy may be born of your sorrow
that it will completely transform

277

La dolor que vos avés ore.
Amis, ne vos esmaiés rien, 5925
Car Merlin prenderés vus bien.
Jo vos dirai tolt son affaire,
Et se maniere, et son repaire.
Cho est uns hom trestols pelus
Et si est com uns ors velus; 5930
Si est isnials com cers de lande.
Herbe, rachine est sa viände.
Chi a un bos u il soloit
Venir boire, quant il voloit,
Mais .v. jors a voie n'i tint 5935
Car l'aigue i falt por quoi il vint.
Li lius est ses, n'i a que boivre.
Se vos le volés bien deçoivre
Faites cho donc que jo dirai.
Vos remanrés, et g'en irai, 5940
Et jo vos di en mon latin
Que jo revenrai le matin. /
Or ne vos soit d'atendre lait:
J'enporterai vin, miel et lait,
En trois vasscials, et car bien fressce. 5945
Tenés chi mon fural et m'esce.
Si faites demain u anuit
Un fu, que trop ne vos anuit.
Le car cuisiés, quant vos l'arés,
Al miols que vos sos ciel sarés, 5950
En rost, sans flame et sans lumiere,
Car donc jetra forçor fumiere.
Et quant Merlins le flaërra,
A la car lués repaiërra.
S'il a humanité en lui, 5955
Il i venra, si com jo cui,
Par la fumiere et par le flair
Del rost qu'il sentira en l'air.
Abandonés li soit li fus,
Et si vos traiés bien en sus. 5960
Li car sera tres bien salee,
Et quant l'ara adevalee,
Et mangie al fu d'espine,
Angoisçols iert por la saïne.
Metés le miel si priés qu'en boivie 5965
Anchois que del lait s'aparçoivie.
Le lait metrés un poi mains pres,

278

the sorrow you feel now.
Friend, don't worry about anything: 5925
you will surely capture Merlin.
I will tell you all about him,
his appearance, habits and hiding-places.
He is a man all covered with hair,
as hairy as a bear.   5930
He is as fleet as a woodland deer.
Herbs and roots are his food.
There is a grove here, where he used to
come and drink when he wanted to,
but he has not been there for five days   5935
because the water he came for was lacking:
the watering-place was all dried up.
If you want to trap him,
do as I tell you.
Stay here, and I will go,   5940
and I promise you
I will be back in the morning.
Don't be annoyed at the wait:
I'll bring back wine, milk and honey
in three containers, and good fresh meat.   5945
Keep my flint and tinder here.
That way, you can make a fire tonight or tomorrow,
so that your stay will be more pleasant.
When you get the meat, cook it
the very best way you know how.   5950
Grill it without open flames:
that way, there'll be a lot of smoke.
As soon as Merlin smells the scent and smoke,
he'll come running.
If there is any human nature left in him,   5955
he will come here, I'm certain,
attracted by the smoke and the scent
of the roasting meat in the air.
Leave the fire to him,
and withdraw to a safe distance.   5960
The meat will be very salty,
and when he has seized it from the
fire of thorn-branches and eaten it,
he will be terribly thirsty.
Place the honey close by so that he will drink it   5965
before he catches sight of the milk.
Place the milk a little farther away:

Car s'il avient qu'en boivie adiés,
Plus enflera, plus avra soi,
Et plus iert tormentés en soi.   5970
Le vin li metés tolt en sus:
Se il en boit, tolt iert confus.
S'i[l] boit del vin, tost iert sopris,
Car il n'est pas del boivre apris.
S'il dort, ainz qu'il soit esvelliés,   5975
Soiés, amis, apparelliés."
Cho dist li blans hom, puis s'en vait.
Si a porcacié entresait
Miel, lait et vin, et car avoec.
Si s'en revient tolt droit illuec   5980
U il Silence avoit lasscié,
Entre .i. bos et .i. plasscié.
Que vos diroie? Tolt li livre,
Se li a mostré a delivre
Le bos u Merlins vait et vient.   5985
Dont prent congié, sa voie tient.

Silences s'en fu a estruit.
Or l'en doinst Dex venir a fruit.
Le miel, le sait, le vin i mist,
Tolt si com li blans hom li dist./   5990
La car salee cuist en rost
Et li fumiere en va moult tost
Par tolt le bos destre et senestre.
Et Merlins qui estoit en l'estre
Flaire la car, met se a la voie,   5995
Quant Noreture le desvoie.
"Ahi!" fait Noreture. "Ahi!
Com cil sont malement trahi
Ki noriscent la gent a faire
Cho que lor nature est contraire.   6000
Quanque jo noris et labor
Me tolt Nature a un sol jor.
Tant a esté noris en bos
Bien deüst metre ariere dos
Nature d'ome, si voloit   6005
Herbes user, si com soloit."
Or est Merlins en male luite.
"Qu'as tu a faire de car cuite?"
Dist Noreture. "Est cho dangiers?
Herbes, rachines est tes mangiers."   6010

280

if he should happen to drink it next,
he will be even more bloated and thirsty,
and extremely uncomfortable.   5970
Place the wine farthest away:
if he drinks it, that will be his undoing.
If he drinks the wine, he will soon be captured,
because he is not used to drinking.
If he falls asleep, be ready to make your move   5975
before he wakes up, my friend."
That's what the white-haired man said; then he went off.
In the interval, he obtained
honey, milk, wine and meat
and came right back to where   5980
he had left Silence,
in a clearing near the grove.
What can I tell you? He gave him everything,
showed him all around
the grove that Merlin frequented,   5985
then took his leave and was on his way.

Silence went about his preparations.
May God bring them to fruition!
He placed the honey, milk and wine
exactly where the white-haired man had told him to.   5990
He roasted the salted meat,
and the smoke soon spread
right and left throughout the woods.
And Merlin, who was nearby,
smelled the meat and was on his way   5995
when Nurture forced him to turn aside.
"Alas!" said Nurture. "Alas!
How badly deceived are those
who condition people to do
what is contrary to their nature!   6000
Whatever I work for and accomplish,
Nature deprives me of in one day.
Merlin was nurtured in the woods for so long
that he certainly should have put
his human nature behind him, and should have wanted   6005
to continue eating herbs, the way he was used to."
Now Merlin felt a fierce inner conflict.
"What have you to do with cooked meat?"
asked Nurture. "Is that what you want?
Herbs and roots are what you eat."   6010

Donques se choroce Nature.
Dist: "Ahi! ahi! Noreture!
Tant anui m'as ja fait, par dis,
Tant gentil home abastardis."
"Ja non fac, voir, ains faites cho,"   6015
Dist Noreture, "plus que jo.
Ki cors a gentil, cuer malvais,
S'il honte fait, qu'en puis jo mais?
Ne jo ne il n'en poöns nient,
Mais Nature dont cho li vient.   6020
Home qui violt a honte tendre
Ne voel, car ne li puis deffendre.
Ains le norris bien a honir,
Puis qu'il n'a cure d'enbonir.
Et mains hom qui tent a honor   6025
N'apreng jo nule deshonor.
Contre un malvais par noreture,
Sont il .m. malvais par nature.
Tu as grant tort qui si m'asals
Car de Nature mut li mals   6030
Dont Adans fu primes honis.
Tes drois n'est pas al mien onis.
Tolte gens sont estrait d'un home
Et d'une feme, c'est la some.

Adans fu li premerains pere   6035
Et Eve li premiere mere.
Nuls hom ne fu devant als mie,
Ki lor apresist felonie. /
Quant par Nature de pute aire
Comencierent le mal a faire   6040
Et al boizier et al pechier
Et Deu lor segnor a boisier,
Trestolt cho fu par toi. Nature,
Et nient par moi," dist Noreture.
Cho dist Nature: "Or doi jo dire,   6045
Cho sache Dex, li nostre sire,
Tu m'oposas del premier home
Ki pecha par mangier la pome.
Dex le fist certes com le suen,
Net, sans pechié, et biel et buen.   6050
Ainc de Nature ne li vint
Que il les males voies tint.
Car se cho de Nature fus.

282

Then Nature grew angry.
She said, "Alas, alas, Nurture!
By the gods, you cause me so much trouble!
You have brought many a good man low."
"No I haven't! You're the one!"   6015
said Nurture. "You do it more than I do!
If a man has a noble body and a vile heart,
what can I do if he acts dishonorably?
Neither he nor I can do anything about it;
only Nature, who made him, can.   6020
I don't want anything to do with a man inclined to evil,
because I can't protect him from his nature.
I'd much rather raise him to be bad,
since he has no inclination to improve himself.
I don't go around teaching dishonor   6025
to those who value honor.
For every man evil because of nurture,
there are a thousand evil by nature.
You are very wrong to attack me like this,
Nature, because you are the source   6030
of that evil which claimed Adam as its first victim.
We are not equally to blame.
All human beings are descended from one man
and one woman, that's a fact.

Adam was the first father,   6035
and Eve the first mother.
There was no man in existence before them,
to teach them transgression.
It was corrupt Nature
that caused them to begin to do evil   6040
and deceive and sin.
and lie to their lord God.
All that was done by you, Nature,
and not by me!" said Nurture.
Nature replied, "Now I must say,   6045
as our lord God well knows,
you have opposed me ever since the first man
sinned by eating that apple,
God most assuredly created him in His own likeness,
pure, without sin, beautiful and good.   6050
Nothing in his nature
caused him to go bad.
For if Adam's original sin

Qu'Adans pecha ensi el fust,
Dont peüst on par cho prover   6055
Et bone provance trover
Que deüst faire el que bien.
Car en Adan n'ot onques rien
Que Dex ne creäst et fesist
Et qu'il en Adan ne mesist.   6060
Dex n'est pas tels qu'en lui lassast
Male nature quil quassast,
Ne nule rien mesavenant
Qui l'empirast, ne tant ne quant.
Car Dex ne fist ainc male choze.   6065
Noreture, car te repoze?
Quanques Adans fist de rancure,
Fu par toi, certes, Noreture.
Car li diäbles le norri
Par son malvais consel porri.   6070
Tant l'enasprist, tant l'enorta,
Que la pome le sorporta.
Quanque gens font de vilonie
Tolt naist de cele felonie.
Tant si delitent li alquant,   6075
Li honi, et li recreänt,
Qu'il font alsi com par nature,
Mais tolt lor vient de Noreture.
Dont l'enemis Adan enbut*
Quant par la pome le deçut.   6080
De cel pechié et de cel visce
Naist envie et avarissce,
Escarsetés et gloternie,
Et malvaistiés et felonie.
Jo te conmanc que tu t'en voises   6085
Et que tu mais ichi n'estoises. /
A Merlin as tu tolt falli."
Et Noreture en enpali,
Et la place li relenqui.
Et Nature, qui le venqui,   6090
Tient Merlin por maleöit fol,
Si l'a enpoint deviers le col
Et tant le coite et tant le haste
Qu'il va si tost enviers le haste
Que les ronsces et les espines   6095
Ronpent ses costés, ses escines,
Si que sor lui n'a point d'entier

284

were the fault of Nature,
that would be clear   6055
and irrefutable proof
that he was meant to do other than good.
Nothing was ever in Adam
except what God created
and placed there.   6060
It is not like God
to leave an evil nature in him to claim him
or anything negative
that would impair him in any way,
for God never did anything evil.   6065
Nurture, why don't you give up?
Whatever evil Adam did
was due to you, Nurture, without a doubt,
for the Devil fed him
evil, rotten advice.   6070
He urged him and inflamed him until
he succumbed to the apple.
Whatever evil men do
all stems from this transgression.
Some, knaves and cowards, for example,   6075
err so much
that it seems like second nature to them,
but all that is due to nurture,
with which the Enemy imbued Adam
when he deceived him with the apple.   6080
From this sin and vice
arose envy and avarice,
gluttony and stinginess,
spitefulness and evil-doing.
I command you to leave   6085
and never return.
You have completely failed with Merlin."
At this, Nurture turned pale
and relinquished her position.
And Nature, triumphant,   6090
treated Merlin like a wretched madman:
she grabbed him by the scruff of the neck
and pushed and shoved him along so fast
toward that piece of meat
that the brambles and thorns   6095
tore his back and sides.
No part of his body was left unscathed,

C'ainc n'i tint voie ne sentier;
Ne s'i tenist pas cers de lande.
Moult est golis sor le viände.   6100
A la car vient, si fait tolt suen.
"Oho!" fait il, "chi fait moult buen!"
Silences el bos se destorne,
Et Merlins al mangier s'atorne.
La car a trestolte envaïe.   6105
Se Dex fait a Silence aïe
Merlins, jo cuit, le paiera,
Anchois que il s'en parte ja.
Tant est golis de la car calde
Merlins, que trestols s'en escalde   6110
De la car qu'il prist sor le fu;
C'ainc ne demanda s'ele fu
Cuite u crue, salee u fresce,
Mais al plain puig a es i pesce.
De la car se refait moult bien.   6115
Or ne violt il fors boire rien.
Encoste garde, et del miel voit,
Met a sa boce et si en boit
Ki miols valut d'un esterlin.
Ki donc veïst enfler Merlin!   6120
Com plus en goit, plus en puet boire,
Et si ne fait fors lui deçoivre.
Ki donc veïst home a mesaise!
Merlins crieve d'anguissce enaise.
Il voit le lait, si en boit donques.   6125
Or n'ot il mais tele angoissce onques.
Ki donc veïst ventre eslargir,
Estendre, et tezir, et bargir,
Ne lairoit qu'il n'en resist tost!
Mar i manja la car en rost   6130
Et la composte al fuer d'Escot.
Jo cuit qu'il iert a chier escot.
Dont voit le vin, se s'i est trais,
Et si en boit a moult grans trais. /
S'est endormis com hom soppris.   6135
Silences salt et si l'a pris.
Ki donc dolans, se Merlins non!
"Amis," fait il, "com as tu non?
Et por quoi me maines ensi?"
"Silences ai non, si isci   6140
De mon ostel por toi tracier.

for she didn't keep to road or path;
a woodland deer could not have stood the pace.
He was greedy for the meat. 6100
He came to the roast and seized the whole thing.
"Oh!" he said. "This looks good!"
Silence hid in the woods,
and Merlin got ready to eat.
He tore into the meat at once. 6105
If God is on Silence's side,
Merlin will pay dearly for it
before he leaves.
Merlin was so greedy for the hot meat
he had seized from the fire 6110
that he burned himself.
He didn't stop to ask whether it was
raw or cooked, fresh or salted —
he dove into it eagerly with his bare hands.
He made an excellent meal of that meat. 6115
Now all he wanted was something to drink.
He looked around and saw the honey,
put the jar to his lips, and drank it,
more than a pound sterling's worth.
Then you should have seen Merlin swell up! 6120
The more he swallowed, the thirstier he got —
all he accomplished was his own undoing.
You never saw a man in greater discomfort;
Merlin was nearly dying in agony.
He saw the milk and drank it then. 6125
He had never been in such pain!
If you ever saw how his belly swelled up,
expanded, inflated and dilated,
you would burst out laughing!
It was bad luck for him that he ate the roasted meat 6130
and the mixture worth a Scottish pound.
I think he'll pay dearly for it!
Then he saw the wine and went for it,
and drank it in giant gulps
and fell into a drunken stupor. 6135
Silence jumped out and seized him.
Now Merlin was sorry!
"Friend," he said, "what is your name?
And why are you doing this to me?"
"I am called Silence, and I left home 6140
in order to track you down.

287

Ta mort te volrai porcacier."
"Ma mort?" dist Merlins. "Tu por quoi?"
"Mes ancestres fu mors par toi,
Gorlains, li dus de Cornuälle.   6145
Tu en morras, comment qu'il alle.
Merlin, assés le me tuas
Quant Uterpandragon muas
En le forme al duc mon a[n]cestre
Et toi fesis altretel estre   6150
Com fu ses senescals avoec.
Uter en menas droit illuec
U il o la feme al duc giut,
Quant a Artu le preu conciut."
Dist Merlins: "Cho fu graindres prels,   6155
Qu'Artus nasqui, qui fu si preus
Qu'il fust damages del duc mie."
Silences dant Merlin enguie.
Merlins ne se fait gaires morne,
Qu'il set ja bien u li viers torne.   6160

Silences dant Merlin enmainne.
A lui mener rent moult grant painne,
Car il le prist moult loig de la
Li rois Ebayns sejornet a.
Se Deu plaist, qui ainc ne menti,   6165
Ki por nos p[e]chiés consenti
Longin son costé a percier,
Or pora l'on bien entiercier
Et conoistre sa felonie.
Se Merlins est tels qu'il le die   6170
Or sera la cose asomee.
Al roi en vient la renomee
Qu'or vient Silences et Merlins.
Por .c. .m. livres d'esterlins
Ne volsist pas li rois adonques   6175
Que Silences repairast onques.
Or est il viers Merlin espris
Por cho qu'il dist ja n'estroit pris,
Se ne fust par engien de feme.
Et moult en est dolante Eufeme.   6180

Or a Merlins moult mal tissu.
Plus de .vii. .c. en sunt issu/
Por Merlin garder a mervelle.

288

I sought your death."
"My death?" said Merlin. "Whatever for?"
"You killed my ancestor,
Gorlain, duke of Cornwall.*   6145
You shall die for it, whatever happens.
Merlin, you as good as killed him
when you transformed Uther Pendragon
into the likeness of my ancestor, the duke,
and you yourself likewise pretended   6150
to be his seneschal and accompanied him.
You led Uther right to the spot
where he lay with the duke's wife,
and she conceived the noble Arthur."
Merlin said, "that was for a greater good: 6155
Arthur was born of it; one as worthy as he
was no disgrace to the duke."
Silence forced Lord Merlin to get underway.
Merlin isn't exactly worried,
for he knows how things will turn out.   6160

Silence brought Lord Merlin back with him.
It wasn't at all easy,
because he had captured him very far
from where King Evan was staying.
If it please God, who has never failed us,   6165
who suffered Longinus to pierce
his side for our sins,
the king's wrongdoing
will soon be revealed and made known.
If Merlin is all he says he is,   6170
the matter will soon be cleared up.
The king heard the news
that Silence and Merlin were coming.
Not for a hundred thousand pounds sterling
would the king ever have wanted   6175
Silence to come back.
And now he was furious with Merlin
because he had said he would never be taken
except by a woman's trick.
Eufeme was also very upset.   6180

Now Merlin was really in a fix.
More than seven hundred people turned out
to gaze in wonder at him.

Trestols li païs s'en esvelle.
Il tienent or Merlin por sot,
Mais il decoverra le pot,
Si fera tels i a maris.
En son la ville en .i. lairis
L'encontrent et Silence avoec
Ki Merlin mainne droit illuec.
Voit Merlins venir un vilain:
Uns nués sollers porte en sa main
Bien ramendés de cuir de tacre.
Merlins le voit de deseur l'acre,
Si en commenche fort a rire
Mais ne volt onques un mot dire
Por quele oquoison il a ris.
Un roi i ot qu'ot a non Ris.
Cil ne li pot ainc tant proier
Si tangoner, ne si broier,
Que l'oquoisons li fist gehir. . .
Dont vient devant une abeÿe
Et voit un mezel tarteler
Et por Deu l'almosne apieler.
Dont rit Merlins, por poi ne derve,
Et quant il les povres enterve
Et cil prient que il lor die
L'oquoison, mais il nel violt mie,
Et cil muerent enaises d'ire.
Illueques ot un cimentire
Joste l'eglize; a un des cors
Voit Merlins enfoïr un cors,
Entre .ii. pieres ensierer.
Uns priestres cante a l'entierer
Et uns prodom i crie et pleure.
Et Merlins en rist en es l'eure.
Assés i a ki li enquiert
Por quoi il rit, n'a quoi affiert,
Mais ne degne un mot respondre,
Son ris esclairier, ne despondre.
Se li tornent a grant desroi.
Dont le mainnent devant le roi,
Se li ont dit de ses ris donques,
Mais il ne volt mot soner onques.

Li rois par maltalent respont:
"S'il orendroit ne le despont,

6185

6190

6195

6200

6205

6210

6215

6220

6225

The whole country was excited.
They thought that Merlin was a fool,   6185
but he was about to lift the lid off the pot,
and make things unpleasant for certain people.
On a hillside above the city,
they met Merlin and Silence,
who was leading him right to them.   6190
Merlin saw a peasant approach,
carrying a new pair of shoes,
nicely mended with brand-new leather.
Merlin saw him in the field below
and began to laugh heartily,   6195
but wouldn't say a word
about why he was laughing.*
A king named Ris was there.
He couldn't force Merlin
by asking or needling or thrashing him   6200
to confess the reason.
Then they came to an abbey
and saw a leper shaking his rattle
and begging for alms in the name of God.
Merlin laughed so hard at this he almost had a fit.   6205
And when he was amusing himself at the expense of the poor
and they asked him to tell them
the reason why, he refused to say:
they almost died of rage, they were so mad.
In that same place, there was a cemetery.   6210
In a corner, next to the church,
Merlin saw a body being buried,
enclosed between two stones.
A priest was chanting the burial service
and a man was weeping and crying there.   6215
Again, Merlin burst out laughing at this.
Plenty of people asked him
why he was laughing and what was going on,
but he didn't deign to answer a word
to enlighten them or explain his laughter.   6220
This made them very angry,
and they took him before the king
and told him about Merlin's laughter,
but he still refused to utter a word.

Vexed at this, the king replied,   6225
"If he doesn't come up with an explanation right here and now,

Gel ferai livrer a martyre."
Et Merlins en comence a rire,
Desor le roi, qu'il n'en a cure.
Ains li promet male aventure:/   6230
Et nonporquant forment se duelt
Que il respondre ne li vuelt.
Dire ne conter ne vos puis
Com rist de soi meësme puis.
Ainc por blecier, ne por quasscier,   6235
Ne por le roi ne volt lasscier,
Et li rois derve enaises d'ire,
Que Merlins ne li volt mot dire.
Dont prent Silence a regarder
Et s'on le deüst dont larder   6240
Ne se tenist il pas de ris,
Mais ne dist mot, tant lor fist pis.
Cil ont veü le roi irier.
Prendent Merlin a enpirier.
L'uns le sache, l'altres le boute.   6245
Or est li cor sor Merlin tolte.
L'uns l'enpaint, l'altres le tangone.
O la roïne ert une none.
Cele va Merlin deruant:
"Oho!" fait ele, "quel truant!   6250
Confaite prophesie il dist!"
Merlins l'esgarde, si en rist.
Tels voloirs de parler li vient
Qu'il a moult grant painne se tient.
Demandent li, mais c'est en vain,   6255
Por quoi [il] rist de la nonain.
"Ahi!" dist donques la roïne,
"Confait vassal! com il devine!
Et confaite bachelerie!
Ahi! et quel chevalerie   6260
D'amener a cort tel devin!
Cil doit boivre moult bien de vin!
Ki tel vassal a amené
Honiement a assené."

Silences respont: "Tort avez,   6265
Dame roïne, et ne savez
Que li rois le fist amener
Et si m'en a moult fait pener.
Vos m'en rendés tel gueredon

292

I will have him executed."
And Merlin began to laugh at this,
right in front of the king, to show he didn't care.
The king continued to threaten him,   6230
and was nonetheless very upset
that he wouldn't answer him.
I can't begin to tell you how hard
Merlin laughed at himself then.
Neither wounds nor blows   6235
nor the presence of the king could make him stop,
and the king was nearly beside himself with rage,
because Merlin wouldn't tell him a thing.
Then he began to look at Silence,
and even if they had burned him alive,   6240
he couldn't have stopped laughing,
but he didn't say a word, no matter how upset they were.
Those who had witnessed the king's fury
now began to attack Merlin.
One shook him, another knocked him down;   6245
then they all jumped on Merlin.
One beat him, another jabbed him.
There was a nun in the queen's entourage
who began to gibe at Merlin:
"Oho!" she said, "what a rascal,   6250
coming out with false prophecies like that!"
Merlin looked at her and laughed.
He wanted to speak out so badly
that he could scarcely restrain himself.
They asked him in vain   6255
why he laughed at the nun.
"Oh my!" said the queen then,
"what a vassal! what a phony!
and what a hero we have here!
My, what an act of chivalry   6260
to bring such a great magician to court!
What an old wine-bibber!
And whoever brings such a vassal to court
has succeeded in covering himself with disgrace."

Silence replied, "You are wrong,   6265
my lady queen. Are you perhaps unaware
that the king ordered him brought here
and that this has caused me tremendous hardship?
And now you reward me thus,

293

U il nen a se tolt mal non. 6270
Mais Dameldex qui tolt cria
Voit bien et set quanque il i a."
Dont respondi la dame fole:
"Silences, trop avés parole!
Vos le devriez avoir plus brieve." 6275
Merlins en rit, por poi ne crieve
Sor la roïne et ne dist mot;
Et il le tienent tuit por sot. /
Ne sevent pas dont li ris naist.
Com plus l'enquierent plus se taist. 6280
Tant li delite li taisirs
Que parlers li est nonplaisirs.
Escoltés dont. Il prist a rire,
Atant a parler, et a dire
Que grief li est a comencier. 6285
Li rois n'a cure de tencier,
N'onques ne pot tençon amer.
Or violt il Merlin afamer,
S'il le peüst par cho destraindre.
En le cartre le fait empaindre 6290
Et sel fait .iii. jor geüner.
Et al quart jor fait aüner
Et ses barons et ses princiers
Qu'il plus ama et plus tint ciers.
Verront quel fin Merlins fera: 6295
U ochis, u pendus sera.
Se il ne dist sa prophesie,
N'en portera, cho dist, la vie.

[M]erlins est menés en la place.
Jo ne cuit pas que tant se hace 6300
Qu'il ne parolt ains c'on le tue.
Li rois tient une espee nue.
Dist li: "U tu diras, dant fol,
U jo te trencerai le col."

Or voit bien Merlins qu'il morra 6305
S'il ne parole, et qu'il pora
Salver sa vie par le dire.
Al roi a dit: "Or oiés, sire,
Jo ne vos puis pas par taisir
Servir a gré, ne rien plasir. 6310
Or ne voel jo mal gré avoir.

294

when the exploit was hardly that unworthy.   6270
But the Lord God who created all things
sees and knows the truth."
To this, the lady harlot replied,
"Silence, you talk too much.
You had better keep your mouth shut."   6275
Merlin laughed so hard at the queen
he nearly died, but he didn't say a word,
and they all thought he was a fool.
They didn't know the cause of his laughter.
The more they questioned him, the more silent he was.   6280
He took such great delight in silence
that speech could offer him no pleasure.
Listen to what happened then: he began to laugh
and then to speak and then to say
that it was too hard for him to begin.   6285
The king didn't feel like arguing;
he never had much use for disputes.
He preferred to starve Merlin,
to see if he could force him to talk by this means.
He had him thrown into prison   6290
and starved for three days.
And on the fourth day, he called together
the most trusted and valued
lords and counsellors of the realm.
They would decide Merlin's fate: 6295
whether he would be beheaded or hanged.
If he did not reveal the truth,
he would not escape with his life, the king said.

Merlin was brought to the place of judgment.
I don't think he is so self-destructive   6300
that he won't talk to save his own life.
The king held a naked sword.
He said to him, "Either you shall speak, Sir Fool,
or I will cut your head off."

Then Merlin saw he would surely die   6305
if he didn't speak, and that he could
save his life by talking.
He said to the king, "Now listen, Sire.
I cannot please you and do your will
by remaining silent,   6310
but I have no wish to incur your wrath

295

Se jo vos di de mo[n] savoir."
"Non avrés vos, amis, par foi!"
"Jo ris, bials sire, oiés por quoi.   6315
Quant ens en la cité entrai,
Un fol vilain i encontrai
Si com il venoit del marchié.
Uns nués sollers ot encargié:
Sis ot fais ramender tols nués   6320
Mais onques ne li orent wés.
De rire oi jo bone oquoison,
Car ains qu'il venist en maison/
Morut li vilains, c'est la voire."
Li rois l'a fait enquerre en oire,   6325
Si l'a tolt altressi trové.
Et donques a Merlin rové
Que li vertés li soit jehie
Por que il rist devant l'abeÿe.
"Sire, por Deu qui tolt conselle,   6330
Jo ris, mais ne fu pas mervelle,
Des povres gens qu'illuec estoient
Et por Deu l'almosne apieloient.
Il demandoient la le mains,
Et li plus ert devant lor mains.   6335
Desos lor piés ot un tresor
Moult mervellols d'argent et d'or,
A .ii. piés et demi sos terre."
Et li rois fait le tresor querre.
Cil ki le quist moult bien le trueve,   6340
Si en fait cho que li rois rueve.

"Merlin, Merlin, li rois a dit,
Or t'ai jo plus chier un petit,
Por cho que m'as dit verité.
Mais, se Dex me gart m'ireté,   6345
Jo te rehac moult d'altre part
Car tu desis que ja par art
N'estroies pris, n'estoit par feme.
Par cele foi que doi Eufeme,
Sor cuer te rai por ta mençoigne,   6350
Car tes dis torne ichi a songe."
Merlins respont: "N'aiés paör,
Qu'al wespre loe on le biel jor.
N'ai soing encore de fuïr."
"Merlin, tu veïs enfoïr

296

by telling what I know."
"You won't, my friend, I swear it!"
"Then I will tell you why I laughed, Sire.
As I was about to enter the city,   6315
I came across a foolish peasant
who was coming from the marketplace.
He was carrying a pair of new shoes:
he had had them made brand-new,
but he would never have any use for them.   6320
I had good reason to laugh,
because the peasant died
before he reached home. And that's the truth."
The king quickly sent messengers to look into the matter,
and found it was just as Merlin had said.   6325
And then he asked Merlin
to tell him the truth about
why he had laughed at the abbey.
"Sire, by God who gives us good counsel,
it's no wonder I laughed   6330
at the paupers who were standing there
begging for alms in the name of God.
They were asking for so little,
when there was so much within their grasp.
Under their feet was a treasure,   6335
huge quantities of gold and silver,
just two and a half feet beneath the surface."
The king sent someone to search for the treasure;
the one who looked for it found it with ease,
and did with it what the king commanded.   6340

"Merlin, Merlin," said the king,
"now I like you a little better,
because you are telling the truth.
But, may God preserve my inheritance,
I still dislike you, on the other hand,   6345
because you said you would never be tricked
or captured, except by a woman.
By the loyalty I owe Eufeme,
I am still disturbed by your lying,
for your prophecy has turned out to be false."   6350
Merlin replied, "Don't fret.
It's always darkest before dawn.
I'm not ready to run away yet."
"Merlin," said the king,

L'altrier," cho dist li rois, "un cors   6355
El chimentire a l'un des cors.
Por quoi en presis tu a rire?"
Cho dist Merlins: "Ja l'orés, sire.
Uns priestres cantoit por le mort,
Et uns prodom i ploroit fort.   6360
Li prodom en deüst liés estre
Car li enfes estoit le priestre,
Ki en deüst par droit plorer
Et li prodom Deu aörer
De cui feme li enfes fu.   6365
Por verité le vos desnu.
[Por verité le vos desneu]
Li prodom n'i fist fier ne cleu
Mais li priestres l'aida a faire,
Et Dameldex li doinst contraire."   6370
"Merlin," dist la roïne Eufeme,
"Com tu ses mesdire de feme!
Quels joies est de ton mesdire?
Ja nel deüst sofrir mes sire!
Ains te deüst faire tuer,   6375
U en .i. malvais liu jeter."

Que que la dame die u face,
Merlins n'a soig de sa manace.
El le tient or por menteör,
Por medisant, por trecheör,   6380
Mais il le fera veritable
Et la dame fera menchable
Ki dist qu'il ne set deviner.
Or primes vient a merliner:
Jo croi bien qu'il devinera   6385
Huimais, et qu'il merlinera
Par tel engien et tele entente
Que la roïne en iert dolente.
Si est ele orendroit moult fort,
Manace Merlin de la mort.   6390

"Tort avés, dame," dist li rois.
"Si uns Escos u uns Irois
Me disist folie u savoir,
Se deüst il bien pais avoir
Chi devant moi. Ne sui jo sire?   6395
Moi lasciés convenir et dire,

"the other day you saw a body   6355
being buried in a corner of the cemetery.
Why did you burst out laughing at this?"
Merlin said, "I'll tell you, Sire.
A priest was chanting for the dead
and a man was weeping bitterly there.   6360
But the man should have been happy,
because the child was the priest's,
who should by all rights have been weeping,
while the man whose wife had the child
ought to have been thanking God.   6365
I will solve the mystery for you:
[line repeated]
it wasn't the man who hammered the nail home:
the priest helped him do it,
may God punish him."   6370
"Merlin," said Queen Eufeme,
"you certainly know how to speak ill of women.
What good will come of your slander?
My lord shouldn't tolerate it.
We should have you killed,   6375
or thrown into some foul place."

Whatever the lady said or did,
Merlin was unmoved by her threats.
She thought he was a liar,
slanderer and trickster,   6380
but he would reveal the truth
and prove the lady a liar
for saying he was a false prophet.
Now he will finally be himself.
I am certain that he will reveal the truth   6385
and show that he is Merlin
with such skill and such results
that the queen will regret it.
But right now she was feeling strong enough
to threaten Merlin with death.   6390

"You are wrong, lady," the king said.
"If a Scotsman or Irishman
were to tell me something, wise or foolish,
he would be entitled
to have peace in my presence. Am I not king?   6395
You will kndly allow me to speak and act

299

Faire mon bon et mon plasir.
Sens de feme gist en taisir.
Si m'aït Dex, si com jo pens,
Uns muials puet conter lor sens.   6400
Car femes n'ont sens que mais un,
C'est taisirs. Toltes l'ont commun,
Se n'est par aventure alcune,
Mais entre .m. nen a pas une
Ki gregnor los n'eüst de taire   6405
Que de parler. Lasciés me faire,
Et vos alés en vostre cambre."
Merlins, ki siet desos le lanbre,
Ki voit et set trestolte l'uevre,
Destemparra ancui tel suevre,   6410
Ki sera tels i a moult sure
Anchois que viegne nuis obscure.

Li rois dist: "Merlin, par ta foi,
Di por quoi resis tu de moi,
De toi, et de Silence puis.   6415
Moult bielement te proi et ruis
Que vertés ne me seit celee:
Et puis de la nonain velee,/
Et savoir voel la verté fine
Por quoi resis de la roïne."   6420
Merlins respont: "Moult volentiers,
Si faites pais endementiers.
Sire, jo ris, bien le savés
Trestolt si con vos dit avés.
N'en puis mais se jo ris de vos,   6425
Car, par la foi que jo doi vos,
N'a home el mont qui ne resist
Por quoi que ses cuers li sesist
Si com li miens cuers siet, bials sire,
Et s'il seüst altretant dire   6430
Con vos orés ains que j'en voise,
Cui qu'il soit biel, ne cui en poise."

Quant cho entendi la roïne
Forment se diolt, la teste encline;
Sue, sospire moult a trait,   6435
Moult crient qu'ele ait tel baing atrait
Qu'ele n'est mie par tolt vraie.
Et li none forment s'esmaie.

300

according to my pleasure.
A woman's role is to keep silent.
So help me God, I think
a mute can tell what women are good for,   6400
for they're only good for one thing,
and that is to keep silent. They are all alike,
and it's hardly a coincidence
that there isn't one in a thousand
who wouldn't earn more praise by keeping silent   6405
than by speaking. Let me handle this.
You go to your room."
Seated in the carved and gilded hall,
Merlin, who sees and knows everything,
is preparing a sauce so spicy   6410
that it will give several people indigestion
before nightfall.

The king said, "Merlin, swear
that you will tell me why you laughed at me,
at yourself, and then at Silence.   6415
I beseech you in all earnest
not to hide the truth from me.
Tell me also about the veiled nun,
and I want to know the real reason
you laughed at the queen.   6420
Merlin answered, "I'll tell you gladly,
if you'll keep quiet during the telling.
Sire, it is true that I laughed
just as you have said.
I couldn't help laughing at you, Sire,   6425
because, by the good faith I have pledged you,
there's not a man in the world who wouldn't have laughed
if his heart had been so full of laughter
as mine was, Sire,
and if he could tell you as much   6430
as I will tell you before I leave,
regardless of how some people may feel about it."

When the queen heard this,
she was profoundly disturbed. She lowered her gaze,
sighed profoundly, and broke out in a sweat.   6435
She was so afraid of being in hot water
that she was no longer completely sure of herself.
And the nun was exceedingly dismayed.

Ne vos puis dire de Silence.
Con le remort sa consiënce. 6440
"Dolans," fait il, "por que amenai
Merlin? com mar i assenai!
Jo ai fait al fuer de serjant
Ki quiert meïsmes le verjant
Dont on le destraint et castie, 6445
C'or ai jo tel coze bastie
Dont g'iere tols desiretez.
Cho est la fine veritez!
Voirs est li respis al vilain:
Mains hom atrait a une main 6450
Par folie desor lui plus
Qu'il puist a .ii. boter en sus.
Si ai jo fait qui Merlin pris.
Par lui perdrai jo tolt mon pris,
Car il fera descoverture 6455
De quanque ai fait contre nature
Jo cuidai Merlin engignier,
Si m'ai engignié. Forlignier
Cuidai a tols jors us de feme.
Cho m'a tolt porchacié Eufeme. 6460
Mais Demeldex, qui tols jors velle
Sor les bons homes qu'i conselle,
Me consalt si con moi estuet
Et com Il set et doit et puet;
Et se la dame a recovré 6465
Selonc qu'ele a tols jors ovré, /
Ja certes ne m'en pesera.
Et jo sai bien que cho sera:
Novielement n'avra garant,
Merlins fait tres bien l'aparant." 6470

Merlins s'estost, dist: "Oiés, sire,
Dirai por quoi jo pris a rire
Primes de vos et puis de moi,
Puis de Silence que chi voi,
De la nonain qui la se cline, 6475
Et en apriés de la roïne.
De nos .v. ris, cho sachiés vos,
Car il n'i a celui de nos
Ki nen ait l'un l'altre escarni.
Mais or vos ai jo, rois, garni. 6480

302

As for Silence, I cannot tell you
how much his secret thoughts and desires were tormenting
    him.   6440
"What a fool I was," he said, "why did I bring
Merlin here? What a catastrophe!
I've acted like the sergeant
who goes himself to fetch the club
with which he will be beaten,   6445
for now I have fixed things
so that I will be disinherited.
There's no getting around it.
There is much truth to the old peasant proverb:*
'By their own folly, many bring   6450
more trouble upon themselves with one hand
than they can push away with two.'
That's what I've done by capturing Merlin.
Because of him, I will lose everything,
for he will reveal   6455
what I have done that is contrary to nature.
I thought I was tricking Merlin,
but I tricked myself. I thought
to abandon woman's ways forever,
but Eufeme has ruined any chance of that.   6460
But may God, the guardian
and counsel of upright men,
counsel me according to my needs,
according to his wisdom, as he has pledged to, as only he can,
and if the lady receives her just deserts,   6465
in keeping with her behavior,
I will certainly not be sorry.
And I know this will happen:
there'll soon be confirmation of it,
for Merlin is clearly doing very well."   6470

Merlin cleared his throat and said, "Listen, Sire,
I will tell you why I burst out laughing,
first at you, then at myself,
then at Silence here,
at the downcast nun over there,   6475
and finally at the queen.
I want you to understand that I laughed at the five of us
because there is not one of us
who has not tricked one of the others.
But now I give you fair warning, King: 6480

303

Li escars nen est pas honis,
Car l'uns de nos en est honis.
Li doi de nos, cho sachiés vos,
Ont escarnis les .ii. de nos,
Sos fainte vesteüre et vaine." 6485
Li sale est de chevaliers plaine:
Oiant trestols Merlins devine
Alques priés de la verté fine,
Mais la parole est moult obscure
Car dite est par coverture. 6490
Ne mais li .iiii. qui i sont
Sevent bien priés qu'ele despont;
Merlins, Silences et la none
Sevent que la parole sone.
Si set la roïne altressi, 6495
Ele le set tres bien de fi.

Cil de le cort s'esmaient fort,
Li uns a droit, l'altres a tort.
Cascuns s'esmaie moult de s'uevre:
Criement que Merlins ne descuevre. 6500
Ne mais icil sont esmaiable
Ki sevent bien qu'il sont copable.
Or conmence mals a monter.
Ne vos puis dire ne conter
Com sont en male sospechon. 6505
Merlins a liute tel lechon
Que s'il le recomence a lire,
A recorder, et a redire,
Et a descovrir tolt le blasme,
Honie en iert al mains la dame. 6510
Et li none en sera honie
Qu'ele n'est pas par tolt onie
As altres nonains par le mont.
Atant li rois Merlin semont/
Que parolt plus apertement. 6515
"Merlin, jo voel savoir coment
L'uns de nos puet l'altre escarnir.
Merlin, tu m'en dois bien garnir,
Et si me fai descoverture
Puis de le fainte vesteüre. 6520
Quel sont li doi qui gabé sont
Et li doi qui gabés les ont?
Quels est li honis, par ta foi?

the share in the deception is not equal for all parties
   concerned,
for one of us is dishonored by it.
Two of us, I'll have you know,
have tricked two of us
by wearing borrowed finery."   6485
The hall was filled with knights,
all listening to Merlin
almost revealing the complete truth,
but obscuring his meaning
by means of veiled statements.   6490
Only the four in question
knew very well what was being said:
Merlin, Silence and the nun
knew what his words meant.
The queen knew as well—   6495
she knew very well indeed.
The courtiers were greatly alarmed,
some with good reason, others needlessly.
Each was worried about his own deeds;
all feared that Merlin would reveal everything.   6500
Those who knew they were guilty
were not more frightened than the others.
The atmosphere became increasingly tense.
I cannot find words to tell you
what dreadful suspicions were aroused.   6505
Merlin has begun to give such a lecture
that if he picks up where he left off
and continues to confirm, affirm
and uncover all the wrongdoings,
the lady will be disgraced at the very least.   6510
So will the nun,
for she is not exactly like
the rest of the nuns in the world.
Then the king admonished Merlin
to speak more plainly.   6515
"Merlin, I want to know how
we have deceived one another.
Merlin, you must let me know what is happening.
Tell me the truth
about the borrowed finery: 6520
which two have been tricked,
and which two are the tricksters?
You swore to tell the truth—who is dishonored?

Merlin, jo voel savoir par toi."
"Sire rois, c'est la verté fine   6525
Que honi vos a la roïne.
Si sarés bien coment, ains none.
Cil doi, Silence et la none,
Sont li doi qui gabés nos ont,
Et nos li doi qui gabé sunt.   6530
Rois, cele none tient Eufeme.
Escarnist vos ses dras de feme.
Rois, or vos ai jo bien garni.
Silences ra moi escarni
En wallés dras, c'est vertés fine,   6535
Si est desos les dras meschine.
La vesteüre, ele est de malle.
La nonain, qui n'a soig de halle,
Bize, *ni* ven*t*, ki point et giele.
A vesteüre de femiele.   6540
Silences qui moult set et valt,
Bials sire rois, se Dex me salt,
Ne sai home qui tant soit fors
Ki le venquist par son effors.
Et une feme, tendre cose,   6545
Vos poet honir et set et ose.
Et c'une feme me ra pris,
Quele mervelle est se j'en ris,
Qu'ansdeus nos ont ensi deçut,
Qu'eles nos ont tel plait esmut   6550
Comme .xx. .m. ne porent faire.
Sire, jo ris de cest affaire."

Or est plus angoissçols li rois
Que nus Escos ne nus Englois.
Enaises que mors fust son vuel: 6555
Onques encor n'ot mais tel duel.
Trestolt l'ont oï li baron,
C'ainc n'i ot dit mot a laron.
Ne lor ert rien fors por le roi,
Car la dame ert de grant desroi,   6560
Et plaine de grant vilonie
Et d'orguel et de felonie./
Moult ot cruels tols jors esté
Et soufraitolse d'onesté.
Poi prometoit et mains donoit   6565
Et moult vilment s'abandonoit.

306

Merlin, I want you to tell me!"
"My lord king, the truth is   6525
that the queen has dishonored you.
You shall know how before noon.
These two, Silence and the nun,
are the deceivers;
you and I are the deceived.   6530
King, this nun is Eufeme's lover;
he is deceiving you in woman's dress.
Now I've spoken plainly enough, King.
Silence, on the other hand, tricked me
by dressing like a young man: in truth,   6535
he is a girl beneath his clothes.
Only the clothing is masculine.
The nun, who has no need to fear the scorching sun
or the north wind's blast that stings and freezes,
is a woman in clothing only.   6540
Silence is wise and valiant,
good Sir King, so help me God,
I don't know any man, however strong,
who could have conquered him in combat.
A woman, a tender little thing,   6545
knows she can dishonor you and does.
And it was a woman who captured me.
Is it any wonder I'm laughing,
when they have deceived both of us like this,
when they have set a snare for us   6550
such as twenty thousand men couldn't?
Sire, I think this is really funny."

Now the king was much more upset
than anyone else in his kingdom, Scot or Englishman.
He almost wished for death: 6555
he had never felt such anguish.
His men had heard everything
and could not even whisper a word.
They cared only for the king's honor:
the lady's wickedness knew no bounds;   6560
she was malicious,
arrogant and perfidious.
She had always been cruel
and dishonest.
She had promised little and given less;   6565
she was vile and depraved.

307

Sor cuer l'avoit la cors trestol[t]e.
Li rois en est encor en dolte.
Fait Merlin fermement tenir
Et dont a fait avant venir   6570
La nonain, sil fait despollier,. . .
Et Silence despollier roeve.
Tost si com Merlins dist les trueve.
Tolt issi l'a trové par tolt.
En la sale ot moult grant escolt: 6575
Nus n'i parla se li rois non,
U s'il nel conmanda par non.
Li rois a dit oiant trestols:
"Silence, moult as esté prols,
Bials chevaliers, vallans et buens;   6580
Mellor n'engendra rois ne cuens.

[O]r te conjur jo par le foi
Que tu dois Dameldeu et moi,
Por quoi tu t'as si contenu
Et coment cho est avenu?   6585
Nos veöns bien que tu iés feme.
Di por quoi se clama Eufeme
Que tu le voisis efforcier.
Son wel te fesist escorcier."
"Sire, se Dex bien me consente   6590
Il n'est pas drois que jo vos mente.
Mes pere fist de moi son buen. . .
Et quant jo ving a tel aäge
Que gent comencent estre sage
Mes pere me fist asavoir   6595
Que jo ja ne poroie avoir,
Sire, ireté en vostre tierre.
Et por mon iretage quierre
Me rova vivre al fuer de malle,
Fendre mes dras, aler al halle,   6600
Et jo nel vol pas contredire.
A .xv. ans vig a cort, bials sire.
Si m'enama lués la roïne.
Ne li vol dire men covine
Ne m'encusast par aventure   6605
Et mostrast avant *ma* nature. /
Ele cuida que jel lassasce
Por orguel, qu'amer nel degnasce.
Venistes en la cambre o nos:

308

The courtiers had no trouble believing the whole thing.
The king still had his doubts.
He had Merlin seized and held firmly,
and then had the nun   6570
brought forward and disrobed,
and he ordered Silence to be undressed.
It was just as Merlin had said:
he found everything in its proper place.
There was complete silence in the hall: 6575
no one would speak except the king himself,
or whomever he commanded by name.
The king said so that everyone could hear,
"Silence, you have been a very valiant,
courageous and worthy knight;   6580
neither count nor king ever fathered better.

Now I conjure you, by the faith
you owe God and myself, to tell
why you have conducted yourself in this manner
and how it came about.   6585
We can see for ourselves that you are a woman.
Tell me why Eufeme claimed
that you were trying to rape her.
Her ill-will might have cost you dear."
"Sire, if God will allow it,   6590
it is only right that I should tell you the truth.
My father did with me as he saw fit. . .
and when I reached
the age of understanding,
my father explained to me   6595
that I could never inherit
in your land, Sire.
And in order to claim my inheritance,
he asked me to live like a man,
to wear men's dress and not protect my complexion.   6600
I didn't want to go against him.
When I was fifteeen and came to live at court, Sire,
the queen immediately fell in love with me.
I didn't want to reveal my secret to her,
for I feared she might denounce me   6605
and reveal my true nature.
She thought I was resisting her
out of arrogance, that I scorned to love her.
And so, when you came into the chamber where we were,

309

Ele se clama lués a vos   6610
Que jo le vol a force amer.
Vos m'envoiastes dela mer.
Cuidastes le, par verité.
Jo me celai por m'ireté;
Ne vos vol pas le verté dire.   6615
Or savés comment il est, sire.
D'altre part ne vos vol irer,
La dame viers vos empirer.
Puis reving jo en vostre tierre,
S'aidai a finer vostre guierre,   6620
Et la dame me rasali.
N'euc cure de parler a li:
Por cho me volt, sire, avillier
Et fors del païs essillier.
La vertés nel puet consentir   6625
Que jo vos puissce rien mentir,
Ne jo n'ai soig mais de taisir.
Faites de moi vostre plaisir."

Li rois a dit .iii. mos roials:
"Silence, moult estes loials.   6630
Miols valt certes ta loialtés
Que ne face ma roialtés.
Il n'est si preciose gemme,
Ne tels tresors com bone feme.
Nus hom ne poroit esproisier   6635
Feme qui n'a soig de boisier.
Silences, ses qu'as recovré
Por cho que tu as si ovré?
Amer te voel *et* manaidier."*
"Sire, cho me puet bien aidier."   6640
"Ses que jo ferai por t'amor,
Que jamais nen oras clamor?
Femes raront lor iretage."
Silence respont come sage:
"Chi a gent don, Dex le vos mire,   6645
Et al fait pert quels est li sire."
Cil del palais en sont moult lié.
Le roi enclinent trosqu'al pié.
Prendent Silence a beneïr
Et dient Dex le puist tehir.   6650

she immediately claimed   6610
that I was trying to take her by force.
You sent me abroad.
You believed that she was telling the truth,
but I was disguising myself for my inheritance,
and didn't want to tell you the truth.   6615
Now you know how things stand, Sire.
I also didn't want to arouse your anger
and compromise the lady's position as queen.
Then I returned to your land
to help put down your rebellion,   6620
and the lady went at me again.
I didn't even want to speak to her,
and that is why, Sire, she wanted to ruin me
and send me into exile.
Truth does not permit me   6625
to keep anything from you,
nor do I care to keep silent any longer.
Do with me what you will."

The king said a few royal words:
"Silence, you are very loyal.   6630
Indeed, the price of your loyalty
is far above that of my royalty.
There is no more precious gem,
nor greater treasure, than a virtuous woman.
No man can assess the value   6635
of a woman who can be trusted.
Silence, know that you have saved yourself
by your loyal actions.
I give you my friendship and protection."
"Sire, I certainly have need of them."   6640
"Do you know what I will do for you,
so that you will never have cause for complaint—
women will be allowed to inherit again."
Silence replied judiciously,
"This is a noble gift. May God reward you for it.   6645
It is by his acts that one knows who is truly king."
The courtiers were very happy.
They bowed deeply to the king,
and blessed Silence,
asking God to exalt her.   6650

311

Li rois ot Eufeme en despit.
Onques ne volt doner respit,
Ne nus nel quist ne demanda.
Si com li rois le conmanda/
I fu la none donc deffaite,   6655
Et la dame a chevals detraite.
Li rois en a fait grant justice.
Or est la roïne as las prise
Dont el volt Silence lachier.
Si vait: tels cuide porcachier   6660
Honte et damage avoec altrui
Ki soi meïsme quiert anui.
Nus hom qui fust ne plainst Eufeme.
Silence atornent come feme.
Segnor, que vos diroie plus?   6665
Ains ot a non Scilensiüs:
Ostés est -us, mis i est -a
Si est només Scilentiä.

D'illuec al tierc jor que Nature
Ot recovree sa droiture   6670
Si prist Nature a repolir
Par tolt le cors et a tolir
Tolt quanque ot sor le cors de malle.
Ainc n'i lassa nes point de halle:
Remariä lués en son *vis**   6675
Assisement le roze al lis.
Li rois le prist a feme puis—
Cho dist l'estorie u jo le truis—
Par loëment de ses princhiers,
Qu'il plus ama et plus tint ciers.   6680
Et dont i vient li cuens ses pere,
Et Eufemie avoec, sa mere.
Grant joie en ont, cho est a droit.
Maistre Heldris dist chi endroit
C'on doit plus bone feme amer   6685
Que haïr malvaise u blasmer.
Si mosterroie bien raison:
Car feme a menor oquoison,
Por que ele ait le liu ne l'aise,
De l'estre bone que malvaise,   6690
S'ele ouevre bien contre nature.
Bien mosterroie par droiture
C'on en doit faire gregnor plait

312

The king despised Eufeme.
He had no wish to spare her,
nor did anyone ask him to.
In accordance with royal decree,
the nun was executed,   6655
and the queen was drawn and quartered.
Thus was the king's justice accomplished.
The queen was caught in the trap
she had set for Silence.
That's how it goes: he who plots   6660
to harm others
seeks his own undoing.
No one was sorry for Eufeme.
They dressed Silence as a woman.
Lords, what more can I say?   6665
Once he was called Silentius:
they removed the -us, added an -a,
and so he was called Silentia.

After Nature
had recovered her rights,   6670
she spent the next three days refinishing
Silence's entire body, removing every trace
of anything that being a man had left there.
She removed all traces of sunburn:
rose and lily were once again   6675
joined in conjugal harmony on her face.
Then the king took her to wife —
that's what it said in the book where I found this story —
on the advice of his
most loyal and trusted advisers.   6680
And then the count her father
and her mother, Eufemie, came to court.
They were overjoyed, as was only fitting.
Master Heldris says here and now
that one should praise a good woman   6685
more than one should blame a bad one.
And I will tell you why:
a woman has less motivation,
provided that she even has the choice,
to be good than to be bad.   6690
Doing the right thing comes unnaturally to her.
I put it to you directly
that one should take far greater account of these circumstances

Que de celi qui le mal fait.
Se j'ai jehi blasmee Eufeme   6695
Ne s'en doit irier bone feme.
Se j'ai Eufeme moult blasmee
Jo ai Silence plus loëe.
Ne s'en doit irier bone fame,
Ne sor li prendre altrui blasme,   6700
Mais efforcier plus de bien faire.
Chi voel a fin mon conte traire./
Beneöis soit qui le vos conte,
Beneöis soit qui fist le conte.
A cials, a celes qui l'oïrent   6705
Otroit Jhesus cho qu'il desirent.

Explicit.

than of the woman who does wrong.
If I have blamed Eufeme today,   6695
a good woman should not take offense,
for if I have censured Eufeme,
I have praised Silence more.
A good woman should neither take offense
nor blame herself for someone else's faults,   6700
but simply strive all the harder to do what is right.
I want to bring my story to a close.
God's blessing on the narrator,
God's blessing on the author.
And as for those — male and female — who listened to it,   6705
may Jesus grant them their dearest wish.

APPENDIX: SUMMARY OF "GRISANDOLE"

AVENABLE, daughter of Mathem, a German duke exiled by Frole, a usurper, disguises herself as a squire called Grisandole, enters the service of Julius Caesar, emperor of Rome, and becomes knight and seneschal of the realm. Merlin, knowing that the emperor is troubled by a dream in which a sow with a golden crown is serviced by twelve wolf whelps, bursts into city and court in the form of a great stag and tells emperor and populace that only the wild man of the woods can interpret the dream. He then vanishes by magic. The emperor promises his daughter to anyone who captures either wild man or stag. One day the stag appears to Grisandole, the only one not to abandon the quest, and tells her to come the following day with five companions, prepare food, and then hide. When the wild man falls asleep by the fire after a huge meal, Grisandole easily captures him. On the way to court, the wild man laughs three times. When Grisandole asks why, he insults her, alluding to her unnatural state. Brought before the emperor, he promises to reveal the reasons for his laughter before all the barons of the empire, and asks that the queen and her ladies be present. He reveals that the emperor's dream was a warning that the queen is deceiving him: all twelve ladies-in-waiting are really men. The emperor has them all burned. Then the wild man reveals that Grisandole is a woman, delivering a diatribe on the deceitful nature of women. After revealing the other reasons he laughed (and inserting a few prophecies), he advises the emperor to marry Grisandole/Avenable, restore her parents' estates, and marry his daughter to her brother. The wild man refuses to reveal the whereabouts of the stag or his own identity. He departs from the hall abruptly, leaving a Hebrew inscription in the doorpost. After a successful campaign against Frole, the marriages take place. Later, a Greek messenger interprets the inscription (whereupon the letters vanish): both stag and wild man were Merlin.

NOTES TO THE OLD FRENCH TEXT

Words in square brackets in the text are Thorpe's emendations. MS = Manuscript, TH = Thorpe, LC = Lecoy, IG = Iker-Gittleman (in personal correspondence), GD = Godefroy, TL = Tobler-Lommatzsch.

2. *a talle*. The expression can mean "made to measure," but also refers to the composition of verse, *tailler la rime*. In poetic treatises of the fourteenth and fifteenth centuries, *taille* is regularly used to designate the form of couplets. Cf. TL, with reference to Paul Meyer, *Romania* 15 (1894), 461–462.

7. LC: *Que* = *qui*, as often in this text.

73. MS *n*.

77. With LC; MS *muire*.

116. With LC; MS *carcre*.

132. With TH; MS *garder et doner*.

146. MS *danor wege*.

192. *corus* MS (otherwise unattested); LC *corlius*.

269. MS *Et lor dist tels* (LC no suggestion).

281. MS *qui*; *qu'i* for *qu'il* as often in this text.

340. With MS (*fories i a*), vs TH.

350. *tolte* MS: I posit metathesis **tolet*; cf. glossary (LC: "me reste obscur").

373. MS *estraint*.

454. *Qui* MS; LC *Cil*.

463. LC; MS *estiuit*.

561. LC; MS *anchois*.

567. LC; MS *il* (as also 567, 597, 2010).

635. LC; MS *lisiet*.

755. MS *amaint*.

805. LC; MS *estoit*.

833. MS *refust*.

835. *El* MS; LC *Ne*. (Depends on interpretation of *dangier*; cf. glossary.)

945. MS *malges*.

954. MS *prendes*.

1403. MS *veu*.

1418. MS *desos*.
1453. LC; MS *cestui*.
1575. LC; MS *tant*.
1638. *il*: LC probably for *el*. (Or is it simply that the narrator has launched into a general statement and forgotten the antecedent?)
1759. LC; MS *poons*.
1848. LC; MS *ki fais degrosse et de delie*.
1890. MS *sa*.
2039. MS *descuser*.
2125. MS *qunt*.
2176. *desirrer* MS; cf. glossary.
2225. LC; MS *m*.
2243. *soolte* MS; LC *sooste* (cf. GD *soiste*).
2308. LC; MS *se nus*.
2318. MS *repent*.
2391. LC; MS *palais*.
2499. MS *ki se*.
2579. MS *Queles ia naie io conte*.
2604. MS *sa*.
2664. MS *con*.
2872. MS *en el grage*. Cf. glossary. (TH *el en grage* = *grange*; LC "2871–72 me reste incomprehensibles.")
2937. LC; MS .
3027. MS *c'on n'ait*.
3100. MS *lenfant*.
3209. MS *colp*.
3232. *cha jue*: sic MS. TH *chaive* is impossible (LC).
3408. LC; MS *seil neuscent*.
3410. MS *molt*.
3629. MS *penset requelt*.
3720. IG; MS *mais maiast* (TH *mals m'aiast*). (Or perhaps *mais* = *mauvais*; *maiast* is then more easily understood as a scribal error: starting to write *mais* again.)
3765. MS *ma*.
3844. LC; MS *se*.
3845. LC; MS *vus*.
3866. MS *Que del enfant*. (TH *Que cil enfans*, which makes no sense.)
3890. LC; MS *moult convenroit esmaier*. 4044. *athace* = metathesis for *atache*.
4102. MS *mabre* (but scribe had written *marbre* for *arbre* in 4101).
4210. MS *tels est ille*.
4756. LC's punctuation (*qui* = *si on*).
5434. MS *Li*.
5479. *le* LC; MS *les*.

5833. *C'om* TH; MS *C'un om*.

5838. LC; MS *en*.

6079. With MS *dont lenemis Adan enbut* (TH *dont, je ne mis Adan en but*; LC *dont le venins Adam enbut*).

6582. *LC; MS conur*.

6606. LC; MS *par*.

6639. MS *amer te voelent*.

6675. LC; MS *ensomis*.

NOTES TO THE TRANSLATION

145 As Thorpe points out (1972, 32), the state of war between England and Norway is found in Geoffrey of Monmouth, although there is no king Begon.

426 The prayer that follows (427–72) belongs to a type common in Old French literature, the so-called "biblical-creed-narrative" prayer (see Koch 1940). The theological points concerning angels (449 ff.) are solidly within the "cur deus homo" tradition from St. Anselm on, as Lecoy remarks (1978, 113). The gratuitous negative remark regarding the Jewish faith (472) is unfortunately formulaic in medieval romance. (Wolfram's *Parzival* is an admirable exception.)

593 Women often appear as healers and physicians in medieval romance. The most famous are undoubtedly Morgan le Fay and Queen Iseut of Ireland. For many examples, see Hughes (1943).

645 The venom of snakes or dragons is frequently associated with the affliction of passionate love. Lancelot, incurably in love with Guinevere, must be healed by the maiden Amable when he drinks from a fountain poisoned by two serpents; Amable in turn is tormented by love for Lancelot. A very funny version is *Le Bel Inconnu*, where a maiden is cursed to appear as a huge snake until the hero will kiss her.

694 The *bos d'Ardane* of Cador's dream is the archetypal forest (originally the *Arduenna silva* of antiquity, later the Ardennes) frequented by outlawed or questing heroes of chansons de geste and courtly romances. Shakepeare's Forest of Arden, though technically on the Avon rather than the Meuse, retains the mythical qualities of its medieval prototype.

837 In taking the initiative here, Eufemie is a typical romance heroine (Lasry 1985). Lavine in *Eneas* sends the hero a love-note attached to an arrow; princess Guilliadun in Marie de France's *Eliduc* arranges a tryst and gives the hero ring and belt. Chrétien's Blanchefleur simply climbs into Perceval's bed.

882–915 The belabored punning is a parody of the famous *mer/amer/amor* of Thomas de Bretagne's *Tristan*.

964 This is the Latin proverb, "Honores mutant mores."

1226 *joi d'amors*: a collective feeling of refined, exalted joy. The lady represents the epitome of courtly values; she is the outward manifestation of the perfection of ennobling love.

1615 The passage is an expansion of the proverbial saying (Tobler No. 105), "Encontre mort nul ressort" (nothing can prevail against death).

1866 For the theme, see Malkiel (1977). Of the many possible sources of inspiration (aside from Alain, of course) Heldris seems to have had Chrétien's Enide particularly in mind:

> The maid was charming, in sooth, for Nature had used all her skill in forming her. Nature herself had marvelled more than five hundred times how upon this one occasion she had succeeded in creating such a perfect thing. Never again could she strive so successfully to reproduce her pattern. Nature bears witness concerning her that never was so fair a creature seen in all the world. In truth I say that never did Iseut the Fair have such radiant golden tresses that she could be compared to this maiden. The complexion of her forehead and face was clearer and more delicate than the lily. But with wondrous art her face with all its delicate pallor was suffused with a fresh crimson which Nature had bestowed upon her. Her eyes were so bright that they seemed like two stars. God never formed better nose, mouth, and eyes. What shall I say of her beauty?
>
> (trans. W. W. Comfort)

2354-55 This is a dig at Perceval, the holy fool raised in sylvan ignorance.

2479 *el a en tine que ferine* (there's something in the barrel besides flour); for this proverb, cf. Morawski No. 627, "El a en tine, dit le suriz, que farine."

2747 *par les serjans de la maizon*, etc.; cf. Morawski No. 194, "Au seneschal de la maison/peust on connoistre le baron."

2761-65 The "Breton *lai*" played on the viele would be a lyric poem with a subject matter like that of Marie de France's short narrative *lais*. "Gueron" (or Guiron) is the "lai pitus d'amur" sung by Iseut in Thomas's *Tristan* (833-945), in which the heart of a lover is eaten by his unsuspecting beloved. Although Mabon, a demoted Celtic divinity, appears fairly frequently in Arthurian romance, chiefly as enchanter, a *lai* of Mabon does not seem to have survived. See Gelzer (1925).

2939 *ki tempre puet ostel avoir*; cf. Morawski No. 2158, "Qui tempre vient a son hostel/ mieulx lui en est a son souper."

3209 *por bien fait col frait rendre*: to return evil for good; cf. Morawski No. 463, "de bien fait col frait."

3257 *vergant*; cf. Morawski No. 1154, "Maint home cuillent la verge dont il sunt batu"; cf. also 6444.

3313 St. Anthony's Fire is a name for a terribly painful skin disease usually identified as erysipelas, although it freqently was gangrenous ergotism.

3326 *sans caperon li ferons cape*, "we'll short-change him," plays with the literal meaning of a proverbial expression (he won't need a hood because his head will be missing). Cf. Morawski No. 1170, Tobler No. 132 "mal fait la chape qui ne fait le chaperon," to do something half way, or TL *doner chape sans chaperon* "etwas Halbes schenken." Cf. also the variant (Tobler note to No. 132), Se il sens perte s'en eschape/ Senz caperon set taillier cape."

3527 The viele of Silence's day was a six-stringed instrument very much like a lute, without the small rosined wheel it acquired in later times and still has today. (This later form of the viele is also known as "hurdy-gurdy.")

3559 This old man is certainly Merlin in disguise, penetrating Silence's disguise and unmasking her, just as he appears later as white-haired old man (i.e., in human form, not stag, as in "Grisandole") to help her with his own capture. Thus, Heldris forges a link between the two parts of the narrative.

3570 The old man would say, with Morawski No. 1285, "Meus vaut science que richece" (wisdom is better than wealth)

3817 Here, and especially 3935–48, the accusation of homosexuality, a great favorite in courtly romances (made, e.g., against Eneas in very crude and graphic terms by Lavine and her mother) is directed against our female transvestite protagonist to far more profound narrative ends (see introduction and Bloch, 1986).

3818 *jovenes sains est vies diables*, proverbial expression, cf. Tobler No. 32, "Qui juenes saintist, vieuz enrage," and variant in note: "qui jeunes saintist, vius est diables."

4243–44 A laundered paraphrase of a proverb; cf. Tobler No. 240: "Quant plus remuet on la merde, et ele plus put"(the more you stir up shit, the more it stinks).

5281 The passage paraphrases a proverb, Morawski No. 883: "Il fait mal nourrir autruy enfant/ car il s'en va quant il est grant" (It's a bad idea to nurture other people's children because they leave when they grow up).

5557–9 These are the realistic-sounding names that Thorpe had no luck tracing. No one else has tried, so far as I know.

5784 The story of Vortigern's tower occurs in *L'Estoire Merlin*, Wace, Geoffrey of Monmouth, and elsewhere (two dragons fighting under the earth were causing the trouble), but as Thorpe notes (1972, 31),

Heldris adds that he took to the woods at that point, prophesying that he could only be captured by a woman.

5892 Aymes de Dordonne was obliged to fight his own sons out of feudal obligation to Charlemagne (in the chanson de geste *Renaut de Montauban* or *Les quatre fils Aymon*).

6145 Here Heldris unexpectedly provides Silence with some Arthurian motivation. The episode of the siring of Arthur is from Geoffrey of Monmouth, 8:18–19.

6191 For details as to how many times Merlin laughed at what in which sources or analogues, see Paton (1907), Thorpe (1972) and Lecoy (1978).

6352 *al wespre loe on le biel jor* (one praises a beautiful day at sunset) = Morawski No. 197; Tobler No. 32 has "au vespre loe on le jour, au matin son oste" (one praises the day at sundown, and one's host at daybreak). Similarly Tobler, notes to No. 12, "Qu'au vespre loe l'en lo jor/ Quant l'en voit que bele est la fin/ Si fet l'en son oste au matin." My translation reverses the imagery, but I preferred it to "all's well that ends well."

6449 *li respis al vilain*: I haven't been able to find this proverb.

PROPER NAMES (PERSONS AND PLACES)

[N.B. For Cador, Ebain, Merlin, and Silence I have listed first and last occurrences and noted where there are clusters or gaps in their frequency.]

Adan 1703; 6031, 6035, 6054, 6058, 6060, 6067, 6079 (Adam).

Ades 583 (one of King Evan's servants—name invented for rhyme).

Aimon 5892 (Aymes de Dordonne in *Les Quatre Fils Aymon* or *Renaus de Montauban*; cf. notes to trans.).

Alemagne 3458 (Germany).

Alixandre, roi 5518 (Alexander the Great).

Alvergne 3458 (Auvergne).

Amor 635, 649, 677, 679, 680, 684, 720, 726, 743, 748, 752, 754, 787, 838, 872, 902, 1058, 1362, 1555 (Love personified).

Ardane, bois d' 694 (archetypal forest; cf. notes to trans.).

Artus 109, 6154, 6156 (King Arthur).

Avarice 39, 88 (Avarice personified).

Beg(h)es/Begon 145, 164, 165, 173, 228 (King of Norway).

Berta(i)gne 2703, 2895, 2920, 2930 (Brittany).

Blois 4496 (Blois).

Blois, li cuens de 4534, 4604 (an adviser to the King of France).

Borgoigne, duc de 3216 (Duke of Burgundy).

Cador 392, frequ. until 1657, then 4422 (King Evan's nephew, dragon-slayer, Eufemie's husband, Silence's father. He becomes Count of Cornwall at the death of Count Renald).

Cestre 293, 337, 537; 5288, 5317, 5321, 5481, 5669 (Chester).

Cestre, li cuens de 1309, 1390, 1399, 1463, 5407 (vassal of King Evan, wily politician, later rebel; cf. Conans).

Clermont 4498 (Clermont-Ferrand).

Clermont, li cuens de 4582, 4597, 4631, 4649, 4771 (sage adviser to the King of France).

Conans, li cuens 5619 (the Count of Chester).

Cornualle 1, 397, 1297, 1450, 1543, 2697 (Cornwall).

Cornualle, li valles de 5556, 5572 (what the French troops call Silence).

Durame 114 (Durham).

Ebain/Ebayn 107 frequ. until 372; 1545, 1690; 2444, 2831; 4081, 4100, 4178, 4320, 4336, 4388, 4427, 4436, 4500, 4506, 4545, 4850, 5104, 5195, 5272 (Evan, King of England).

Englet(i)er(r)e 107, 147, 237, 277, 315, 1735, 2449, 2695 3483, 4883, 5186, 5226, 5262, 52 63, 5273, 5287 (England).

Engletiere, li rois d' 4769 (the king of England).

Englois 111, 140, 3712, 6554 (Englishman).

Escot 6131, 6392, 6554 (Scot).

Espagne 3329, 3457, 5391 (Spain).

Eufeme 165, 229, 3703, 5242, 5680, 5804, 6180, 6348, 6371, 6460, 6531, 6587, 6651, 6663, 6695, 6697 (daughter of King Begon of Norway, wife of Evan, temptress and enemy of Silence. N.B. called Eufemie 5206 to rhyme with *mie*).

Eufemie 402, 549, 593, 606, 797, 830, 833, 879, 901, 937, 984, 985, 987, 1018, 1063, 1312, 1441, 1501, 1508, 1597, 1633, 1671, 1958, 2145, 3014; 6682 (daughter of Count Renald of Cornwall, skilled physician, wife of Cador, mother of Silence).

Eufemie 5206 (= Eufeme).

Eurincestre 338 (= Winchester).

Eve/Evain 1704, 6036 (Eve).

Faintise 1550 (Deceit personified).

Fort(i)gierne 5784, 5910 (King Vortigern of Britain).

Franc(h)e 100, 3455, 4253, 4381, 4966, 4977, 5105, 5209 (France).

France, li rois de 4253, 4289, 4303, 4654, 4677, 4895, 4905, 5253, 5338, 5357 (the King of France).

Francois/Franchois, li 4418, 5299, 5334, 5369, 5387, 5522, 5527, 5533, 5550, 5557, 5569, 5576, 5581, 5642, 5672 (the French).

Galtier 1740 (posthumous and short-lived child of a nobleman and Cador's cousin. After his death, his mother is midwife to Eufemie and nursemaid to Silence).

Gascoigne 3215 (Gascony).

Gorlain 6145 (Gorlois, Duke of Cornwall, whose shape Uther assumes — through Merlin's enchantment — to sleep with the Duchess Ygerna and engender Arthur).

Gueron 2762 (the title of a *lai*; cf. notes to trans.).

Gui de Calmont 5557 (one of three French knights who rescue King Evan in battle).

Hantone 4885 (Southampton).

Heldris de Cornualle 1, 6684 (Master Heldris of Cornwall, author of *Silence*).

Herincestre 538 (= Winchester).

Honors 1557 (Honor personified).

Honte 1558, 1563, 1568, 1570, 1571, 1574 (Shame personified).

Hyebles de Castiel Landon 5559 (one of three French knights who rescue King Evan in battle).

Irois 1302, 4222, 6392 (Irishman).

Izeuls/Izelt 3700, 3701 (Yseult [Isolde] beloved of Tristan).

Jhesus Cris 1702, 1972, 2070, 5688, 6706 (Jesus Christ).

Jordan 437 (the river Jordan).

Jozeph 3705 (the Biblical Joseph, who is tempted by Potiphar's wife).

Judeu, Juis 436, 443, 472 (Jew[s]).

Londres 4900 (London).

Longin 6167 (Longinus, who pierced Christ's side with his spear).

Losenge/Lozenge 71, 1552 (Flattery personified).

Mabon 2765 (title of a *lai*; cf. notes to trans.).

Malduit 3177, 3576 (pseudonym of Silence).

Malroi, bos de 559 (the wood where Cador killed the dragon).

Merlin 5792, 5794, 5808 with high density until 6573 (Merlin).

Monjoie 5555, 5643 (the battle-cry of the French).

Monmartre 4257, 4403, 4979 (Montmartre).

Mont Loon 5265 (Laon).

Mors, uns 5539 (a Saracen).

Nantes 2936, 2941 (Nantes).

Nature 1027, 1228, 1679, 1799, 1805, 1825, 1835, 1851, 1866, 1869, 1893, 1900, 1902, 1916, 1918, 1921, 1927, 1943, 1956, 2020, 2254, 2257, 2268, 2294, 2295, 2298, 2300, 2346, 2423, 2500, 2527, 2540, 2544, 2550, 2590, 2594, 2604, 2605, 2614, 2619, 2655; 5154; 5607; 6002, 6005, 6011, 6020, 6030, 6039, 6043, 6045, 6051, 6053, 6090; 6669, 6671 (Nature or Heredity personified).

Navers 4497 (Nevers).

Nav(i)ers, li cuens de 4629, 4650 (adviser to the King of France).

Noreture 2267, 2275, 2293, 2299, 2348, 2374, 2424, 2547, 2587, 2607, 5153, 5996, 5997, 6009, 6012, 6016, 6066, 6088 (Nurture or Environment personified).

Norois 231 (the Norwegian King [Begon]).

Noroise 209 (the Norwegian princess [Eufeme]).

Norwege/Norouege 146, 157, 227 (Norway).

Noviel Testament 1716 (New Testament).

Paris 5106, 5135 (Paris).
Pentecoste 5133 (Pentecost, Whitsuntide).
Pharaon 3706 (Pharaoh).

Raison 2609, 2625 (Reason, Common Sense personified).
Renalt 397, 1298, 1451, 1505, 1525, 1527, 1611, 1619, 1625, 2144 (Count Renald of Cornwall, Eufemie's father).
Ris 6198 (name of a king invented for rhyme).
Rogiers de Bialmont 5558 (one of three French knights who rescue King Evan in battle).
Rome 2814 (Rome).

Sains Amans 1330, 1368 (Love personified as a saint).
Saint Germain 5137 (Saint-Germain-des-Pres).
Saint Juliien 2718 (Saint Julian the Hospitaller).
Sainte Marie 503, 3494 (the Virgin Mary).
Sainte Paciensce 2068 (Patience personified as a saint).
Saint Pere 313 (Saint Peter).
Sathanas 3699 (Satan).
Silence 2067, 2396, 2497, 2609 frequ. until 6698 (the heroine, Silence [var. Scilence, Silensce]).
Scilencia/Scilentia 2078, 6668 (Silence, the feminine form of her Latin name).
Scilenscius/Scilentius 2074, 2126, 2530, 2532, 2533, 2537, 2542, 6666 (Silence, the masculine form of her Latin name).

Tamise 4900 (the Thames).
Tintaguel 2892 (Tintagel).
Tintaguel, le vallet de 4378 (= Silence).
Tristran 3700, 3701 (Tristan).

Uter/Uterpandragon 6148, 6152 (Uther Pendragon, King of Britain).

Valors 1555 (Worth personified).
Verites 1553 (Truth personified).
Vilonie 1551 (Baseness personified).
Virgene, le 431 (the Virgin Mary).

Wincestre 114, 4981 (Winchester [var. Eurincestre, Herincestre]).

GLOSSARY

GD = Godefroy, LC = Lecoy, TH = Thorpe, TL = Tobler-Lommatzsch; Fr = French, L = Latin; conj = conjunction, intrans = intransitive, reflex = reflexive, subj = subjunctive, trans = transitive.

aase 3031 (cf. *ase*).

abonir, s' 2425 to devote oneself to.

acaigne 1615 (*acaindre aceindre*) to encircle, hem in, try to win over (subj).

acesmer 1665, 3229 to arrange beautifully, dispose tastefully, prepare.

acointier: to inform (acquaint with the facts) 571; to meet (make the acquaintance of) 1536, 4950; encounter in battle 5461, 5581.

aduit 1802 *aduire*, to train, instruct: knowledgeable, informed.

aente: (cf. *ente*), 3352, 3376.

afoler: to destroy, mutilate 4437, 5625; cause to behave foolishly 4469; to become frenzied (the berserk-rage of the warrior in battle) 5448.

aforee 1551 *aforer* to value highly (to set the market- price of).

agaise [*argaise*] 5889 wasteland.

agoisse 412, 1128 (= *angoisse*).

ahoce 2116 *ahocier* to let dangle.

aie 5404, 5417, 5519 aid, help, support.

aiue 2163 aid, assistance.

alie 1847 trans., crab-apple; lit., sorb-apple, fruit of service-tree: something of very little value.

amoier 1334 to direct toward a goal (by moderation).

amordre: cause to become familiar with, habituate someone to, 1626, 2552; *s'amordre a*, to become used to, make something a habit 331, 2612, 5618.

amortie 2973 *amortir* to be dead in color.

anne [*ane*] 3863 wild duck.

ante 1738 aunt.

anter [*hanter*] 792, 2597 to frequent, keep company with.

aoues (cf. *ues*).

apetizier [*apeticier*] 1645, 2064, 2094 to diminish (trans/intrans){petit}.

ase/es [*aise*], *a*: at ease with regard to 55, 1062; close to achieving; *mis a es* 1520 put at ease/placed adjacently (the author is playing on both meanings as

331

well as the expression *aise du lit*, pleasures of love); *al plain puig a es i pesce* (Merlin is attacking the meat with voluptuous enjoyment {L *adjacens*}), 6114; cf. also *aase* 3031 opportunity, ease.

asmes 850 asmer [*esmer*] to decide.

assener: provide accommodation for (stable horses) 2755; act in such a manner as to 4200, 6264; give advice, guidance to {general sense: aim toward, act with a goal in mind}.

atirer 3339 to plot, arrange to injure someone.

ator: determination, force of character 1480; possessions 2723; materials 5788 {general sense: what one is endowed with}.

atrais [*atrait*] 5281 the way one is, one's nature, essence (trait of character).

auferrans 5361 warhorse {orig. "spirited," attribute of a destrier}.

avoec 6661 (and elsewhere) = *ues*: with regard to.

awapie 95 awapir [*agapir*] insipid {vapid}.

baldor 3320 presumption (high spirits) {bold}.

balle [*baille*] 2236 nurse.

ballier [*baillier*: to hand over, pass on to 325, 2235, 3538, 4350, 4367, 4943, 4946; to lay hands on 61, 3121.

bargir 6128 to swell up, be bursting.

bastonage 2871 (not in GD, TL) being in a position of servitude.

belizor 1847 more beautiful.

berser 2881 to hunt with bow and arrow.

bestorner 2259 to invert, turn from its proper direction.

blos solement 19 "one single solitary."

bolt [*bot*, *bout*], de, 4816 immediately, without hesitation, thoroughly.

bon: *dire (son) bon*, to speak from the heart, reveal one's innermost desires, thoughts 1066, 1076 [MS *bien*] 1190; *faire (son) bon*, do as one pleases 6397; *de lor bon* 1122 with all their hearts.

bresiller 1928 to tint red {brazil wood}.

bruhier [*bruier*] 94 buzzard.

bruir 360, 409 to burn.

buer [*boer*] 4969 in a lucky moment {L *bona hora*}.

buletiel [*buretel*] 1809 sieve (for flour).

bulette 1812

buleter [*bureter*] to sift.

busce [*busche*] 1818 bit of straw (in the flour).

caiel [*chael*] 3255 puppy.

caieles/chaieles/kaieles/kieles, heavens! for pity's sake! 309, 2803, 3252, 5604.

camp male [*champ mesle*] 290 duel, armed combat as legal means of settling dispute.

cantiel [*chantel*] 5150 *porter l'escu en cantiel*: carry one's shield to one side, not covering one's chest.

casti [*chasti*] 5464 castigation (chastisement).

chant 5616 side (L *canthus*); *torna en chant* to be turned aside (TL 2:226). Cf. *cantiel* [*chantel*] 5150.

c[h]astiement 1266 proper guidance (chastisement).

chierissement 3884 raising the price of something, as at an auction.

cifler [*chifler*] 348 joke, chat.

cleu 6368 *n'i fist fier ne cleu*, "had nothing to do with," double-entendre with a proverbial expression.

cois [*chois*]/*quois*/*kiuls*/*kius* 799, 975, 981, 1009, 1073, 1240 choice.

coisir [*choisir*] 3045, 5671 to observe.

coitier/*qoitier*: to hurry 2938; to hurry someone on 6093.

confes/*confies* 3808, 3809: *se faire confes*, to confess; *faire confes*, to grant absolution.

conisance [*conoissance*] 5494 coat of arms (displayed as sign of recognition on helmets and shields, on pennants fluttering from lances, etc.).

contoier [*cointoiier*] 5148 to display one's (knightly) prowess.

corlius [MS *corus*] 192 messengers.

cosinain 1767, 2112 cousin.

covine: true nature, character 3872, 4974; conduct, behavior 4048: *por quoi nos fais tu tel covine?* "why are you spoiling things for us by acting this way?"

coze 2501 *cozer* [*choser*] to scold, nag.

crois 5444 crash/clash of weapons.

crosler [*croler*] 4921 to shake (one's head).

cuerine: grief, sorrow, uneasiness 3878; *avoir en cuerine*, to have a grudge against 3923.

cuivre 481 attack.

dangier: caprice 993, 3731, 3777; *faire dangier de*, to refuse, deny, treat scornfully 2760. I interpret *faire dangier a* (835) as "to grant someone his heart's desire," keeping the MS reading. LC, by emending *el* to *ne*, clearly understands it as synonymous with *faire dangier de*. The problem is that *dangier* means an arbitrary act— negatively, whim or caprice; neutrally, something based on or subject to individual judgment or discretion: *a grant dangier*, e.g., can mean "unwillingly" or "to one's heart's content"; cf. Tobler's comments (*Li proverbe au vilain*, p. 117).

delie/*delie delier* [*desliier*] 1832, 1833, 1837, 1848 that which is well separated (here, by sifting).

delis delir 5782 dejected, sad.

deloie 952 *deleer* [*delaiier*] to hold back (subj).

denai 5077 *doner*.

deporter: to leave unfulfilled, neglect 1257; spend free time with 2848; to spare, let someone off 4324, 5489; *s'en deporter*, to do without 422.

deruant 6249 *deruer* [*desreer/desroier*] to attack (disconcert).

desirrer 2176 [otherwise unattested] I suggest 'to put on the wrong path' [*dis + iterare*]; cf. *desvoie/desvise* 2255/56? [TH 'to take care of' (without explanation); LC *'egarer le jugement'* referring to 2181–82.]

desjuer/desjoer 33, 3238, 3932, 5505 to spoil one's good mood.

desmentir, se 1912 to depart from.

desnu/desneu 6366, 6367 *desnoer* to solve {*denouement*}.

desparellier 63 to make uneven (here: spoil the nice round sum by spending some of it).

despondre: to mean, signify 3578, 4429, 5843 etc.; to explain the significance of 5809, 6220, 6226.

desroi 2874 advance, a pushing forward.

desserrer 489 to tear open.

desseus 3570 *dessavoir*: ignorant.

destemperra 6410 *destremper*, to prepare.

destroite 4275 savage, cruel.

detrier (*se*) 4080, 5644 to hold back, delay.

detuert 591, 2102 *detordre*, to wring one's hands; *se detordre* 4162, 4398 to writhe in agony.

deviser: to plan, devise 2175, 3211; to decide 2981; to have in mind 3560; to tell, say to someone 3595; *nus ne devisa qui jostast* 5440: cf. *joste devisee* (TL 2: 1880) a fight between evenly matched opponents.

diviers/diverse: perverse 16; deeply divided 2663, 2681; diverse, different 1899; *diversement* 2662 in conflicting ways.

dosnoier [*donoiier*] 44 to woo ladies in courtly fashion. *eente* cf. *ente*.

enbarer [*embarrer*] 5515 to smash in, split open (a helmet).

enbonir: to seem good to 852; to improve (oneself) 6024.

enbronc 5451 leaning forward in saddle, ready for the shock of contact in battle.

encrees 3642 *encraier* to treat with chalk. New fur was treated with powdered chalk to make it seem whiter; unscrupulous merchants, to pass off old cloth as new, would rechalk it (LC with ref. to *Romania* 59: 491–92).

encrieme 4087 rascally.

encuser: *accuse* 4072; betray 6605.

enerre 2321 *enerrer* to pay a deposit on {Fr *verser des arrhes*}.

engagne 264, 3144, 4248 anger, chagrin.

engier 1460, 1472, 1759, 3974, 5308 to endow, provide. *engragne* 967 *engragner* [*engraignier, engrangier*] to increase.

enmiodrement 3269 improvement.

enprieme 2308 *enpriembre* to impress, put its stamp on.

entamee 1550 tin-plated, gilded, silvered (of a mirror), a variant of *estamee*. Cf. TL 3,1:557 *entamerie* for *estamerie*, with ref. to Bloch, *Romania* 47 (1913) 580–581, where the verb *entesmer* is also found attested.

ente: *a ente/aente/eente* 2730, 3027, 3352, 3376, 4077, 4116, 4184, 5629: *estre a ente a*, to be a cause of anxiety, pain to; as adv, painfully.

enterver 2160, 2246, 3322, 3497, 3574, 5649, to understand, find out, to wonder, to ask; 6206 to act malicious toward (cf. noun *enterve*, used [GD] of demons.

entoillier 1856 to trick, trap, deceive.

entruel [entroeil] 1922 space between the eyes.

envis [enviz] with difficulty 2332, 3022; reluctantly 4432 {counter to one's will}.

escalle [eschaille] 1818 chaff.

escars [eschars] 6481 ridicule, shame.

es, a 1120, 1520, 6114: cf. *ase*.

esce [esche] 5946 tinder (cf. note at *fural*).

*esciller, s' 4210 est ille] to dishonor oneself [*essillier*].

esgrocier [cf. *grocier*] 306 to pick a fight with someone.

eskiver [eschiver] to refrain from (refl) 3024; to go astray 4888.

esmier 699, 1829, 1831 to break or hack to pieces.

esniie 1830 for *esnie esneier*, to purify.

espagnent, s' 225 *s'espandre [espeindre]* to put to sea, sail out to sea.

espanir 3507, 3668 to carry off as plunder, kidnap.

essillier 4622 to kill, have killed [exile].

estalcier (s') [estaucier] 2055, 2559 to tonsure, be tonsured; have one's hair cut short.

estolt 1500, 1501, 1618 rash, imprudent.

estossir, s' 1405, 6471 to cough.

estreloi 4840 outrage, injustice.

estruit 5987 preparation.

estuier 1877 to hold in reserve.

fais, a un 3079 all together, all at the same time.

fait, a 748 vigorously, forcefully.

faiture 1955 character, disposition (makeup).

falose [faloise] 123 trickery.

faltre [feltre, fautre] rest for lance (padded with felt).

fausnoier 1439 mislead, deceive.

fierne 5783 *ferner*, to blame (subj).

forcor 608, 5952, *fortre* 408 stronger: synthetic comparative [L *fortior*].

fordine 790, 4793 lit., sloe (a small sour wild plum); something of no value.

forlignier: to cause to be degenerate 2298; behave in a degenerate manner 4156; throw off the influence of (deviate from) 6458.

forssalent forssalir 757 to slip away somewhere: cf. TL *forsaillie*, 'Entweichen'.

fortre cf. *forcor*.

francois, savoir son: to know one's man 2227; know what one is about, what (whom) one is dealing with 3324.

fretel [*frestel*] 1359 agitation.

frois, a un 5443 at the same time (at one blow).

fuer 2520 true nature (i.e. real value); *a(l) fuer de* 1302, 2361, 2459, 2503, etc., just like, in the manner of; a *nul fuer* 4150, 4710, 4993 etc., at no price {general sense: price, market value, equivalent value}.

fural [*fusil, foisil*] 5946 flint: cf. GD 4:45c "prent le fuisil, si a de l'esche prise." This form not in GD, TL.

*gage 2872 [MS *grage*; cf. notes to text] *avoir en gage*, to have as security.

gagnon [*gaignon*] 5258 like a vicious dog, eager for prey, pillage.

gargherie [*jargerie*] 91 noxious weeds.

gas [*gab/gap*] 4345, 4752 joke, pleasantry.

gentiors [*gencior*] 5511 most valiantly.

giens 2900 in no way.

gient 686 *geindre* [*giembre*] to groan, moan (cf. *jaindre* 719).

gloze 789 gloss.

glozer 990 to gloss.

golis [*golif*] 6100, 6109 greedy.

goloser/golozer 248, 1340, 2345, 3330 to lust after, want badly.

gordine 2649 curtains draped about the bed (translated as 'bedcovers').

gorgie 83: *dire sa gorgie*, to pour out one's innermost thoughts.

gragne 968 *graignier*, to grind one's teeth, be angry.

grant, en 2204, 3925, 4009 desirous of.

haitie 177, 1674, 2404 well, in high spirits.

halsage [*haussage*] 565, 4806 haughty behavior.

harponciel [*harpon*] 3792 brooch.

houes cf. *ues*.

huissiere 4112 porter, doorkeeper (translated as "locksmith").

iolt 621 *oloir*, to smell of.

ivuelle 1271 *ivueller* [*iveler*] to make equal.

jaindre 719 = *geindre*, cf. *gient*.

jehi [*jehui*] 6695 today.

kieles, cf. *caieles*.

kiuls, kius, cf. *cois*.

lachier [*lacier*] 6659 to snare, entrap.

lairis [*larris/larriz*] 6429, 6188 fallow land, brush.

lambre 614, 825, 2109, 4104, 6408: floor or ceiling beautified by some decorative covering; by extension, marble or other decorative material, as in 2109 *vassiel de lambre*.

larder 6240 to burn alive (by extension, from larding before roasting).

lassor [*loisir*] 2491, 5692 opportunity, occasion, leisure.

leust 5083 *loisir*, to be possible, permitted (subj).

loche 2115 *lochier* [*logier*] to wobble, dangle.

loir 128 = *lor*: to rhyme with *valoir* (Picard forms).

lues 593, 723, 4392 on the spot, immediately; 4673 (conj) from the instant that.

malhaitie 3713 unwell, indisposed.

malle [*mal*] 5161 feeble.

mallet 2210 diminutive *masle*: little male.

manaidier 6639 to treat mercifully.

maniere [*manier*] 2843 (adj) skillful at. But the poet is playing with *maniere*, good manners, conformity to social norms.

manieres, de 250, 618 of many different sorts.

margerie 92 daisy.

mence 1676 *mentir*, to be lacking (subj).

menchable [cf. *menchonchable, mencongeable* GD 5:231] 6382, lying.

meriane 693 siesta.

merir 5620 to pay for.

mervalt 738 *merveillier* to be surprising (subj).

mest 2147, 2687, 2707 *manoir*, to stay, remain.

mois 274, 562 simpleton.

moitiier 3396 equal sharer.

mon 5891 absolutely, indeed.

morjoie [*murjoe, musgode*] 84 strongbox, safe (originally, cellar for provisions).

ne mais: except 625, 2198, 3241, 4500; no longer 2561; no more 4576; however 4837; *ne mais c'* [*que*] 4784 except in so far as, only to the extent that.

oire [*erre*] 218 journey; *en oirre* 217, 977, 1704 etc. in haste, immediately.

oirre 3737, 4738 *errer,* to act, proceed.

oni/honi 2643, 3804, 6032, 6481, 6512 equal, uniform.

onor 2623 fief.

ordie 3170 *ordier/ourdier,* GD 5:, '*observer, epier*', to keep a close watch on.

ordist 269 *ordir,* to set up a web/loom for weaving.

oriere 5876 edge of a wood, forest.

ostoir 93, 233, 3863 goshawk.

oues cf. *ues.*

paint 3229 *pener*, to make every effort to (subj).

parconier(e) 811, 5234 sharer.

parmenterie 2324 finery (*parement* is a long rich ceremonial surcoat): *soiller la parmenterie*, to disgrace one's lineage.

pepie 2414 pip (disease of birds—it produces mucus that chokes them).

peule 2172 = *pueple* (Picard form).

pie 2413: *ne valoir une pie* (magpie), to be worthless.

piure 4359 = *puire puirier* to hand over, offer (by metathesis).

pire [*piere*] 3332 way, road.

plait: 4243, 5482 situation, conflict.

plaseis [*plaisseis*] 2224 palissade.

plasscie [*plaissee*] 5982 open space enclosed by hedges.

polcier [*polz*] 1923 thumb.

posan, a 976 next year {L *proximo anno*}.

pot 6186: *decovrir le pot aus roses*, to reveal the truth.

prover 4242: *pris prove*, caught in the act, in flagrante delicto.

pue 354 = *puee* (subj) *povoir*.

puis piece 4428 a little later.

pule 4830 = *pueple*.

raes, rese 1497, 1553 *rere*, to shave, tonsure.

redos 211 support (as in 'to put new backing into').

riviere 2912 low area, hunting ground: *de povre riviere*, badly off, from a poor background.

roiogne 1419 *rooignier* [GD 'couper en rond']: to tonsure (the truth).

rote 349 troop, company of armed men {Fr *routier*}.

rue, a 353 in a circle {L *rota*}.

ruee, une 2711, 2725 for a stone's throw around (cf. ruer, to hurl, throw).

saine 5964 thirst.

sans 465 except (relatively rare but well attested use of *sans* [LC]).

sensablement 2366 sensibly (rare form).

sinple 3972 downcast.

sivable 4682 *sivre* [*siuvre*]: what follows from.

soivre 527 *sevrer*, to cut off.

solroit/solle 1384, 1415 *soldre*, to recompense.

son [*som*] 529 tip of spear (in general, highest point) {L *in summo*}.

son [*sonc*] 127 according to.

soneis 5424 sounding of horns.

sontre [*soentre, soventre*] 687 next in the sense of following.

soolte 2243 [otherwise unattested] company, friendship. [LC: *sooste*].

sopple 4785 submissive: *fait l'un de nos vers l'altre sopple*: 'causes each of us to bend to the other's will.'

sordens 3253 extra tooth (GD 10:729c). I have translated somewhat freely.

soshaidier: wish, desire 1067, 1448, 5372; to cause someone to be present by wishing 5250, 5251.

suevre [*soivre*] 6410 spicy sauce.

tagne 4247 *taindre* (subj): *ne taindre a rien*, to have nothing to do with anything.

talle [*taille*] 2 measure; cf. notes to text.

terchuel/tercuel [*tercoeul*] 1814, 1822 bran.

tezir [*tesir*] 6128 to swell up.

tolte 350 seizes, grabs. I posit **tolet*, pres. indic. 3 *toler*, an attested variant of *tolir/toldre* (cf TL 10:366), with metathesis for rhyme.

trait, a 894, 1310, 6435 distinctly, with deliberation, protractedly.

[*ues, a*] *aoues/houes/oues/wes* 1873, 3586, 3745, 4035, 4317, 6320 for, towards, of use to.

verror 1156, 1984 etc. truth.

viaire: face 4011, 4456; opinion (way of seeing things) 4012, 4643, 5000.

vials [*vels*] 49, 817, 829, 2849 etc. at least.

vias [*viaz*] 2099 at once.

voisos/eus/ies 1399, 1646, 2117 wise, prudent, clever.

wes 3586, 6320 cf. *ues*.

SELECT BIBLIOGRAPHY

The Manuscript: Editions and Textual Studies

Cowper, F.A.G. 1959. "Origins and Peregrinations of the Laval-Middleton Manuscript." *Nottingham Medieval Studies* 3:3–18.

Lecoy, Félix. 1978. "Le *Roman de Silence* d'Heldris de Cornualle." *Romania 99:* 109–25.

Stevenson, W.H. 1911. *Report on the Manuscripts of Lord Middleton at Wollaton Hall, Nottinghamshire.* Historical Manuscripts Commission.

Thorpe, Lewis, ed. 1972. *Le Roman de Silence.* Cambridge: Heffer. (First published in *Nottingham Medieval Studies* 5–8 (1961–64) and 10–11 (1966–67).

Critical Studies of the Roman de Silence

Allen, Peter. 1989. "The Ambiguity of Silence: Gender, Writing and *Le Roman de Silence.*" *Sign, Sentence, Discourse: Language in Medieval Thought and Literature,* ed. Julian N. Wasserman and Lois Roney. Syracuse: Syracuse University Press, pp. 98–112.

Bloch, R. Howard. 1983. *Etymologies and Genealogies: A Literary Anthropology of the French Middle Ages.* Chicago: University of Chicago Press. [*Silence* discussed pp. 195–97.]

_____. 1986. "Silence and Holes: The *Roman de Silence* and the Art of the Trouvere." *Yale French Studies* 67: 81–99.

Brahney, Kathleen J. 1985. "When *Silence* was Golden: Female Personae in the *Roman de Silence.*" *The Spirit of the Court. Selected Proceedings of the Fourth Congress of the International Courtly Literature Society* (Toronto, 1983), ed. Glyn S. Burgess, Robert A. Taylor, Alan Deyermond, Dennis Green, Beryl Rowland. Cambridge: Brewer, pp. 52–61.

Cooper, Kate Mason. 1985. "Elle and L: Sexualized Textuality in the *Roman de Silence.*" *Romance Notes* 25: 341–60.

Ferrante, Joan. 1988. "Public Postures, Private Maneuvers: Roles Medieval Women Play." *Women and Power in the Middle Ages,* ed. Mary Erler and Maryanne Kowalski. Athens and London: University of Georgia Press, pp. 213–229.

Gaunt, Simon. 1990 "The Significance of Silence." *Paragraph* 13: 202–16.

Gelzer, Heinrich. 1917. *Nature. Zum Einfluss der Scholastik auf den altfranzö-sischen Roman.* Halle a. S.: Max Niemeyer.

———. 1925. "Mabon." *Zeitschrift für französische Sprache und Literatur* 47:73–74.

———. 1927. "Der Silenceroman von Heldris de Cornualle." *Zeitschrift für romanische Philologie* 47: 88–99.

Lasry, Anita Benaim. 1985. "The Ideal Heroine in Medieval Romances: A Quest for a Paradigm." *Kentucky Romance Quarterly* 32: 227–43.

Lloyd, Heather. 1987. "The Triumph of Pragmatism: Reward and Punishment in the *Roman de Silence.*" *Rewards and Punishments in the Arthurian Romances and Lyric Poetry of Medieval France,* ed. Peter V. Davies and Angus J. Kennedy. Cambridge: Brewer, pp. 77–88.

Perret, Michèle. 1985. "Travesties et transsexuelles: Yde, Silence, Grisandole, Blanchandine." *Romance Notes* 25: 328–40.

Other Primary and Secondary Sources

Bonilla y San Martin, Adolfo, ed. 1904. *Libro de los enganos y los asayamientos de las mugeres.* Barcelona: L'Avenc.

Brunet, Charles and A. de Montaiglon, ed. 1856. *Li Romans de Dolopathos* [by Herbert]. Paris: P. Jannet.

Castets, Ferdinand, ed. 1909. *La Chanson des quatre fils Aymon.* Montpellier: Coulet.

Comfort, W.W., trans. [1914] 1975. "Chrétien de Troyes." *Arthurian Romances.* Reprint, with introd. and notes by D.D.R. Owen. New York: Dutton, Everyman's Library.

Crosland, Jessie. 1956. "*Dolopathos* and the Seven Sages of Rome." *Medium Aevum* 25:1–12.

Curtius, Ernst Robert. 1967. "The Goddess Natura." Chap. 6 of his *European Literature and the Latin Middle Ages.* Trans. Willard L. Trask. Princeton: Princeton University Press, Bollingen Series 36, pp. 106–27.

Davis, Natalie Z. 1975. "Women on Top." Chap. 5 of her *Society and Culture in Early Modern France.* Palo Alto: Stanford University Press, pp. 124–51.

Economou, George D. 1972. *The Goddess Natura in Medieval Literature.* Cambridge, Mass.: Harvard University Press.

Felman, Shoshana. 1981. "Rereading Femininity." *Yale French Studies* 62: 19–44.

Gilleland, Brady B., trans. 1981. Johannes de Alta Silva, *Dolopathos.* Binghamton (N.Y.): Center for Medieval and Renaissance Studies.

Godefroy, Frédéric. [1881–1902] 1961. *Dictionnaire de l'ancienne langue fran-çaise et de tous ses dialectes.* New York: Kraus Reprints (Cited as Godefroy).

Hilka, Alfons, ed. 1913. *Historia septem sapientium. II. Johannis de Alta Silva Dolopathos sive De rege et septem sapientibus.* Heidelberg: Carl Winter.

Hughes, Muriel. 1943. *Women Healers in Medieval Life and Literature.* New York: King's Crown Press.

Keller, Heinrich, ed. 1836. *Li Romans des sept sages.* Tübingen: L.F. Fues.

Koch, Marie Pierre. *An Analysis of the Long Prayers in Old French Literature with Special Reference to the "Biblical-Creed-Narrative" Prayers.* Washington, DC: Catholic University of America Press, 1940.

Lida de Malkiel, María Rosa. 1977. "La dama como obra maestra de Dios." In her *Estudios sobre la literatura española del siglo XV.* Madrid: Ediciones José Porrúa Turanzas, S.A., pp. 179–290.

McConeghy, Patrick M. 1987. "Women's Speech and Silence in Hartmann von Aue's *Erec.*" *PMLA* 102:772–83.

Morawski, Joseph. 1925. *Proverbes français antérieurs au XVe siècle.* Paris: Champion.

Paton, Lucy A. 1907. "The Story of Grisandole: A Study in the Legend of Merlin." *PMLA* 22: 234–76.

Riese, Alexander, ed. 1973. *Historia Apollonii Regis Tyri.* Stuttgart: Teubner.

Roloff, Volker. 1973. *Reden und Schweigen. Zur Tradition und Gestaltung eines mittelalterlichen Themas in der französischen Literatur.* Munich: Wilhelm Fink. [nothing on *Silence*]

Rokseth, Yvonne. 1935. "Les femmes musiciennes du XIIe au XIVe siècle." *Romania* 61: 464–480.

Ruberg, Uwe. 1978. *Beredtes Schweigen in lehrhafter und erzählender deutscher Literatur des Mittelalters.* Munich: Wilhelm Fink.

Sacks, Sheldon, ed. 1979. *On Metaphor.* Chicago: University of Chicago Press.

Salverda de Grave, ed. 1925, 1929. *Eneas, Roman du XIIe siècle.* Paris: Champion.

Singer, Samuel. 1895. *Apollonius von Tyrus: Untersuchungen zum Fortleben des antiken Romans in späteren Zeiten.* Halle a. S.: Niemeyer.

Sommer, H. Oskar. 1909–16. "Grisandole." In *The Vulgate Version of the Arthurian Romances.* 7 vols with index. Washington: Carnegie Institution, 2: 281–92.

Thompson, Stith. 1966. *Motif-Index of Folk Literature.* 2d ed., rev. and enl. Bloomington: Indiana University Press.

Tobler, Adolf. 1895 *Li proverbe au vilain.* Leipzig: Hirzel.

Tobler, Adolf, and Erhard Lommatzsch. 1925–. *Altfranzösisches Wörterbuch.* Berlin: Weidemann (Cited as Tobler-Lommatzsch).

Williams, G. Perrie, ed. 1929. Renauld de Beaujeu. *Le bel inconnu.* Paris: Champion.

Yunck, John A., trans. 1974. *Eneas, a Twelfth-Century French Romance.* New York: Columbia University Press.